THE ROAD TO THE TOP OF THE MOUNTAIN

THE ROAD TO THE TOP OF THE MOUNTAIN

RECOVERING FROM A TRAUMATIC BRAIN INJURY WITH
THE HELP OF FREESTYLE SKIING, COOL RUNNINGS AND
THE BRISTOL STOOL CHART!

ANNE MASSON
AND MATT MASSON

The Book Guild Ltd

"From signing a poster for a hospitalized fan, to meeting him in person in a walking frame, and many years later go skiing the slopes of Chamonix together as friends, the story of Matt Masson has been an incredible journey to partake in – a reminder that true passion helps us overcome even the largest of obstacles... buy this book..."

JACOB WESTER,

Swedish Freeskier

"This is a story of resilience, positivity, adaptability and love."

CLARE BALDING

"Whatever might be the path that life brings you on, you've got to own it rather than let life own you. Matt could have given up. Given up on walking, given up on skiing, given up on studying, given up on so many things that "normal" people do on a daily basis. Get owned. I mean, who would have resented him for it. Instead he pushed through and accomplished things that "normal" people dream about. I'm sure that the thought of giving up never crossed his mind. He owns it big time!"

MARKUS EDER,

Freeride World Tour Ski Men's
Champion and Olympian

"As a passionate skier and physio, meeting Matt was really inspiring... to see the power and faith in coming back so strong after such a gnarly accident and willing to ski again really put everything in perspective... and having the chance to help him walk/ski around was for me a great pleasure!"

ARIANNA TRICOMI,
Three-Time Freeride World Tour Ski Women's Champion

"Lit by the beacon of wisdom C.R Johnson left him with, Matt shaped an unfortunate event into miraculous achievements."

PHIL CASABON,
Two-time X Games Real Ski winner

"Matt has taken ownership of a bad situation in an immensely inspiring way. I could not help but be in awe of how he overcomes his difficulties and does his job and does it well."

DAVID WISE,
American Skier and Two-time Winter Olympic Gold Medallist

"A truly remarkable story of incredible courage and tenacity from a young man determined not to let a life-changing injury stop him from fulfilling his dreams. As a medical professional, I gained a deep insight from Anne's account of how traumatic brain injury affected her son Matt and them as a family. It is an invaluable read and I would highly recommend it, especially to all medics to understand the impact of our words and the uniqueness of all patients."

DR. TANIA AHERN

First published in Great Britain in 2021 by
The Book Guild Ltd
9 Priory Business Park
Wistow Road, Kibworth
Leicestershire, LE8 0RX
Freephone: 0800 999 2982
www.bookguild.co.uk
Email: info@bookguild.co.uk
Twitter: @bookguild

Typeset in 11pt Minion Pro

Printed and bound by CPI Group (UK) Ltd, Croydon, CR0 4YY

ISBN 978 1913551 247

British Library Cataloguing in Publication Data.
A catalogue record for this book is available from the British Library.

Dedicated to the memory of CR Johnson
10th August 1983 - 24th February 2010

Thank you for showing us the way
and allowing us to hope

CONTENTS

Foreword   xi

One   A Life is Changed   1
Two   Not Meaning to Brag, but...   4
Three   Too Many Missed Calls   10
Four   The Critical Phase   21
Five   From ICU to HDU   36
Six   Matt Enters the Twilight Zone   44
Seven   Back in the Land of the Living   57
Eight   A Little Bit of Brain Info   69
Nine   The Hard Work Begins   76
Ten   Home Leave   91
Eleven   It's Up to Us Now   100
Twelve   Heading for the Winter   111

Thirteen   Back on Real Snow   116

Fourteen   Some Serious Training for Some   129
                  Serious Torchbearing

Fifteen   Matt's Feeling Very Olympic Today!   134

Sixteen   Slow and Steady   141

Seventeen   Surely the Best Ski Season Ever   149

Eighteen   The Hidden Injury   172

Nineteen   A Season in Cham   181

Twenty   "No head injury is too severe to despair   189
                  of, nor too trivial to ignore" – Hippocrates

Twenty-One   California Skiing on a Winter's Day   196

Twenty-Two   Marathon Training   209

Twenty-Three   The Amsterdam Marathon   215

Twenty-Four   Matt Decides on his Future   225

Twenty-Five   London's Air Ambulance   233

Twenty-Six   "I Bet I'm The Only Person on My Uni   239
                  Course to Empty the Clip of an AK-47
                  On Their Work Experience!"

Twenty-Seven   The Wobbly Journo   247

Twenty-Eight   Some Final Thoughts as We Look   251
                  to the Future

Afterword   260

Glossary of Terms   264

Acknowledgements   266

References and Sources Consulted during   270
the writing of this memoir

FOREWORD

BY ROY TUSCANY

FOUNDER & CEO OF HIGH FIVES FOUNDATION, CALIFORNIA, USA

It is not often you meet a person who understands all the good that you are trying to do in this world, but that is the case with Matt Masson; he speaks the same language as me. Unfortunately, an accident had to happen for our worlds to come together, but out of tragedy comes triumph, and that is exactly the process of friendship that I have built with Matt and his family. It started with an email from a concerned mother who wanted to find an answer about a commemorative jacket in memory of free-ski legend, CR Johnson. Inside the jacket was the phrase '*Reign Supreme*' – a term used by CR Johnson to express his daily gratitude to the world after sustaining a traumatic brain injury (TBI) and getting a second chance at life. That was the common tie between Matt and me; this jacket that was designed to honor my friend and his hero, CR Johnson, who unfortunately passed away from a second head injury.

Matt, like CR, suffered a devastating head injury from a fall. His old life stopped that moment. He decided to use his life's passion – skiing – to fuel his recovery. This fall to his head changed everything in his world and he had to start over, but he used skiing as his ultimate goal to show the people in his life that he could return to the sport he loved, regardless of how his life had changed from this TBI. When Matt got back to skiing, it showed that anything was possible, and I truly believe that Matt has only just started to show his accomplishments to this planet post-injury.

Life is a journey and those that have a second chance find that journey to be enriched with the ability to love life every day. The experiences that I have gotten to accomplish with Matt personally have been some of my life's best moments: fly-fishing, skiing, NASCAR and touring America. In 2017 Matt interned with my organization, High Fives Foundation, where he learned new skills and got to immerse himself within a community of like-minded individuals who shared a common tie: life-changing injuries.

Matt gets life; he understands that his second chance is there for him to chase his passions, to empower others and to reign supreme. Don't judge a man by his physical scars, but by his internal drive to heal.

ONE

A LIFE IS CHANGED

There is a building in the Waterloo area of London that houses the Emergency Operations Centre for the London Ambulance Service. It is a most unprepossessing building – a large grey rectangle with a flat roof and featureless windows – not worth a second glance from a passer-by. We should know better than to judge a book by its cover though, for behind that boring façade is the world's busiest ambulance control room. Dial 999 to request an ambulance in London and this is where your call will be handled. For most medical emergencies, the familiar ambulances with their blues and twos will be dispatched from one of the seventy ambulance stations spread across five operational sectors in London.

In the most extreme of emergencies, where lives are in the balance, the services of the bright red helicopters of London's Air Ambulance will be called upon. They are based at the Royal London Hospital in Whitechapel. On board the helicopter will be a pilot, a highly skilled paramedic and a trauma doctor –

often of consultant level. The specialist skills of these teams can make the difference between the patient living or dying. Many procedures that would normally have to wait until the patient's arrival at the accident and emergency department of a hospital can be carried out at the scene quickly and efficiently. Their patients are often at the edge of life, and these men and women will do everything in their power to save them.

An LAA advanced trauma paramedic is based at the Emergency Operations Centre to monitor incoming calls and decide if the air ambulance should be deployed. There are certain triggers that call for its immediate dispatch, with no need for further questions. These include falls from higher than two floors, serious road traffic accidents and traumatic amputations.

At 1.30 in the early hours of the morning of Saturday 27th November 2010, such a call was received. In Camden Town, a young man had fallen from a height and was unconscious at the scene. This was flagged up as needing an urgent response from the LAA. During the hours of darkness it is considered too dangerous for the helicopter to fly, so the calls are attended using one of the rapid response cars attached to the LAA with the same highly skilled trauma team on board.

A car was mobilised and on the scene by 1.43am. The situation was quickly assessed and a serious head injury was diagnosed. In addition, the patient's airways were compromised by his tongue, which was down the back of his throat. The initial head injury was bad enough, but what they then needed to do was prevent any further damage to the brain from a secondary head injury. This can occur if the oxygen supply to the brain is interrupted. Ordinarily, the brain consumes 20% of the oxygen carried in your body's blood. If this blood supply is interrupted for even just two or three minutes, the brain cells are starved of oxygen and will start dying. By 1.50am (within seven minutes of arrival), the team had cleared the patient's airways and anaesthetised him. He was now in an induced coma with a tube down his throat supplying that vital oxygen, which would give him the very best chance of survival.

By 2.30am, the young man had been transferred to the Royal London Hospital by road ambulance. The A&E team were standing by, having been fully informed of the treatment he had already received and of what he would then need on arrival.

TWO

NOT MEANING TO BRAG, BUT...

At the tail end of 2010, our son Matt was nearly halfway through his 23rd year and living the dream. Always the eternal optimist, he had seized life firmly with both hands and was just seeing where it would take him. So far, it had taken him to some pretty good places as he pursued his love of travel, the sea and, above all, the mountains.

Matt is the youngest of our two sons, with Tim being the eldest. My husband, Nick, had worked for international companies, which meant that we had been lucky enough to have moved around Europe with our young sons as they grew up, living in France, Germany and Switzerland, before returning to the UK in 2002.

Geneva in Switzerland had been our favourite place, with both sailing on the lake and skiing in the mountains on our doorstep. It was a fantastic experience and I never lost sight of the fact that it was a real privilege to live in such a beautiful country. Tim and Matt were twelve and nine years old when we first moved there. Their journey to school was a feast for the eyes as the school bus took them through the Swiss vineyards bordering the lake, with the Jura Mountains as a backdrop; then looking across to the other side of the lake were the magnificent snowcapped French Alps. If they missed the bus, then I would have the pleasure of driving them to school – and it was a real pleasure as we drove up the lakeside road.

"Oh, boys, just look at those views. How lucky are you two to see this every day!"

"Mum," wailed two voices in unison. "You say that every time you drive up this road."

"Well, it's true and one day you'll look back and appreciate all this."

Clearly, that day wasn't going to be anytime soon.

As non-skiers, we had to learn to ski – after all, we were in Switzerland, so it was almost obligatory. During the winter weekends, the canton emptied as everybody escaped to the mountains. We came to the conclusion that if you can't beat them, join them, and that's exactly what we did by buying an apartment in the mountains as proof of our newfound commitment to mountain life. We found a real gem in the little alpine village of Le Tour near Chamonix, just over an hour away in the French Alps. Over the course of the following years, we would spend many happy hours up there perfecting our skiing skills and just enjoying life in the mountains.

When Matt finished school, he really hadn't got a clue what he wanted to do, so it seemed that a gap year might be a good option.

"Andy's doing a ski instructor course in Canada over the winter. I think that would be cool for me too," he announced to us very enthusiastically. Great, that was the first part of the puzzle in place – now he just needed to fill in the remaining part of the year. He decided to keep with the instructor theme, but this time it would be watersports in Vassiliki, Greece.

He then took us completely by surprise when he decided that he should go to university after the gap year. "Darryl's going to Bournemouth, so I might as well go there." Nick and I weren't convinced that more studying was the best option for him, but only time would tell. At least he put his newly gained watersports qualifications to good use that summer by teaching at a sailing school on the Isles of Scilly, in the freezing cold waters of the Atlantic, off the Cornish coast.

He dabbled with university life in Bournemouth, while supposedly studying Leisure Marketing. Unfortunately, Matt was far more interested in the leisure part than the marketing and dropped out after a couple of years. He'd had fun, made a load of friends, but seemed to have entirely missed the point of why he was actually there. It was clear that his heart wasn't really in it and he needed to be out in the big wide world pursuing adventures. Nick and I weren't too upset, as we'd never quite been able to picture him in an office anyway. Things always had a habit of working out for Matt and we felt that he'd find his way in life eventually. No doubt, he'd end up doing something entirely unexpected and take us all by surprise. He was bright and personable and, when he was doing something he enjoyed, he would throw himself into it with great gusto and do a good job.

His Scilly Isles sailing had already become a regular summer season job, so he just needed to complement it with something to occupy him for the winter season. That didn't prove too much of a problem, as he managed to find seasonal bar work in Courchevel in the French Alps. He had decided against teaching skiing at that point, as he figured that bar work would free him up for many more skiing adventures during the day. Instructing was something he could always come back to at a later date. He was soon part of the local *saisonnaire* scene, which consisted of all sorts of people from all walks of life – his roommate was an ex-RAF fighter pilot. Life was pretty sweet, as Matt himself would say.

His first winter season was rounded off in fine style as he and a couple of friends decided to cycle home to the UK. The bike they found for Matt was a very old, bright pink, drop-handled racing bike – not at all suitable for such an epic adventure. It was made even worse when one of the pedals broke in half at the beginning of the journey, so he peddled most of the way on one and a half pedals. He eventually arrived home with his customary huge grin and an equally huge hole in the sole of his shoe from the sharp edge of the broken pedal.

Following another summer of sun and sea on the Scillies, the end of 2009 saw him heading off to the sunshine in Sydney, Australia, to teach sailing down under. Once again, he made some very good friends and no doubt got up to all sorts of harmless mischief and had many great experiences. These new friends would soon prove to be absolutely solid friends-for-life sort of friends.

Matt's approach to life was very simple, and looking back at those times, he later explained to me, "Not meaning to brag, but my life was pretty good. My one rule was that you don't need to earn loads of money as long as you live and work in a place where people pay to go on holiday!"

There's a lot to be said for the Matt Masson Philosophy of Life. He was earning enough money to keep himself, he was very happy and in between seasons, he would come breezing back home for a few weeks before the next adventure. At the end of every season he would be super-fit, tanned and, at the end of the summer season, his long dark hair would be bleached by the salt water. No need for gym memberships or fancy hairdressers in order for him to get that healthy, sun-kissed look. He was always accompanied by a heap of dirty washing, presents for us all and lots and lots of funny stories.

2010 was the year of Matt's endless summer, as he returned from the Australian summer ready to get straight back to the Cornish summer on the Scilly Isles. However, by the end of that third consecutive summer, the mountains were definitely calling to him once more. He had managed to line up another bar job in Courchevel, despite my well-meaning mum advice when he went for his interview. He had come home after the summer with an extreme beach bum look, so I suggested that a bit of a trim might be in order before he met the bar owners. He took my excellent advice and was smiling when he returned from London after the interview.

"How did you get on?"

"Really well. I've got the job."

"Great! When do you start?"

"Beginning of December, but do you know what the lady said?" He was looking at me with a twinkle in his eye.

"No, what?"

"She said that she was a bit disappointed that I'd cut my hair. She liked my hair in the photo I sent."

Luckily for me, Matt was never one for bearing a grudge. He was once again anticipating a season of great skiing and further expanding his already considerable circle of friends. In Matt's world, life couldn't possibly get any better than this.

Before heading off to France, he had planned a bit of a road trip to catch up with various friends from previous seasons. His new job was due to start in December, so at the end of November he got into his trusty Citroen C2 and set off on his travels. His trip started in London, where many of his pals were now based, and it was due to end in Devon about a week later. Undoubtedly, there would be at least one more load of dirty washing to be put through the machine before he finally set off for his 2010/2011 winter adventures.

In his usual whirlwind fashion he had just chucked all his stuff into the back of the car, and with a cheery "See you next week, Mum!" and a slam of the door behind him, he was gone. Once again, the house was an oasis of peace and calm.

As I savoured the quiet all around me, little did I know that I would see him well before the next week, but he wouldn't be seeing me again for quite a while.

THREE

TOO MANY MISSED CALLS

Matt's road trip came to an abrupt end two days later in Camden Town. Back on the West Sussex coast, Nick and I had enjoyed an uninterrupted night's sleep, blissfully unaware of what the approaching day would hold. I vividly remember feeling totally energised that Saturday morning in anticipation of the busy weekend that lay ahead. I can even remember what I chose to wear that day. I had looked out of the bedroom window first thing to see a clear blue sky above a white frosty lawn and, beyond that, the blue sea with the sunlight twinkling off it. The cold and frost meant that it was the ideal day to debut my new cosy white winter jumper.

The picture-perfect view from the upstairs window is the first of several images that will forever stay etched in my mind concerning that day. It was one of those 'good to be alive' sort of days. December was just a few days away and, for us, that meant the beginning of the ski season. Matt would soon be off to the

French Alps to start his new bar job and Tim would be teaching skiing and snowboarding in the Swiss Alps. There were lots of good things to look forward to and, at that precise moment in time, life was looking good for the Masson family. It was hard to imagine that anything could possibly spoil such a beautiful day.

"Come on. Let's go," said Nick, impatiently heading for the car, ready for our planned shopping trip to Chichester.

"Hang on a sec. I just need to switch my phone on. Maybe Matt's sent one of his funny texts."

The phone rang immediately. It was a voicemail. I couldn't really make out what was said, except for the last four words: *It's about your son.*

Nick saw the puzzled look on my face. "Who was that?"

"I don't know. Someone with a message about our son."

"Did they say which one?"

"No, maybe this is them again," as the phone rang out for a second time.

I listened to the second message and my stomach went into a tight knot.

"It's about Matt. He's somewhere in London – Royal something or other. I think he's in hospital."

I looked again at my phone and saw that I had thirty-five missed calls – all after 3am. That wasn't normal. Nick grabbed the phone and disappeared into his office. By then, my brain had frozen; this didn't make any sense at all. Matt was staying with friends in London. What possible harm could he have come to?

Nick came back into the hallway, where I was still glued to the spot. He looked shaken but calm. "He's in the Royal London Hospital. They couldn't give me any details over the phone, but he's in intensive care and stable and we need to get going."

"What about the dogs? Can you go and ask Brian to let them out at lunchtime?" Lunchtime was as far ahead as I could manage to think at that time.

In the few minutes that Nick was away, I began to absorb a bit more of what we had been told. I have watched enough hospital dramas on TV to know that stable means nothing – it could be good stable or bad stable. It just meant his condition wasn't changing. In the space of less than fifteen minutes, my perfect winter's day had turned into my worst nightmare. Standing in our hallway, looking at that phone and not being able to make any sense of it is the second unforgettable image I have from that day.

It was all so confusing and unbelievable. I suspect that the human brain is only capable of taking in a limited amount of bad news at a time and, as a coping mechanism, it has an uncanny ability to block out the worst of it. That's what my brain appeared to be doing anyway.

My brother, John, lives in London and I felt I should call him. He and Matt get on really well, bonded by their shared love of football.

"Matt's in hospital." I got straight to the point.

"What? Is it serious?"

"I think it probably is. He's in intensive care in the Royal London."

"Christ, what happened?"

"I don't really know. They wouldn't tell us, we're heading up there now."

"Would you like me to go there?"

"Yes, please. It would be good to think that Matt has someone there for him."

"Right, I'm leaving now."

That was the shortest telephone conversation I've ever had with my brother.

We just fled from the house with no thought of how long we might be away or when we would be back to feed the dogs. I was incapable of thinking straight – this definitely wasn't my normal sort of day; indeed, it was so far beyond any normal parameters that it was hard to even believe it was actually happening.

Nick had given up smoking many years ago, but stopped at our local Co-op to buy a packet of cigarettes to get him through the journey. After three hours on the road, all twenty of the cigarettes had been smoked. At some point during the journey, I called Tim to let him know that his brother was in hospital but didn't tell him how serious it was. He would join us there.

As the seemingly endless journey continued, dark thoughts kept popping into my head. What if they were just waiting for us to give permission to switch off a life support machine? I told myself not to think about such things – this was Matt we were talking about. He is the luckiest guy around; only good things happen to him. Bad things never happen.

The journey was very weird. I can still picture Nick and me sitting in the car, him driving and smoking, and me feeling as if I was almost having some sort of out-of-body experience. It felt as if I was holding my breath, just waiting for my world to come crashing down completely – I knew it was well on its way there already.

I think that Nick and I both made the decision during that journey not to discuss what we were each expecting to find on our arrival. I know I definitely wanted to keep my deepest, darkest thoughts to myself. I somehow thought that if I were to mention out loud the possibility of Matt dying, then it could become a reality, so it was best not to say anything.

It was not until well after the event (maybe two or three years later) that Nick admitted to me that the nurse he had spoken to on the phone earlier that day had emphasised the need for us to get there as quickly as possible. Apparently, they had been trying to reach us all night, but our bedside phone was not working and our mobiles were downstairs. We also found out later that a policeman had been sent to our house in the early hours of the morning to provide us with a blue-light escort to the hospital. Fortunately, we hadn't heard the doorbell. I say fortunately because I kept telling myself during the journey that if it was really serious, they would have sent the police around. As far as I was concerned, no one had been to the house, so maybe it wasn't that bad. It was almost as if I had two people in my head. One was worried sick and very afraid, the other was arguing the case for it all being a big fuss over nothing.

*

We finally arrived in Whitechapel after what seemed like the longest journey of our lives. I had managed to speak to Matt's friend Darryl on the way in, who explained that Matt had fallen off a balcony and was in a pretty bad way. Strangely enough, at that time, neither Nick nor I had the slightest desire to know the details of Matt's accident. It wouldn't have made any difference to the situation. Whatever had happened had happened, and it was the present we needed to deal with.

The area around the Royal London at that time was one giant building site. The old buildings were scheduled to be replaced by a very fine new one, so all the surrounding side roads seemed to be full of portacabins and sheets of metal acting as walls blocking off the site. We left the car alongside one of the metal walls and made our way through the maze of building equipment and pedestrian diversions until we found the old hospital building. I guess we must have enquired at reception as to Matt's whereabouts and then gone up the old stairwell to the Intensive Care Unit on the 4th floor. I didn't really take in any details of the surroundings on that day.

When we reached the Intensive Care Unit, we saw a little huddle of people waiting anxiously outside in the corridor. My brother, John, was there with my nephew, Charles, and a few of Matt's friends from the night before, who were all looking very tired and shocked. That provided the third unforgettable image in my head.

None of us really knew what to say to each other. Darryl vaguely introduced us to the people we didn't know and pointed us in the right direction: "He's through there." His tone of voice told us everything. He might as well have said, *He's through there, but it's going to be tough to see.* John supported this sentiment with a sad little smile.

We went through to the ward in a bit of a daze. Sally and Charlotte (my sister-in-law and niece) were there beside Matt's bed and, finally, I burst into tears as I saw Matt. He was lying there with I don't know how many tubes and wires going into him. There was a bank of machines surrounding him with flashing lights and bleeps and lots of numbers and graphs. He had obviously tried to break his fall by putting his left arm out, resulting in a broken wrist, which was now in a plaster cast. This was the least of his problems, though, and it was his head that was causing concern. His ears were full of blood, there was blood on his eyebrows, but the most shocking thing was the bolt in his head, which was there to measure the pressure on his brain – intracranial pressure, or ICP. I always describe this as a bolt, but I have since learnt that it is more of a special tube and it is officially called an intracranial pressure monitor. Whatever it was, to us it looked like something out of a Frankenstein movie. This was the worst moment of our lives, and it was the fourth and final image of the day that will be with me forever. After that, everything became a bit of a blur as the dreadful reality of the situation began to hit us.

Matt had a lovely Irish nurse called Claire looking after him. Her kind smile and reassuring manner were both much appreciated by Nick and me. In the ICU, the nursing is one-on-one and the nurses are fantastic. They work 12-hour shifts and barely more than a couple of minutes go by without them having to adjust some knob or tube. The lives of these patients are literally in their hands, and it goes without saying that they will always do everything they can to keep them alive.

As the afternoon progressed, we learnt a little more. Matt had somehow managed to fall over 20 feet through a corrugated plastic roof next to the balcony of a club in Camden and sustained a severe traumatic brain injury (TBI). I will never understand why he did that and he certainly can't explain it. He suspects he might just have been showing off, but we'll never know. He was unconscious at the scene, which is not a good thing. We learnt all about the Glasgow Coma Scale (GCS), which measures the patient's degree of consciousness. It comprises three tests: eye, verbal and motor responses. These are graded as follows:

Eye Response

1. No eye opening
2. Eye opening in response to pain stimulus (e.g. squeezing on a fingernail)
3. Eye opening in response to speech
4. Eye opening spontaneously

Verbal Response

1. No response
2. Incomprehensible sounds
3. Inappropriate words
4. Confused
5. Oriented (i.e. coherent, appropriate response)

Motor response

1. No motor response
2. Involuntary muscle straightening and extending
3. Abnormal flexion to pain
4. Flexion/withdrawal to pain
5. Localises to pain
6. Obeys commands

You add up the scores from the three categories (represented by the numbers on the left) and anything below a 9 is classified as a severe brain injury. The lowest possible score is 3 (deep coma or death), while the highest is 15 (as in a fully awake person). At the scene of the accident, Matt was 1+1+1=3. Not good, not good at all.

At some point during those first couple of hours, we were handed a leaflet about dealing with shock and grief. I couldn't understand how this was in any way relevant to us. I had to keep telling myself that everything would be fine. I still couldn't fully accept that this really was about as bad as it could get.

Later on during the afternoon of that awful day, a consultant and his registrar came over to talk to us. I remember them both looking almost apologetic and very concerned. It was painfully obvious that they must spend a lot of their time delivering difficult news to anxious relatives and it probably never gets any easier for them. I guess they never know how people will react, or even how much they are capable of taking in at such a difficult time. The consultant was an older man and looked as if he'd just come from watching a rugby match, with his slightly crumpled cord trousers and old tweed jacket. The registrar was a much younger man, who was hanging on to every word his boss said, while occasionally looking across at us to give us an encouraging, kindly smile.

Nick and I were sitting on one side of Matt's bed and they came and sat down on the opposite side. I can remember the consultant saying, "Well, it's a bit of a mess in there. We've done a scan, but there's too much blood for us to really see what's going on. We can see that he's fractured his skull." Then he added, "We'll just have to wait and see what happens." As I recall, Nick and I just sat there. It didn't seem like real life, especially when he said, "He obviously had a few beers." Funnily enough, that shocked me more than anything. Despite Matt being twenty-three years of age, we had never seen him drink alcohol. At home, he never accepted offers of a beer or a glass of wine from us. I remember his eighteenth birthday party when we gave everyone champagne for a birthday toast. As soon as he thought I wasn't looking, he tipped his into a plant pot.

Although he had been deeply unconscious at the scene, he was then put into an induced coma to protect his brain until his brain pressures came down. The consultant informed us that we were in for the long haul and could have weeks or even months of hospital visiting ahead of us. I really couldn't take this in – surely Matt would just get better quite soon, wouldn't he? He had a job lined up in Courchevel starting the next week and he wouldn't want to miss that. When the consultant then started talking about rehab and physiotherapy, I got really confused. What did he mean? I thought rehab was for drug addicts and alcoholics – what had it got to do with Matt getting better? As for physiotherapy, that's for people who have tennis elbow or broken legs. Why would you need that with a damaged brain?

Both Tim and Matt had always been adventurous, constantly leaping off or over things. It was a characteristic that I rather liked. Boys should be bold. As a consequence, we were used to hospital visits for the odd broken bone or deep cut. Breaking their brains, however, was not something that I had ever worried about. At that time, I knew very little about the workings of the brain, but I did know that it was essential to everything we do.

Despite the consultant having already told us that we'd just have to wait and see, we must have asked him for some sort of prognosis, as I vividly recall his answer: "I really can't even hazard a guess. I've seen people with worse injuries who have walked out of here after a couple of weeks. But then I've also seen people with seemingly lesser injuries who have never regained consciousness." He shrugged his shoulders. "I'm sorry I can't give you more than that."

I was sorry too, but I immediately reassured myself that Matt would be in the former category and soon life would be back to normal.

When Tim arrived to see his brother, he breezed in with a ski magazine he thought Matt might like to read. The shock on his face was clearly visible as he immediately realised that Matt wouldn't be reading anything for a while. Nick decided that he needed to make a quick visit back to our house and get a few changes of clothes for us, as it was now obvious (even to me) that we wouldn't be going back home that night or even the next.

The long day dragged on. I just sat next to Matt feeling utterly helpless. I couldn't do anything to help him – a Band-Aid on his head or an antiseptic cream weren't going to sort this one out.

At 8pm, it was time for a change of shift for the nurses. John and I went to the pub next door for a hot chocolate while the nurses went through their patient handovers. Little did we realise that this was going to be very much part of our daily routine over the next few weeks. After our hot chocolate, we went back into the ward to meet the night staff and spend a last half-hour with Matt before visiting hours were over at 9pm. That night, Matt had another Irish nurse with him called Lisa. All these nurses were to become the most important people in our lives.

Although their patients were often completely unresponsive, they still chatted to them and informed them of everything that they were doing for them. It became very important for us to spend that final half-hour with Matt each night, rather than just leaving at 8pm. We needed to know exactly who was looking after our son through the night, even though we had complete confidence in each and every one of them.

That evening, we all met back at John and Sally's house in Highgate, where Sally had a delicious meal waiting for us. Nick had returned from collecting our clothes and had also found a home for the dogs. They were now safely lodged with Fiona, the lady who always looked after them when we were on holiday. Tim also stayed with us. I don't think any of us slept well that night. All I wanted was to be back at the hospital to make sure Matt was safe.

We had all just been through the most emotionally exhausting day of our lives and it was only the first of many more to come. The only thing that we knew with any certainty was that we had to stay strong for Matt and for each other and to be prepared for anything that lay ahead – not that we had a clue what that might turn out to be.

FOUR

THE CRITICAL PHASE

In those early days, it was very difficult to leave the hospital at the end of each day. What if something awful happened overnight and we weren't there for Matt? Our lives had been completely transformed, and all that mattered to us was Matt and that one bed in the Intensive Care Unit at the Royal London Hospital. In less than the space of 24 hours, our world had shrunk right down to one tiny area in the East End of London. The rest of the world and what went on in it were now irrelevant to us. We were in our own little bubble and I remember on our daily journey to and from hospital seeing people going about their business, eating in restaurants or drinking in bars and just not being able to relate to it at all. We were in a very different place, and I remember wondering to myself how were these people able to laugh when our son might never laugh again? It didn't seem right – the rest of the world should have stopped too.

The next few days passed in a bit of a blur. On Day 4, Sally suggested that I keep a diary, which turned out to be a brilliant idea. It proved to be very therapeutic to sit quietly at the end of the day and write it all down. Simply walking down to Highgate village to choose my journal was a welcome distraction in itself. Later, it would serve as a reference point to measure Matt's progress. However, as I attempted to start the diary and describe those first few days, I found that I could barely remember what had happened, such was my state of mind.

We were all in a state of shock and experiencing levels of stress way beyond the norm. Matt would be wheeled away for CT scans or ECGs and various other tests. We would wait anxiously, only to be told that they had revealed nothing conclusive and there had been no change. In those early days, it was just a case of getting through each day and being there for Matt. We had turned into a bit of a zombie family, simply existing. We didn't really discuss how each of us were feeling. It wasn't necessary. It was clear that Nick, Tim and I all felt the same – absolutely terrified and as if in limbo. Our worlds had simply stopped turning.

Those of Matt's friends who already knew what had happened turned up to lend their support. They would often bowl up quite cheerfully and then leave looking just as anxious and shaken as us once it hit them just how seriously ill their friend was. When people heard that 'Matt's had a head injury', it didn't really convey anything. We see footballers rolling around on the pitch every week with 'head injuries'. Ninety-nine percent of the time, it's a fairly innocuous knock on the head with no ill effects. I hasten to add that all head injuries *should* be taken seriously, but sometimes I find their obvious play-acting disrespectful to people who really have suffered a serious head injury.

Matt's head injury was life-threatening and, at the very least, life-altering. Having seen so many Saturday afternoon head injuries on the television, it came as quite a shock for everybody to see the results of a serious head injury. We all suddenly found ourselves on the steepest of learning curves. Seeing Matt lying completely still, dependent on a bank of machines to keep him alive, was very upsetting for all of his friends. This lively, chatty young man was reduced to a lifeless empty shell and no one knew how long this might last. Would we ever see his cheeky grin again?

In spite of the dire circumstances, the splendid nurses somehow made a very abnormal situation seem as normal as possible. One particular morning, Lisa (the nurse from the first night) made us laugh when she proudly announced, "I've given Matt a wee makeover. He has had a good wash, hair shampoo and a wee shave!" It was only a few days in and I think maybe they hadn't wanted to do too much to him in those first 48 hours, but now all the dried-up blood had been washed away by Lisa and he did look pretty smart, actually. It certainly brought a smile to our faces. I'm willing to bet that she would have chatted away to him all the time she was doing it.

Visiting hours started at midday and we were there on time every day. The mornings were the very worst times – what would we find when we got there? It was like waiting for Christmas Day as a child, but in a completely opposite way. The anticipation was huge, the waiting felt like forever, but in this case, there was no excitement – only dread.

Over the next few days, I gradually contacted people. I believed that Matt needed a huge gang of supporters to cheer him on. *I* knew that he wanted to live, but *he* needed to know how many other people also wanted him to live. In my head, I was building Team Matt, and it would be the best team in the world and succeed in bringing him back to us. When you find yourself in a situation that is really completely out of your control, you need to feel that there is something you can do and something that you can control. I think this was why building Team Matt became so important to me.

*

There is a special waiting room in the ICU where friends and relatives sit together. It is a strange place, full of anxious, stressed, unhappy people. Some people are tense and silent, others weep. Some have been there for weeks, or even months, and have settled into a surreal routine; some are only there for a few days. We now found ourselves part of that motley crew, consisting of people of different ages, different nationalities, different backgrounds, and together we formed some sort of weird exclusive club to which none of us really wanted to belong. As far as I was concerned, these people were the only people who could truly understand what it was we were going through. The first real conversation I had there was with a Rastafarian man and a Chinese lady about curry recipes. The lady had been there for two months and said she had made some good friends. She came bustling in every day, pulling quite a small but heavy-looking case. She explained to me that, "I have a portable DVD player in there and I sit and watch DVDs with my husband."

Her husband was lying unconscious in the ICU, but she was looking on the bright side and hoping that he could sense her presence there with his favourite movies. Looking on the bright side was something we all needed to learn to do.

The Rasta man was someone we saw and chatted to on most days and we would compare notes on our son and his daughter. He was a very gentle, kind soul who often seemed like an oasis of calm in the midst of turmoil. Tim would often seek him out to chat to when things got too much.

All around us were tragic stories. A surprising number of people had fallen off balconies, some had actually been thrown or pushed off by others, one young mother had thrown herself off a seventh-floor balcony. She had survived, but had broken virtually every bone in her body and caused herself horrendous damage. What sort of future lay ahead of her? I wondered. People had been stabbed, shot, had overdosed, been beaten up and goodness knows what else. On occasion, armed police were on duty outside the ward in order to prevent already heightened emotions from spilling over into dangerous situations, especially if gangs had been involved in the incident. I felt almost pleased that Matt had just had a stupid accident while out enjoying himself – there was no tragic backstory or conflict involved. His injury had most likely been caused by overzealous alcohol consumption on a fun night out, leading to impaired judgement.

One thing is for sure: time spent by a bedside in the ICU must provide one of the most intense experiences possible. You are truly living life on the edge. Every day when you wake up, you know that the day holds the possibility of delivering the best news possible or the worst news possible. Most days, it provides no news. You are in such close proximity to others also going through this that you are fully aware of all that they are going through and their stories. When someone receives good news and finally walks out of there with their loved one restored to them and going home, you feel their joy, but, at the same time, you can't help but feel a tiny bit (or even a lot) jealous as you ask yourself, *Why can't that happen to us?* When someone dies, you witness their family's grief and feel upset for them and just hope that won't be your family tomorrow.

When I look back on that time, it's difficult to describe my feelings. I think all three of us – Nick, Tim and I – were just tense and endlessly waiting to see what would happen. I remember on one occasion a young woman confronted me in the waiting room. "Why are you so calm? Your son is lying there and you don't know if he's going to live or die. You should be in bits!" 'In bits' was exactly how I *should not* have been. We were certain of only two things – Matt was either going to live or die. Should the latter happen, we would all have been devastated and definitely 'in bits'. However, we preferred to cling on to the first possibility for as long as possible.

No one knows how much, if anything, a coma patient might be aware of, and we couldn't risk him picking up on any feelings of grief or sadness from his visitors. Everyone was under strict instructions to chat to him as they would have before the accident. Insults, teasing, jokes – they were all good. After all, it was their big chance to chat to Matt without getting any cheeky comments back from him. His friends proved to be brilliant at this and we would often peep in to see very animated one-sided conversations going on during their visits.

Of course we shed tears and of course we were worried sick, but never in front of Matt. In the hospital, we all felt safe and protected. It was only when we were away from it that dark thoughts entered our minds.

Matt's neighbour for the first week in the ICU was a young man the same age as him, also with a brain injury. We had chatted with his large family and felt we were all fighting the same battle. Sadly, he lost his. One of my abiding memories from that time is meeting his parents a couple of days later and, despite their obvious grief, they were proud and smiling. Fifteen people had benefitted from his death as he had donated his organs. For his parents, this meant that his death hadn't been completely meaningless. His lovely dad wished us luck and said that he had a feeling that Matt would be one of the lucky ones. We grabbed that thought and clung on to it.

Every night at eight o'clock, we went next door for our change-of-shift refreshments. As more people came to visit Matt, they joined us and we would sit there and exchange funny stories about him (and there were many). Matt is famous for his prowess at sleeping, so many jokes were made about how he was just having us on and taking advantage to get a prolonged kip. It was definitely not all doom and gloom, and there really was a fair amount of laughter to relieve the ever-present anxiety we were all feeling. It was heartwarming for us to see that nobody could talk about Matt without a smile on their face.

The winter of 2010/2011 was to be the coldest and snowiest for years. On the first Tuesday (30th November), we woke up to snow. I really thought that just might be enough to cause Matt to wake up so that he could get his new skis out and test them. Unfortunately, even the prospect of fresh snow didn't make him stir from his deep sleep. Somehow, though, the snow made me feel better. Snow played such an important part in Matt's life and now here it was in London, in November. That was a rare event, so surely it must have been some sort of sign. As far as I was concerned, the world was definitely a better place with some snow in it.

*

Every day was much the same. The many machines by Matt's bed beeped away constantly, telling the nurses what was going on. All sorts of stuff was being pumped into him, and other stuff was being pumped out. The worst machine was the ICP (intracranial pressure) monitor. As we all know, the brain is encased in the skull, with the skull protecting the brain. Normally, it fits pretty snugly and all is well. However, in the case of severe trauma where there is bleeding and bruising, the brain can swell and push against the skull, thereby causing further damage. If this happens, the doctors need to know so that they can intervene to relieve this pressure, hence the need for the 'bolt'. On the ICP monitoring machine, there are two parallel horizontal lines, and a line giving the pressure readings is being continually drawn between these lines. As long as that line stays between the two parallel lines, we're okay. However, every so often, there would be huge spikes. If they came back down again, we were still okay. If they stayed up, then Matt was in trouble. Nick was mesmerised by the machine and couldn't look away. It made for pretty stressful viewing, and sometimes it just became too much for him and he had to leave the ward. Conversely, I felt I needed to be there all the time, but I took the nurses' advice and didn't constantly look at those lines. As long as I was holding Matt's hand and willing him to live and passing positive energy through to him, I felt as if I was doing something. On those days when the ICPs just kept going up, I have to admit that we were all terrified.

Tim was very upset and just wanted his brother back. Tears poured down his face as he told me how much he needed Matt. "I miss my brother. I know he's younger than me, but *I* look up to *him*. He's so much better than me and it's not fair that this should happen to him. I don't understand why, what harm has he ever done to anyone? Everyone loves him." Of course, it wouldn't have been any better had it happened to him rather than Matt. We loved both our sons.

Unfortunately, no one knows why bad things happen to good people, they just do. It was, however, strangely comforting to hear Tim admit to his feelings for his brother. In my experience, young men are not normally that open about their feelings, but at times like these, all emotions are heightened and laid bare.

We were introduced to the Family Relations lady, who gave us a booklet about Intensive Care. It was probably the same one that they had given us on Day 1, and I still didn't like it – especially the bit informing us that *sometimes patients may die*. This was something that I really didn't need to hear. All I was interested in were positive stories about people who had defied the odds. Unfortunately, no one would tell me any. No one dared to raise our hopes. All we were told was that they couldn't tell us anything and every case is different. I didn't want to be told the bad things. I knew them already and they were in my head all the time. I wanted some optimism, hope, positivity – why was no one willing to give us any? Basically, I just wanted someone to lie to me and tell me that it would all be fine.

For me, what makes a severe brain injury especially unique is that it is as if you have two people lying in the bed in the ICU. It all depends on who's looking at them. The medical staff see a seriously injured person lying unconscious, unable to give them any indication of the sort of person they were before the accident. The family and friends do see the seriously injured person, but what they also see is their son/daughter/father/mother/friend and clearly remember how they were just hours or days before. That will be the person they focus on – the pre-accident person – and that will be the person they want to see again. That's all they're interested in. Somehow, the professionals and the family need to come together and understand each other's point of view. It's a tricky situation and I don't know the solution. I only know that I wasn't ready to listen to the professionals in those early days. I know for them it's a fine line between false hope and being realistic, but I desperately needed hope.

So, what if there really is no hope? I always say that, if it had become obvious that Matt would never recover, I would have accepted that and taken the advice of the neurologists. But would I really? Would we as a family have been able to do that? It's impossible to predict how anyone might react in such a dire situation. There's no manual or self-help website for this particular problem.

*

I soon saw my Chinese friend again. As before, she came purposefully marching in with her little case on wheels behind her, and as she sat beside me, she said very firmly, "You know that you and I have been chosen for this task. God has chosen us to face a trial and we will both win our trials. We just need to keep fighting." I quite liked the sound of that. I decided there and then that I would be a winner and that Matt was definitely a winner. He's the most competitive person I know and could never bear to lose. I will never know whether or not she went on to win her trial; I really hope she did.

I was more and more touched by the number of people turning up to see Matt. Everyone wanted to will him back to life. The constant trail of Matt's pals provided a refreshing lift for us all. They all had tales to tell – some of which I am not sure that I really wanted to know. I was especially horrified to hear of Matt skiing down some escalators. Maybe he had been lucky to have escaped serious injury until now. I also got rather more information than a mother needs regarding his success with the ladies. If you don't want all your secrets revealed to your nearest and dearest, don't go into a coma.

My brother's family were amazing. Sally cooked wonderful meals for us every night and John ran us around to and from the hospital. Charlie and Charlotte were there every evening telling us about their days and reminding us that normal life did still exist outside the hospital. Meanwhile, in the outside world, chaos reigned as snow fell across the country – I couldn't believe that Matt was missing this. He would have been so excited.

Our days were very much up and down. Those pesky ICPs were on the up, and they were worried that Matt might be having seizures so, as a precaution, he was put on anti-epilepsy drugs. Epileptic fits are not unusual soon after a severe head injury. It was so scary. My heart was once again pounding and we were told not to panic, but that was easier said than done. As usual, the brilliant nurses did their best to reassure us. Fortunately, when a CT scan didn't reveal any bad news, they decided to lower the sedation. This was a huge step and we took it as a sign of progress.

As Christmas was just around the corner, it was a welcome relief to hear the nurses planning their Christmas parties. One of Matt's nurses, Mark, was in charge of the Secret Santa. He was also a pretty good cook apparently and was planning what cake he was going to bake on his day off. In the middle of all these machines and medication, it was very comforting to discuss home baking, not that the nurses' attention was ever distracted very far from their patients. It was a constant routine of adjusting knobs, turning the patient, washing them, checking the ebb and flow of whatever was going through those pipes, monitoring heartbeats and ICPs.

From Day 5, tiny things began to happen. Matt moved his tongue – such excitement! We were also convinced that one eye was slightly open. This may have been our imaginations working overtime, but it gave a little ray of hope for us to cling on to and discuss at our nightly get-together at The Urban.

At some point during that first week, I decided that, just maybe, Matt wouldn't be able to make it out to France in time to start his job at the bar in Courchevel, so I rang the bar owners to explain what had happened. They were very understanding and hoped that maybe he would be able to join them a little later in the season, as indeed did I. I figured if the doctors didn't know how bad he might be when he woke up, then they didn't know how good he might be, either.

*

The Intensive Care Unit at The Royal London was a very large department consisting of various different wards. The beds were fairly crammed in. In Matt's section, there were beds lined up against the walls either side of the ward, and then Matt's bed was pushed into the middle with its head near the end wall, creating a sort of M-shape. I was told by one of his nurses that this was the section for the most seriously ill, which was alarming. It was not good to be top of the list of the most seriously ill in a place where everyone looked bad. Having said that, Matt actually looked fine if you ignored all the tubes going into him. Prior to his accident, he had been getting fit for skiing by jogging up and down the promenade in Bognor. Only two weeks before, we had returned from a lovely holiday in Mauritius, so he was looking tanned and fit. Sometimes, I foolishly thought that maybe they had it all wrong. If only they'd just switch off all those blasted machines, he would wake up, say, "Hello, Mum," and zap off to his job in France.

During the many hours that I sat there fervently believing that it would be all right, but also having to allow a tiny piece of me to acknowledge that it might not be, I took comfort from knowing one thing: Matt had lived his life to the max. He loved his lifestyle of travelling and pursuing his love of water and winter sports. It used to annoy me when friends asked me, "When is he going to get a proper job?" They *were* proper jobs, and thank goodness he had lived the life that he wanted to live. If this was to be it, then he had not wasted a single minute doing things he didn't want to. He was an intelligent young man who did well at school, but drove his teachers completely around the bend because his heart wasn't really in the academic side of things. Sport was his overwhelming interest. At the end of his sixth-form year, the pupils all voted for their peers in different categories. Matt won the vote for 'Most Sporty' and 'Funniest' and that just about sums him up. Whenever he and his friends were around, the house was full of laughter. If he was talking on the phone, every few minutes you would hear an explosion of laughter. It was this zest for life that made me believe that he would come back to us. Maybe all his friends were right and he was simply taking advantage of the situation to have a good sleep.

As it became obvious that Matt was not going to wake up anytime soon, they decided to replace the pipe that was going into his mouth to help him breathe with a tracheostomy. This is a pipe that goes straight into the throat and would be much more comfortable. It involves a small operation, as a hole needs to be cut in the throat. Such was the pressure on the staff in the unit that this had to be delayed as there was simply no one available to do it. In such a busy unit full of seriously ill patients, life and death procedures will always take priority over the more routine ones. When Matt did eventually get this done, it was so much better to see him without all the tapes and tubes that had obscured his face. However, the fact that they had felt it necessary to do this reinforced the message that he was in a deep coma with no signs as yet of coming out of it.

Our roller-coaster ride in the ICU continued for eleven days altogether. Evenings were spent answering the many phone calls from concerned friends. I was delighted to hear that his boss, Rich, from the Scilly Isles, was coming over to visit, and also his best friend from France, Greg. I was convinced that Matt would be so surprised to hear their voices that he would immediately wake up. Unfortunately, that didn't happen. Rich emerged looking very serious and concerned, and when Greg came out, he just burst into tears. I told him it would all be okay, because I couldn't really contemplate the alternative. As time went on, as well as Matt's friends whom I already knew, I got to know a whole load of new ones. The one thing that they all had in common was that they were all lovely people. It's just a shame that Matt had to land on his head before I was introduced to them.

Because the doctors can't really tell you much that is positive, I decided to adopt the ostrich approach – bury my head in the sand and not even consider any bad options. However, after eleven days with Matt still in a coma, I finally plucked up the courage to ask the nurse if this was quite normal.

"Umm, I know Matt has been unconscious for a while now, but you hear about people all the time who are in a coma for months and then wake up and are absolutely fine. That's true, isn't it? We shouldn't really be worried yet, should we?" There, I'd asked the question, then came the reply:

"Unfortunately, we have no idea of when Matt might wake up or even if he will ever wake up. As the consultant has told you, it's just a waiting game."

Well, that really wasn't the answer I was hoping for. Why had I dared to lift my stupid head out of the sand? I can't even begin to describe how it felt to be told that. I knew they had to be realistic, but just the tiniest hope of a chink of light at the end of the tunnel would have been good. My head went straight back into the sand and remained firmly there. It was a very long time before I asked any more questions.

Day 11 proved to be significant in more ways than one. It had been quite easy contacting school, university and sailing friends for Team Matt, but it was proving difficult to get hold of his ski buddies. I had met a few of them but only knew their first names. At the scene of the accident, the police had taken away Matt's possessions, including his phone, so I didn't know how to contact them. Then Tim suddenly remembered that when they had been to the London Freeze in October (a ski/snowboard event), he had met Financial Dave and his friend, who had given Tim his business card. Bingo! We called Dave 'Financial Dave' as he worked in finance, and to differentiate him from the other Daves Matt knew. I managed to relay a message to him via the friend, which started the ball rolling. Financial Dave rang me and said that he would tell Pilot Pete (Matt's fighter pilot mate from Courchevel). Apparently, Pilot Pete was very organised and would have everyone else's numbers. The ski set subsequently also proved to be brilliant friends who pitched in with their support and further swelled the numbers of Team Matt.

The other major event on Day 11 was Matt having the bolt removed from his skull, as the doctors felt that his pressures had settled. He was ready to be moved to the High Dependency Unit where he would still receive a high degree of care, but not as intensive every minute of the day. We should have seen this as a positive thing, but we didn't. In the ICU, he was watched over one-on-one for 24 hours a day. We had complete trust in the nurses there and just wanted Matt to stay there until he was completely better, which was completely unrealistic, of course.

Matt had been getting infections and his temperature frequently soared, so he had to be wrapped in a refrigerated blanket to cool him down. This was something that couldn't be done to a conscious person; the shock would be too great. To us, he hardly seemed well enough to leave this closely monitored environment. The HDU had only one nurse per four patients, as opposed to one nurse per patient in the ICU. We all felt very nervous.

Nevertheless, later on that afternoon, we said goodbye to all those wonderful nurses and doctors in the ICU. We left behind that strange waiting room full of the only other people who we felt could truly understand what we were going through. With great fear and trepidation, we entered the world of the High Dependency Unit.

FIVE

FROM ICU TO HDU

The Royal London Hospital was founded in 1740, although at that time it was simply the London Hospital. It wasn't until 1757 that it moved to Whitechapel, and in 1990 it was granted its royal title by Queen Elizabeth II. Back in 2010, it was a rather scruffy, rundown building, but you could still recognise it as once having been a very grand, impressive place, full of character; a redbrick building with an imposing Georgian façade, featuring five arches as you approached its main doors. Originally, these arches were also reflected above the entrance with imposing arched windows. However, by 2010, only one of those windows remained, the rest having been replaced at some point by less decorative rectangular windows. The imposing Roman-style columns and triangular pediment remained, giving the impression of a Roman temple. I imagine that the original architect had maybe thought of it as a temple of healing.

Its situation in London's East End meant that it was at the heart of all the hustle and bustle of that busy area. Coming out of the tube station, you were immediately immersed in the busy market stalls that lined the side of the road opposite the hospital. The first impression was that you had somehow landed in an eastern bazaar. It was a complete contrast to the world we were about to enter every day – the quiet, ordered world of the hospital ward.

Looming up behind that old building was what was destined to be a state-of-the-art 21st-century hospital, all in gleaming blue glass and seventeen storeys tall. If Matt had had his accident one year later, that is where he would have been. However, we will always have a soft spot for the original building. It is steeped in history, and if its walls could talk, what tales it would have to tell! Thomas Barnado (as in Dr Barnado's) had been a medical student there. Joseph Merrick, aka the Elephant Man, had been a patient there. Rather more infamously, Jack the Ripper claimed one of his early victims in the hospital grounds, which made it a bit of a spooky place after dark.

The present-day Royal London is one of the capital's leading trauma and emergency care centres. So, although Matt was very unlucky to have had such a serious accident, he was extremely fortunate to have ended up in the very best place possible in order to give him the very best chance of recovery.

*

When we arrived in the High Dependency Unit, we were pleasantly surprised to see how modern it was, compared to the rest of the hospital. Apparently, that part of the building used to house the administration offices. Now, following their move over to the new hospital, the space had been refurbished to provide a light, airy modern unit – quite a contrast to the overcrowded, rather scruffy area of the ICU.

By now, we had worked out that a brain injury is very different from any other injury. There was no medical intervention available beyond the initial stabilisation processes. Unlike a broken bone, it couldn't be fixed by surgery. Unlike a failing heart or kidney, it couldn't be replaced. Unlike a disease, there were no drugs available to treat it. A scan can reveal the extent of bruising and bleeding around the brain, but the only way of really knowing what damage has been done is to wait until the patient wakes up and then find out what they can or cannot do. No one can yet see right into the brain to work out what is going on in there. Many conditions are only revealed after death by performing an autopsy, which is a bit late for the person involved.

Could you imagine turning up to A&E with a broken arm, only to be told that, "You'll just have to wait and see what happens"? It might heal; it might not. Only time will tell. That is more or less what happens with a brain injury.

Tim and I felt very upset as we stood by Matt's bed. Without his own dedicated nurse at the end of his bed, he seemed very vulnerable. He was still all wired up, and his bed was right in front of the nurses' station, where he was closely monitored by a bank of machines. We couldn't help but feel very nervous, though. It was an unfamiliar place to us. Matt's breathing wasn't right. It sounded strange and uneven, and his skin was covered in blotches. Tim and I both ended up in tears. We just wanted to take Matt and run straight back to the ICU, which had seemed such a safe, protective environment. Of course, we would soon learn that we were in equally safe hands in the HDU.

The visiting hours were shorter in the HDU – 2pm until 7pm – as opposed to 12pm to 9pm in the ICU. As we left for the evening that first day, a very smart young man went dashing past us and I just had a feeling that he might be Matt's pal from Courchevel, Financial Dave, and indeed it was. Although he'd missed the official visiting hours, they kindly let him in for half an hour anyway.

After his visit, he joined us in The Urban and we soon realised that we had found yet another solid supporter for Team Matt. While we were there, another Courchevel pal, Ben, rang to say he would be coming up soon with two more friends, Freddie and Amy. They had all been with Matt on his epic cycle ride back from Courchevel. Pilot Pete was also now in the picture, so Team Matt was continuing to grow. Long-lost friends from schooldays were also turning up. They all added to the huge amount of positive energy surrounding Matt. I just hoped he could somehow sense it.

The 8th December was Matt's first full day in the HDU. Nick and I had recently moved into a flat belonging to John and Sally. As things had settled down slightly, we decided that we could now have the dogs with us, so Nick had gone down to West Sussex to collect them.

Tim and I went to see Matt on our own and were met by the sister in charge of the ward, who was yet another lovely Irish lady called Grainne (pronounced 'Gronya'). The nurses would frequently joke about Matt waking up with an Irish accent, which would be fine with me; I love an Irish accent. She sat us down and explained everything to us. Matt was away from the ward having an electroencephalogram (EEG) to see what was going on in his head. An EEG is a recording of brain activity. Special sensors are attached to the head and are linked by wires to a computer. The brain activity is shown as wavy lines on the recording, which can then be examined and analysed by a doctor. In Matt's case, they never seemed to reveal very much at all. Apparently, his temperature and raised heartbeat were due to 'storming', which is part of the healing process. I had always thought of brain storming as a group of movers and shakers sat around a table coming up with brilliant ideas. This, though, was a very different sort of brain storming.

'Sympathetic Storming' is a common complication following a TBI and is associated with a set of distressing and uncomfortable symptoms, including elevated body temperature, increased heart rate and perspiration. It is caused by excessive, uncontrolled activation of the Sympathetic Nervous System (SNS). The SNS is overstimulated and the bloodstream is flooded with chemicals normally associated with stress. The storming can take a seemingly peaceful individual into a state of chaos. This increased activity is thought to be a stage of recovery from a severe TBI and can occur within the first 24 hours after injury or up to several weeks later. It usually affects patients with a Glasgow Coma Scale score of between 3 and 8. Untreated storming can increase the risk of secondary injury to the brain due to the increased risks of cardiac arrest, cerebral haemorrhage or elevated cerebral temperature. It is, therefore, very important to get it under control, and this is usually achieved with the use of medication.

At the time, I only heard the bit about it 'being part of the healing process'. I remained blissfully unaware of the very real dangers involved in the process until long after the event, which is just as well, as things were going to get a lot worse before they got better. There are occasions when ignorance really is bliss and I was getting better and better at ignoring a lot of things.

Grainne also explained to us what might happen in the future. She gently asked,

"Has anyone explained to you what to expect in the future?"

Tim and I looked at each other and I mumbled, "Well, not really. We've just been told to wait and see if he wakes up first."

"You need to realise that he could wake up as a very different person. He may not be the Matt you are used to. People often have a completely different personality after a TBI. He could be very aggressive and you need to be prepared for that."

I wasn't enjoying hearing any of that, but then she continued, "Once he is well enough to leave hospital, there will then be a long period of rehab. He will most likely need to relearn a lot of his basic life skills. You have to realise that it's not like it is in the movies. He won't leap out of bed and just get on with life."

"That's what I was rather hoping for," I said, before once again bursting into tears. Any mention of rehab really, really upset me. I think I was picturing some sort of dark Victorian asylum-like place, and I couldn't bear to think of Matt there.

*

One day, Matt was being looked after by a very jolly male nurse who declared that he would make a Tottenham supporter out of him. It seemed as if Matt heard that as he blinked several times, obviously in sheer panic as a diehard Manchester United supporter. Later, he also squeezed my hand when requested. We were seeing the first tiny glimmerings of awareness. When a doctor from the ICU came down to give Matt a pain test, he grimaced in response and she declared that to be "Brilliant!" It appeared that his GCS scores were going up. Remember, 'flexion, withdrawal to pain' scores 4 on the motor response section of the GCS, as opposed to the 1 that he originally scored with his complete lack of any reaction.

Matt had a lot of visitors that day, including his friend Sam who came and 'chatted' with him for a long time. Sam instantly declared how much more he preferred the HDU to the ICU, where he'd been on several occasions, but had never been able to stay long as he always felt a bit faint after about 10 minutes. He was not the only one affected like that by the ICU. Some people just couldn't face it at all. It certainly wasn't the jolliest place to hang out in. Sam's visit was followed by that of Darryl and Chris who kept peering at Matt, trying to figure out if he could see them or not. Nick arrived at the end of visiting hours after his trip down to the south coast to retrieve our dogs, and was rewarded with a hand squeeze from Matt. Afterwards, we went back down to the car, where Bobby and Benji were waiting to come back to Highgate with us. Things were definitely ever so slightly on the up.

As we sat next to Matt's bed in the HDU, we could clearly hear the air ambulance helicopter taking off from or landing on the roof as it continued to bring yet more seriously injured patients into the hospital. We knew that some other family was about to get that awful telephone call and have their lives turned upside down. It was so strange to think about these scenarios that only a few weeks ago, I would never have given a moment's thought to.

The first week in the HDU was a sort of transition point for all of us. Now that Matt appeared to be out of immediate danger, we tried to get back some sort of normality into our lives. As the dogs were with us, instead of sitting around fretting all morning, I could now take them for a walk around Highgate village, which was looking particularly idyllic at Christmas time with all the lovely decorations, and the little squares all had their beautiful Christmas trees. It was another reminder that normal life was still going on in the wider world.

Various celebrities live locally and one day I spotted the actor Jude Law in the High Street. Matt had had a brief encounter with him once during his career as a windsurf instructor, and I felt very tempted to ask him to join Team Matt. However, my better judgement took hold and I realised that he probably wouldn't remember Matt and would think I was some sort of crazy woman, so I held back. I did count seeing him as a good omen, though. I would cling on to anything that I could interpret as a good omen or a positive sign. At times, these were very few and far between.

In the HDU, Matt seemed to have more of a routine. His life was busier, or at least as busy as you can be in a coma. He had started to have a little bit of physiotherapy. Physiotherapy when you are unconscious and a deadweight involves at least a couple of physiotherapists in order to haul you around and move various bits of you. He was also frequently turned by the nurses in order to avoid bedsores. He had a tube put down his throat at regular intervals to clear out his lungs, which seemed to be a particularly unpleasant procedure. Usually, when all these things were happening, the curtains were drawn around his bed and we were asked to wait outside. This was because it was actually quite upsetting to see. When Matt was lying horizontal in bed he looked quite peaceful, but when he was moved around you got a real sense of how truly disabled he was – a completely floppy young man unable to do anything. We knew that if he remained like that, we would do our best to deal with it, but we prayed that we wouldn't have to.

Somehow, we had to try and remain positive.

SIX

MATT ENTERS THE TWILIGHT ZONE

On Day 14, we had a breakthrough. On our arrival, we were met by an excited Grainne.

"I have to tell you that the physios have had Matt out of bed, sitting in a special chair. The best news is that he was responding to commands. When they asked him to open his eyes or stick out his tongue, he did it! And then he did a 'thumbs-up'. I think he's going to be all right."

On hearing that, Nick just broke down in tears – all the pent-up emotion came pouring out. Tim and I weren't far behind.

Matt was now able to squeeze our hands and do a thumbs-up (or 'tums-up' as Grainne pronounced it in her Irish accent) on a regular basis. The thumbs-up became his party piece for visitors. It was very strange to witness him doing these things sometimes, despite not being really conscious; yet he was obviously aware on some level now.

I have since discovered that this odd twilight zone is known as post-traumatic amnesia or PTA. It is a higher level of consciousness than a coma, but less than full consciousness. People can be fully awake during PTA, but be very confused about things like dates and time and what is actually happening. They will not be able to store memories and they can be either agitated or passive. After the PTA has passed, they usually remember nothing about it. Matt was only ever partially awake, and then only very rarely, and he definitely remembers nothing about any of it, even those few moments when he did briefly appear to be understanding and responding quite lucidly. These are known as 'memory islands' and indicate that the patient may be emerging from PTA.

PTA is another tool used as an indicator of the severity of a brain injury using the Westmead PTA Scale, which measures the duration of the period of PTA, and it is worked out as follows:

PTA less than 5 minutes = very mild injury
PTA between 5 to 60 minutes = mild injury
PTA between 1 to 24 hours = moderate injury
PTA between 1 to 7 days = severe injury
PTA greater than 7 days = very severe injury

As with the Glasgow Coma Scale, Matt managed to achieve the worst scores, as his PTA lasted for several weeks.

We always talk about Matt having been in a coma for 6 weeks, but I suppose in retrospect he was in a coma for about 3 to 4 weeks and then in a state of post-traumatic amnesia for about another 3 weeks. At times, it was hard to tell the difference, as mostly he was still fast asleep and never really showed any signs of knowing what was going on, apart from one memorable occasion when his friend Sam came to visit him. He suddenly became extremely animated and was smiling as they talked about football. I say 'talked', but he couldn't actually speak. It was all done through thumbs up, nodding and shaking the head on his part. I was so excited, I thought that was it – problem over. However, he soon lapsed back into sleep and non-activity. I realise now that it must have been a memory island. It was not at all surprising that his most vivid memory island would involve football.

The day following the breakthrough day was not so good. Matt was running a high temperature, which was obviously causing the doctors great concern judging by all the tests they were doing, trying to find out what was going on. Once again, we were terrified. When Matt left the ICU, we assumed that we had left the worst behind us, but obviously that was not the case. When someone is already so weak, they really don't need additional problems thrown at them. This was the roller-coaster ride we were now on, constantly up and down, up and down. Nick vividly remembers the consultant saying to us, "It's a long way back from this." I have no recollection of that, only of someone saying that, "We're fighting hard for him." I really had developed the fine art of only hearing what I wanted to hear and blanking out all the bad stuff. I don't think I was ever able to fully grasp exactly what was happening during that awful time. I was simply waiting for Matt to get better. Matt was now getting so many visitors that we had to issue a temporary ban while he got over this latest hurdle. Getting his temperature down seemed to be a priority and they were constantly taking blood samples and also doing chest X-rays. It just seemed to us as if his poor body was being assaulted as much as his brain. Fortunately, after a couple of days, he did manage to rally round. As if to celebrate his recovery, he managed to raise his arms about 2 inches above his bed. For us, this was the equivalent of Usain Bolt breaking another world record – it was huge.

In the bed next to him was an elderly lady with a very friendly daughter who always made a point of coming across to chat to Matt. She told us that she had arranged for a mass to be said for Matt in her church. It was very touching just how many people were saying prayers and lighting candles in their churches for him. When I was in the hospital shop that raises money for the air ambulance, the lady there told me that she too would light a candle for him. She herself had been in a coma in the ICU at the Royal London, and she told me that my son would be having wonderful dreams. I really hoped he was.

Matt's friends were all busy thinking up different tactics to try and wake Matt up. Darryl brought in a Manchester United book to read to him. Skier Ben brought in his laptop with Matt's favourite ski DVD on it, *Claim*. He was very excited when he saw me come in at the end of his visit. "Anne, I brought *Claim* in to watch with Matt and he was definitely watching it. We used to spend hours in Courchevel watching it over and over again. He really seemed to know what it was." Ben was smiling with delight and, there's one thing for sure, if Matt had been going to watch anything, it would have been that movie.

On 17th December, the snow returned to London. Highgate was really looking like a picture on a Christmas card now. It was a real feast for the senses walking the dogs in the cold and the snow. The crisp fresh air and picture-perfect surroundings provided a welcome contrast to the overheated hospital wards, and always managed to raise my spirits for a brief time.

Back at the Royal London, we continued to watch for any signs of progress. Slowly, different bits began to move: the odd toe wiggled, a finger moved, eyes opened briefly. Although his eyes were now occasionally open, they didn't seem to register anything. We had taken in toiletries for him and he was now regularly having his hair washed and a good bed bath. Surely that would make him feel better.

As time went on and Matt remained in his twilight zone, he appeared to be experiencing more pain and discomfort. He sometimes seemed really sad and even a bit grumpy. The plaster cast on his broken wrist was obviously very uncomfortable, as the skin would have been itching underneath it. However, any awareness of anything is regarded as a good thing, as it is a sign that the levels of consciousness are slowly rising.

*

On 19th December, we were just about to go to bed when the phone rang. It was someone from the hospital informing us that a bed had become available in the Intensive Care Unit in St Richard's Hospital, Chichester (our local hospital). They were intending to move Matt overnight. Nick nearly had a fit. There were severe weather warnings all over the TV and radio. The roads were treacherous with the snow and ice and there was no way we would allow our seriously ill son to be transported in such conditions. Mercifully, they did agree not to do it.

When we went in the next day, Grainne was furious that anyone had contemplated moving Matt overnight and assured us that it wouldn't happen like that next time. She did, however, explain to us that Matt no longer needed neurological intervention. There was nothing that the doctors or surgeons could do to improve the state of Matt's brain. It was now simply a matter of waiting while he slowly came to. This could be done just as effectively in an Intensive Care Unit in Chichester, while the bed in the HDU in London could be used more effectively for a patient in need of brain surgery or other specialist neurological services. That all made perfect sense, but we still wouldn't have wanted Matt driven down the A3 in the dead of night in such icy conditions. Now that the situation had been explained to us, we would be prepared next time.

Having missed that particular slot in Chichester, we had no idea when the next opportunity would be. The good news was that Grainne also informed us that there was an excellent Neurological Rehabilitation Unit in the grounds of St Richard's Hospital. This felt like a real piece of good fortune for us and, of course, especially for Matt.

That same day, I saw Matt in his 'special chair' for the first time. The special chair was a wheelchair with extra support for his head and neck and everything else. It was not a happy experience for me. It was quite shocking to see how thin, floppy and helpless he was. He was now obviously severely disabled and couldn't even hold his own head up. He had lost so much weight that he looked like a famine victim who you might see on a television appeal for Oxfam. It was just so awful to see a previously fit and healthy young man in such a poor state. He had no strength, no control and no awareness of anything. It was heartbreaking.

They had now started to wean him off his tracheostomy tube for short periods of time. This was the tube in his throat through which he was able to breathe. It would take a week or so, but once it was gone, he should be able to speak and eat by himself. I have to say at that time it was very difficult to imagine him being able to do any of those things – trachy tube or no trachy tube. As far as I was concerned, that would take a miracle, and we seemed to be a bit short of those.

At that stage, I was still setting deadlines in my head for Matt to wake up by, which was not a good idea. My first deadline had been my birthday, which was just a week after the accident. When, to my surprise, he did not wake up and stroll out of the hospital, I revised it to two weeks, which didn't work out, either. My next deadline was now looming – Christmas Day. That would be the fairytale ending – what a fantastic Christmas present for us all that would be.

Christmas Day 2010 was a very different sort of Christmas for us. We spent most of it sat by Matt's bed. There were no decorations in the HDU ward for fear of infection, in contrast to other parts of the hospital, which were quite festive and jolly. The patients had all been given little gifts from the nurses in the form of shower gels or shampoo. Needless to say, Matt didn't meet my Christmas Day deadline and remained resolutely out of it.

When we returned to the house that night, we discovered that Sally had made a supreme effort. She had somehow found the time to decorate the house beautifully and prepare the most delicious Christmas dinner. I have to say, even in those most unusual circumstances, we had a lovely evening. It was very special for us all to be together as a family and, once again, we found our spirits being lifted just by the kindness and support that surrounded us.

The days following Christmas saw Matt getting increasingly agitated. He had begun pulling at the various tubes that went into him, most notably the one in his nose through which he was fed. Sitting by his bed was no longer a quiet, passive affair. There was no point in taking a good book with me, as I had done previously. Now visiting involved a lot of wrestling and holding his hands down in order to prevent him from making a grab for his tubes. He was pretty good at it and quite cunning. He would slowly start moving his hand up, and then, when he thought no one was looking, he would make a lightening grab for them! We were informed that this agitation was a good thing, as it was yet another sign of his ever-increasing awareness.

"I don't think it will be long before he joins the mitten club," said one of the nurses with a smile on her face.

"What on earth is the mitten club?" asked Nick, intrigued by this club none of us had heard of.

"Oh, it's a very exclusive club for patients who are getting too lively and constantly trying to pull out their tubes. We put their hands into a big pair of mittens and tape them up so that they can't pull them off. It's then impossible for them to grab anything."

"Okay, well, that will be something for Matt to look forward to then."

Sure enough, on the 28th of December, Matt became a fully-fledged member of The Mitten Club. I think the mittens were actually a pair of padded oven gloves. It may well have been seen as a positive thing by the nurses, but it was actually quite upsetting to see someone you love flailing around in obvious distress as their efforts to pull out those annoying tubes were thwarted.

•

Soon, 2010 turned into 2011 and I found myself getting increasingly despondent and less positive about everything. I hated the way Matt's eyes were open, but there was nothing behind them. To coin a phrase, the lights were on, but nobody was at home. He had even graduated on to doing high fives with people now, but yet there was no real sign of life, no real animation. It was a very bizarre state to witness and difficult to describe. I just longed for a real smile of recognition, but there was nothing. Seeing Matt every single day without him really being there made me miss him more than if he had simply been away somewhere for a few weeks. His body was there, but his spirit and personality had gone. As the days went on like that, it became harder to remain hopeful, despite all my initial resolve to remain positive. It just seemed as if he had too much of a mountain to climb.

Tim, meanwhile, set off for Switzerland to start his new job as a ski instructor. It was obviously very difficult for him to say goodbye to his brother, and he really didn't want to go at all, but we persuaded him that there was nothing more he could do in London and, if he was working, it would be one less thing for us to worry about.

Our intense roller-coaster ride continued, as during the first week of the New Year, Matt developed a lung infection and needed a bronchoscopy to sort it out. This is a procedure where a short thin tube with a mini camera built into its tip is inserted into the airways to examine them. As before, in a hospital with so many life and death emergencies, it was not easy to find time for more routine things such as this, and that in turn was delaying having his tracheostomy tube removed, and also delaying his physiotherapy treatment. It was a nightmare. Much to our relief, he was able to have the bronchoscopy a couple of days later and they were able to decide on an appropriate course of treatment.

•

As often happened on our roller-coaster ride, after a down moment there would frequently be an up. The next up moment was on the 7th of January and it was quite amazing as far as I was concerned. I arrived to visit Matt to find his pal Darryl there. One of the nurses had given him a small sachet of Matt's food supplement to sample. Darryl is a big guy, 6' 4" or more, and he looked fairly comical sipping away through a straw from the small sachet. To add to the comedy factor, we proceeded to have a rather silly conversation about Bobby and Benji. Sadly, I can't remember the details of this conversation, but it must have been funny, as at some point during this daft conversation we looked down at Matt and realised that he was actually laughing at us! At that particular moment in time, that seemed to me to be THE most exciting thing that I had ever, ever seen in my entire life.

That was indeed a turning point. Matt really did seem to be slowly coming to. He started smiling and laughing and doing lots of thumbs-ups and high fives with his visitors. Not all of the time; often he would slip away again, but there were definite signs of an active, thinking brain there now. Grainne told us that in her opinion, she expected him to make a good physical recovery, but she thought that he might have difficulty with speaking. They had tried him with a speaking valve, but so far, he had failed to produce any words. I didn't worry too much about that, as it was impossible to think that Matt would not talk again. He always has plenty to say.

On day 46 (10th January), we had another major highlight. I was with Matt on my own when one of the regular nurses, Sarah, came up to the bed. "Matt, do you have any pain anywhere today?"

He nodded very solemnly.

"Can you show me where the pain is?"

Another nod as he lifted up his hand and pointed to me and broke out into a huge grin.

Sarah and I both looked at each other in amazement and then burst out laughing.

"Did you see that? Matt made a joke! His first post-accident joke," I spluttered. I had not been expecting that. Looked like he was going to be just fine.

The next day, his trachy tube was at last removed, leaving a hole that would heal in time. He had had this in for a lot longer than they would have liked, but as always, due to the extreme pressure they have on their resources, there had been no one available to do it before then.

Visiting time was now getting to be more and more like a game of charades, with his visitors having to try and guess what Matt was trying to say. It was certainly a lot more entertaining for everyone now after several weeks of very one-sided passive visiting. There was a lot of signalling from Matt and we would write down various words to see if any of them might be what he was trying to say. It was often extremely frustrating for poor old Matt as he failed to get his message across. He would inevitably just shrug and give up.

When I left the HDU on the 11th of January 2011, although I didn't realise it at the time, it was to be for the last time. We were given no warning of Matt's imminent departure, so weren't able to say goodbye and thank you to all the wonderful men and women who had cared so diligently for our son. Over the previous couple of weeks, they had shared in our excitement at the slowly increasing amount of awareness and movement we had been witnessing. We could see that they were genuinely pleased for us.

The treatment Matt had received there must have run into I don't know how many tens of thousands of pounds and yet, thanks to our wonderful National Health Service, it hadn't cost us a penny. I honestly believe that, had we had the fortune of Bill Gates himself, we could not have bought better treatment. Maybe the NHS can seem to be a bit slow and unreliable if you're waiting for a routine operation, but if you are seriously ill or injured, it will not let you down. It is a most impressive service, staffed by wonderfully dedicated people to whom we will be forever grateful. The words just don't exist that could properly express how grateful we are to them.

As well as the wonderful staff, we also left behind the other patients whose fates we will never know. In particular, there was a young Albanian man in the next bed who had also fallen from a height. He was about the same age as Matt with a dedicated band of friends constantly by his side, including a devoted girlfriend. He, too, stubbornly refused to wake up. There was also a young Chinese man who just lay there, day after day, never moving, never having any visitors. There was a young man who had been hit by a bus, who continued to be very much up and down. I wonder what happened to them all. And why were they all young men?

According to statistics, every year in the UK, there are between 10,000 and 20,000 severe traumatic brain injuries, and men are twice as likely as women to sustain these injuries. The group most at risk is 15-24-year-old males. This would certainly fit in with what we saw in the Royal London and is a pattern that seems to be repeated the world over. Studies in the USA and Australia are in line with these observations. They conclude that this is due to various factors such as:

- inexperience with new situations, such as driving
- desire for experimentation and thrill-seeking (particularly in relation to alcohol and drugs)
- risk-taking tendency
- strong influence of peers
- overconfidence in their own abilities and a sense of invulnerability

That would all appear to make sense to me.

When I look back, I realise that this six-week period was like no other that I have ever experienced or ever will experience again (hopefully). It was a time of acute anxiety, but also a very unique time. We saw things we never want to see again – people dying, people in the depths of despair and grief. Fortunately, we also saw one family wildly celebrating the rapid recovery of a loved one, which gave us all hope. We stood in awe as the wonderful medical staff performed miracles every day. They will have saved countless other lives since then, but we will always remember them for saving our son's life.

We experienced so many acts of kindness and friendship from Matt's friends, our friends, and even complete strangers.

During those few weeks, we grew much closer to my brother and his family as we spent time with them in Highgate. As with most families, under normal circumstances, we would all be busy doing our own thing, but for those few weeks they took care of us and supported us and, despite the circumstances, gave us a wonderful Christmas.

It seemed strangely appropriate to me that, as Matt lay fighting for his life, it should be one of the coldest, snowiest winters in years. He didn't make it out to the snow that year, so the snow came to him. London looked wonderful under its white blanket and that was also comforting, and I somehow knew that it would be all right in the end.

Never again will I see London as just a big city. It is so much more than that. It *is* a big city, but one with a huge heart and many caring people.

SEVEN

BACK IN THE LAND OF THE LIVING

On Wednesday the 12th of January 2011, it had been 48 days since Matt had fallen so spectacularly through the roof with such devastating consequences. It started uneventfully enough with me walking the dogs, pootling around the flat and killing time until I could set off on my daily journey to visit Matt. Nick had gone to Geneva on business, as now that the immediate crisis was over he felt he could resume his work.

At 10.30am, I received a call to say that Matt was being transferred to Chichester that morning. This time, we were prepared for it to happen with very little warning, and I was quite happy. Matt was definitely beginning to re-enter the land of the living, albeit rather slowly. We knew there was an excellent rehabilitation unit there, which would give him the very best chance of getting back to full health, or as close as possible. The sooner he could get started with full-on physiotherapy, speech and language therapy, and any other therapies they might have on offer, the better. It was also slightly scary, as we were about to face the moment of truth. Now that Matt was more or less awake, we were on the verge of finding out how he would react to his new situation. Will he have changed? Will he be angry, depressed, or aggressive as they warned us he might be? Only time would tell, and that time was very close now. This was our 'Sliding Doors' moment – which door would Matt decide to go through?

It's quite amazing how much junk you can accumulate in just seven weeks, so I took a leaf out of Matt's packing manual and just threw everything into bags and then into the car, together with Bobby and Benji. On the journey down, Grainne rang to say that Matt had gone off in great humour and given them a big 'tums-up'. I certainly felt a lot better on my journey back down to Chichester than I had felt all those weeks ago on my way up to London with Nick. Maybe now we would at last be allowed a little bit of hope.

Matt's new home was going to be St Richard's Hospital in Chichester. Now that he was without his trachy tube, he no longer needed specialist care, so he was going to an ordinary ward until a bed became available in the rehab unit. His new visiting hours were 3pm to 5pm and 6.30pm to 9pm, and I made sure that I was there for the 6.30 visit. As before, when he had been moved from Intensive Care to the High Dependency Unit, it all seemed strange and unfamiliar, as of course it was. The big difference this time was that Matt would now be able to register his surroundings. He still couldn't speak and his left side seemed to have reverted to being completely immobile, despite having previously shown small movements, but at least he was awake. He had absolutely no recollection of the ambulance journey down or anything else to do with his stay in London.

He looked very sad and lonely in his little metal hospital bed. It was a far cry from the all-singing, all-dancing high-tech bed in the Royal London. He had lost over 20 kilos in weight and, as he had got thinner and thinner, his eyes seemed to have got bigger and bigger in his head and he gazed at us with a doleful expression. However, he had obviously grabbed the attention of two of the young nurses who were fussing around him.

"Hello! You must be Mum," said one of them. "Don't you worry about Matt. We're taking good care of him."

"Yes, I can see that."

"We've ordered him a new bed, which will be much better for him. It's one that you can adjust. He probably had one of those in London."

"Yes, he did. Thanks for doing that. How's he settling in?"

"I've been singing to him!" piped up the second one. "I can't get him to join in with me, though."

Matt looked at me with a rueful sort of a smile on his face and rolled his eyes up to the heavens, but I could see that he was going to be very well looked-after. Unfortunately, I couldn't stay for too long, as I needed to pick Nick up from the station. I was determined to be back there on the dot of three the next day. Now that Matt was fully conscious, he must also be very confused about how he ended up there.

As I went to bed that night, I thought about Matt's bed number 6 in Ward AW4 at the Royal London. Someone else would now be playing out their personal drama in that bed. They should be reassured that they were in the very best place, with the very best doctors and nurses caring for them.

The next day, Matt had a couple of VIP visitors: Rich (his boss from the Scilly Isles) and his wife, Amelia. They had been on their way to visit him in London but had had to divert to Chichester instead. As Matt couldn't speak, the hospital had provided him with picture cards and they spent a couple of hours 'chatting' with the aid of these cards. They were much better at it than I was. Rich, who had last seen Matt in the ICU, was very happy and excited about Matt's progress. Amelia, who was seeing him for the first time since his accident, was very upset after the visit. The last time she had seen him was back in September when he had been an extremely fit, lively and funny young man. Quite a contrast to the non-speaking, weak and skinny fellow she was seeing on that day.

While they were with Matt, Nick and I took the opportunity to visit the Donald Wilson Neurological Rehabilitation Centre, which was located within the hospital grounds. Immediately, all my fears and apprehension regarding rehab were dispelled. It is a modern, bright, airy building with a very positive feel. There was a waiting list for beds at the unit, but we hoped it wouldn't be too long before Matt joined them as a patient.

Meanwhile, at home, life was slowly getting back to normal. I had come home to a huge pile of abandoned ironing dating from our pre-accident holiday in Mauritius. That now seemed a world away. Matt had been with us then, playing tennis and golf, swimming, sailing and full of life and energy. We just had to believe that one day he would once again be able to do all those things. I couldn't help but smile to myself as I remembered how Matt and I used to swim out to the bathing platform and he would coach me in the art of the 'corkscrew 360' – a ski trick. Needless to say, I was hopeless at it, but we had fun. On another occasion, he followed a hobbling Nick back to the room, very keen to tell me how his dad had attempted to intercept a lob on the tennis court and had fallen back in a particularly hilarious fashion. He was grinning like a Cheshire cat and could barely tell me for laughing. All very typical Matt – just enjoying life and seeing the funny side of everything.

As always, the nurses in the ward were brilliant and were very aware of the fact that Matt was a young man in a ward full of old men. Consequently, he was rather spoilt and they allowed us to stay a little bit longer than was strictly allowed for visiting, and they encouraged us to bring in food for Matt as he wouldn't eat the hospital food. This was hardly surprising, as in the course of one day he had gone from being fed liquid through a tube to suddenly being presented with 'normal' food. I didn't think his system was quite ready for that yet, so we prepared him liquidised meals in order to slowly wean him back to eating solid food. Little by little, he began to eat more and we hoped that he would soon begin to put on some much-needed weight. He is 6' 1" and now weighed less than 55kg. His pre-coma weight had been 75kg. I have to admit that Nick and I did get a little competitive in the meal stakes, competing to see which one of us could prepare the best received meals. I like to think it ended in a draw.

We also took him in a small portable DVD player so that he could watch films. It was obvious that he was going to be very spoilt over the next few months as we tried to make sure that he would feel that it really had been the right decision on his part to finally wake up.

Unfortunately, during the first week in this ward, Matt definitely slumped. Even visits from friends didn't seem to raise his spirits much. We were desperate for him to get over the road into the rehab unit to start his activities. He received a little bit of therapy on the ward but, as usual, resources were spread very thinly and it wasn't enough. The consultant from the Donald Wilson Neurological Rehabilitation Unit came across to visit and assess him and said that he felt quite optimistic about Matt's chance of a good recovery. Yes! Yes! Yes! Someone had actually used the word optimistic in relation to Matt's recovery. He also thought that he would be joining them in the unit within a couple of weeks, which was very good news indeed.

*

On day 53, Matt spoke for the first time since November! It was strange to think that I had spent nearly every single day since the 27th of November with Matt, and during that time he had been completely silent. He was trying to whisper something and eventually succeeded. He said, very quietly, "I don't think I'll be in here forever." Again, at the time, it seemed like one of the most exciting moments of my life.

Tim, who was on a brief visit from Switzerland, heard it too. We just grinned at each other. I replied, "I don't think you will be, either!" Hardly very profound, but he'd rather taken me by surprise and I didn't have time to come up with a better line.

That was all he said until we were once again leaving the ward the next day when he said, "Say hi to the dogs." From then on, he gradually began to say more and more.

The return of his speech was not like a toddler learning to speak; it was more like someone learning a foreign language. He'd have a go at putting sentences together, but he would often get the words in the wrong order or even use completely the wrong word. I remember him once asking me if I had seen the 'goal of the munch' on TV. He obviously meant goal of the month. Fortunately for all of us, he still had his sense of humour and would join in the laughter when he realised he'd said completely the wrong thing.

As he began to talk, it became very apparent that his short-term memory had gone. He constantly repeated things and also got obsessed by certain things. His main obsession was skiing. There were three things that he constantly demanded:

- I want to get out of here.
- I want the plaster off my arm.
- I want to go skiing!

On day 57, he finally had one of his wishes granted when he had the cast removed, which he then decided to give to Tim. Bearing in mind that it had been on his arm since the 27th of November, it did stink a bit. I think Tim was, nevertheless, thrilled to have been chosen for this unique gift.

His friends continued to come visiting, even though Chichester was well out of the way for most of them. Matt could not believe it when I told him how many people had been to see him. At the back of my diary, I had got all of his visitors to write messages to him. I read these aloud to him and he sat there grinning from ear to ear, as most of them were very funny and cheeky. Once again, it hit me just how important it is to have friends at times like this.

Now that he was speaking again, he was able to surprise people by phoning them on my mobile. He was not yet allowed his own phone, as it was vital for him to rest and to avoid overstimulation. The odd surprise call on my phone was permissible, though. As you might imagine, some of the reactions were quite emotional when people realised who it was on the other end of the phone. There certainly was the odd tear. His sense of humour had returned after that brief grumpy interlude and he seemed to realise just how lucky he was to still be alive and he was now determined to appreciate every second of every day – much like he had always done really.

One of his friends from the Scilly Isles had somehow arranged for a signed photo from Jacob Wester to be sent to him. Jacob is one of Matt's ski heroes and he had written a special message for Matt on the photo – *Welcome back, Matt*. Matt was very excited and told everyone about it. Every passing nurse and doctor was summoned over by Matt, who would then ask them, "Have I shown you my photo of my favourite skier and his message?"

The problem was that, due to his short-term memory problems, he was calling over the same nurses and doctors again and again and again. They would reply through clenched teeth, "Yes, just a few times!" I think all the nurses and doctors will probably remember the name Jacob Wester for quite a long time to come.

His recovering brain soon began to play tricks on him. One evening, the nurse on night duty called to say that she was a little concerned about Matt. He was getting frightened at night and seeing small children floating around. He was also worrying a lot about his memory and how he couldn't remember things. His poor battered brain was still very confused and he wanted to know what had happened to him. Although he had been told many times, he was unable to retain the information due to his memory problems. He was worried about his car in case he had had a car accident. We reassured him time and time again that it wasn't a car accident and his car was fine, but then he would forget and ask again.

As with everything connected with Matt's brain injury, my curiosity was piqued by these apparent hallucinations and I wondered why they were happening. It would seem this is not an uncommon experience for people suffering a brain injury or coming out of a coma. It is a form of psychosis and for some people it can continue long after the brain has healed.

Brain scans of hallucinating patients have shown that the visual cortex is activated during these experiences and, for the patients, these visions are extremely real. Dr Oliver Sacks, the renowned neurologist, explains that the reason hallucinations seem so real is that they deploy the very same systems in the brain as do actual perceptions. He put forward the theory that when someone is surfacing from a coma, as the cortex is returning to full function, it is over-activating itself and thus producing these hallucinations. Matt's brain was obviously raring to go!

For people who have been heavily sedated, the hallucinations can simply be put down to a reaction to the medication. Fortunately for Matt, his visions were quite short-lived.

Over the course of the next few months, we were about to witness just how complex and crazy our brains can be. We were at the very beginning of an extremely long, and often fascinating, learning curve that stretched out ahead of us.

*

Life for Nick and me was exhausting. Our main focus of attention was Matt, of course. We were constantly up and down to the hospital taking him his meals, visiting and generally thinking of ways to keep him motivated and make life more interesting for him. In addition, normal life had to go on with its mundane but necessary chores. Dogs had to be walked, and Nick was slowly returning to his work. His clients had been very understanding, but he couldn't expect them to wait forever. I don't think I had ever experienced true exhaustion before, but you keep going because you have to.

We were rewarded by seeing Matt begin to recover. He now sat for short periods in one of those special chairs, which supported his head and various other bits, but it would soon become very uncomfortable for him. Happily, he was already looking a lot better than he had in his special chair in London, although it was now even more obvious that he had real problems with his left side, as he couldn't move anything on that side of his body. His speech was slurred and muddled, but we knew there was room for improvement there. Sometimes, though, he was unable to find the words and it became like a bizarre game of 20 Questions as we sought to help him express himself. Often, we just couldn't figure out what it was he was trying to say.

His friends were all doing what they could by visiting and talking about things they had done together. His friends in far-flung places such as Australia responded by sending photos to jog Matt's memory. To our great relief, he did appear to remember and recognise all of them.

Quite soon after his arrival in Chichester, he had another visit from Greg, which really cheered him up. They had been best buddies since the age of nine, when we first moved to Geneva, and shared a passion for football. Within a very short time of meeting, the pair of them were practically joined at the hip, always talking about football. The last time Greg had seen him, Matt was unconscious and in Intensive Care, so he was thrilled to see Matt sitting up and chatting. He was accompanied by his girlfriend, whom we had not met before, and we were very excited to meet her. Greg told Matt how he had got hopelessly lost in the Royal London and then found himself in the Maternity Unit instead of Intensive Care, which made us all laugh. Then he disappeared off to the loo in St Richard's and, to Matt's great delight, got lost again. It made Matt's day and he chuckled away with the rather strange, very quiet, little laugh he had now developed.

Matt loved these visits from friends and it always amazed me how he accepted the fact that, after the visit, they would return to their busy lives, while he was left behind in hospital. I always felt a little bit sad for him, but he never showed any self-pity.

He had two further VIP visitors in that ward – Bobby and Benji, our Westies. One of the nurses wheeled Matt out by the door and he was able to pat and stroke them. Every reminder of life outside the hospital was invaluable and showed Matt what was waiting for him when he was ready.

The next day, things continued to go well in Matt's world as he watched his first football match in over two months – Manchester United v Southampton and his team won 2-1. During the match, one of the nurses came in with more good news – on Monday, he would be transferred to Donald Wilson House, the Neurological Rehabilitation Centre.

This move would be a very important one for Matt. The fantastic staff at the Royal London had given Matt his life back; now we were hoping that these, at present unknown, people in Donald Wilson would be able to put the quality back into that life. All our hopes were pinned on them. At this stage, Matt could talk, but not brilliantly. He could eat and drink with help, but he couldn't walk, sit up by himself, wash, go to the loo or very much else really. He had an awfully long way to go. He was still 100% dependent on other people and we all wanted him to be 100% independent. No one was prepared to promise us that would happen, as in the world of brain injuries, nothing is certain when it comes to the future. We were getting that message loud and clear by now.

We were so grateful to have Matt back with us, but we wanted so much more for him. We refused to contemplate anything less than a full recovery, even though everyone was telling us that would be impossible with such a severe injury. Whatever the future may hold, we were determined to aim high. If we were ultimately to fail, we needed to fail knowing that we had tried absolutely everything.

Matt has slightly hazy memories from those early days of being back in the land of the living:

> Trust me, it really wasn't like a movie. I didn't just suddenly wake up from the coma. It was a pretty gradual process. At that point, my short-term memory was shocking, so I don't think I was properly forming memories.
>
> The first thing I remember was my old boss, Rich, and his wife, Amelia, who had come to visit from the Scilly Isles. This first meeting sort of set the tone for the whole recovery. Rich was just laughing, joking and messing around with the picture cards everyone had to use to communicate with me.

That was the start of a pretty steady stream of visitors every day. I know it sounds ridiculous, but I genuinely wasn't really allowed to be sad or worried. I was seeing friends, some of them I hadn't seen for years, and they were all bringing me presents.

Another thing I remember was that I thought people were famous. I thought the guy in the next bed was Karl Pilkington (the hilarious northern guy off TV). He obviously wasn't, though. I was also sure that my occupational therapist was famous. I think in these early stages, my brain was definitely playing tricks on me. I vaguely remember thinking the hospital was in France during the war!

I'm sorry that I don't have more deep and meaningful thoughts about such a dramatic event in my life, but that's the thing with brain injuries – your brain is injured. So I think my brain was a bit busy warming up, for the hard work that was about to begin!

EIGHT

A LITTLE BIT
OF BRAIN INFO

So what exactly were we dealing with here? At the time, I focussed very little on what had actually happened and just concentrated on getting Matt back to some sort of life. I have since come to understand the enormity of it all and realise that most people, unsurprisingly, understand very little about head injuries, which can make the survivor and their family feel very isolated.

I can remember one occasion when I was at a friend's birthday party. I was making small talk, as you do, when the lady I was talking to asked a perfectly reasonable question: "What do your sons do?"

"The oldest one is in Switzerland working as a ski instructor. Unfortunately, the youngest has had a serious head injury, so he's in rehab."

Always a slightly awkward answer that can put quite a damper on the conversation. This lady was not at all deterred, though. "Oh my God, how awful. I know exactly what you are going through. My son is in the school rugby team and he's hurt his knee badly and it's quite likely that he won't be able to play for the rest of this season. It's very difficult, isn't it?"

"Er, yes, it is. Excuse me, I just have to go and find my husband," as I smiled weakly and walked off.

What I really wanted to say was, *NO, NO, NO, you stupid woman. You have no idea what we are going through. There is no comparison between an injured knee and an injured brain. Your son will be able to lead a normal life, but my son might never be able to do that.*

There was one other memorable occasion when Matt was still in rehab. This time, it was a barbecue, and I admit that I probably did go around with a permanent worried frown on my face at that stage. As a consequence, some helpful jolly soul, who did know about Matt, told me to, "Cheer up! It might never happen." But it had already happened. I just ran out to the car in tears with a startled Nick running behind me. I decided there and then that my socialising days were over for the time being at least. It was just too upsetting to risk hearing these upsetting remarks, and most people just don't have a clue. Why should they?

So let's do something about that and start with a little bit of basic information about the brain. The brain is surrounded by the skull, which is a hard, protective, rounded shell of bone. At the front of the skull, there are a number of bony ridges. These can do a lot of damage when the brain is shaken around in an accident. The brain is connected to the spinal cord by the brain stem, which is the cable that carries messages to and fro and controls various bodily functions, such as breathing, swallowing, heartbeat and blood pressure. Damage here is thought to cause concussion and loss of consciousness.

The brain is surrounded by a viscous cerebrospinal fluid, and during normal movement such as walking or running, the brain bounces around quite happily in this fluid and will bounce back as it bumps into the skull.

Also in your brain are the neurons and axons. There are about 100 billion neurons and they are the command centres of the brain. The axons are the messengers that relay the commands. Neuroscientists know that the brain is divided up into different areas and that these different areas are responsible for different functions. Despite knowing what each area controls, they don't know what each of these 100 billion individual neurons control, although the huge amount of research that is presently being carried out may yet shed some light on that.

The cerebral cortex is the largest part of the brain and that is divided into two halves. The left half affects the right side of the body and the right half affects the left side of the body. The cerebral cortex is further divided into four lobes, each of which is responsible for different functions. The frontal lobe is responsible for such things as thinking, planning and personality. The parietal lobe includes perception, arithmetic and spelling. The occipital lobe is responsible for vision. Finally, the temporal lobe is responsible for memory, understanding and language. In the middle of the cerebral cortex are a number of nerve centres, each of which controls different aspects again, such as appetite, thirst, fear, anger and panic.

Long scientific tomes have been written about the brain and how it works, so the summary that I have just given is just that: a summary, and a fairly basic one at that. The brain is infinitely more complicated, but I am not a neurologist, and even the best scientific brains on the planet have not yet acquired a complete understanding of how our brains work. There are still a lot of mysteries waiting to be unlocked.

Matt suffered a diffuse axonal injury, which meant that the injury was widespread. As he fell and hit the ground, his brain was shaken about way beyond the normal parameters. This violent movement will damage the connections into the brain and break up communication pathways. Furthermore, the soft brain tissue will be lacerated along the sharp bony ridges on the underside of the skull in front of the brain. As the brain moves violently around in the skull, there will be damage and bruising to both the front and back of the brain.

Immediately following such an accident, the oxygen supply to the brain can be interrupted, with serious consequences. As previously stated, the brain consumes 20% of the oxygen carried by the blood. It is therefore vital to ensure that the patient is able to breathe, either on their own or on a ventilator. This is why the speedy intervention of London's Air Ambulance at the scene of Matt's accident was so vital in order to lessen the chances of secondary damage. After the immediate consequences of an accident, the brain can continue to bruise and swell. There is also the danger of blood clots. All this must be closely monitored, as it was for Matt in the Royal London.

Every brain injury survivor becomes a pioneer in their own life. As they set out on the road to recovery, they can have no idea of what lies ahead of them. Their brain and their brain injury is unique to them and, therefore, their capacity to recover is also unique to them. It will be dependent on many things, including their age, health and fitness pre-accident, as well as the extent of injuries suffered.

The fact that Matt's injury was diffuse meant that it was anybody's guess as to which bits would work again and which bits wouldn't. He had suffered a closed head injury – although he had multiple skull fractures, nothing had actually gone through it into the brain. Sometimes people will suffer a penetrating injury, which is when something goes through the skull and damages one specific area, such as might happen in a collision when a piece of metal could pierce the skull. In these cases, because it is more specific, it is easier to give a prognosis as to possible outcomes. For example, if the occipital lobe is penetrated, there is obviously a very high chance of vision being affected. However, with a diffuse injury, only as the survivor continues on their road to recovery can they begin to see which parts of the brain have been affected. Strong motivation and a positive attitude are vital, but what if the bits of the brain that control those functions have been destroyed? Unfortunately, it is true that people can undergo a complete personality change following a brain injury because of damage done to those bits of the brain controlling personality and emotions. Depression is a common occurrence in brain injury survivors, and this is hardly surprising in view of the enormity of the challenges they face and the uncertainty about what sort of life may lie ahead of them.

Once our brain cells are destroyed, they don't regenerate – when they're gone, they're gone. The good news is that the brain has a certain amount of 'plasticity' and it can rewire or change in response to repeated learning (hence the 'use it or lose it' mantra). Other areas take over from the damaged ones and new nerve pathways can be established using the undamaged brain cells in those areas. Fortunately, the brain has a lot of spare capacity and, with this rerouting, it is possible to get a lot of functions back. Possible, but by no means certain, and many people do remain severely disabled following a serious head injury. We knew that we would just have to wait and see what would and what wouldn't work again as far as Matt was concerned.

*

In order to fully appreciate the task that lay ahead of Matt, I would ask you to place yourself in his shoes and try to imagine relearning a range of basic skills with a damaged brain. To you, those skills are simply part of life's routine, but what if you woke up one morning and couldn't remember how to do any of them? Or even if you did know what to do, your body just wouldn't do it. On top of that, as soon as anyone told you anything, you would inevitably forget it within about 15 minutes. Often, you would struggle for the right words needed to try and express yourself. To the onlooker, it would appear as if you were fumbling around in a state of confusion. They would often suspect that you were drunk. Even when you eventually learnt to walk again, your balance was shot and, when you tried to move, you wobbled all over the place. You didn't dare look ahead as you tried to walk, but instead kept your eyes firmly fixed towards the ground in case of any trip hazards. That, combined with lowering your centre of gravity to try and maintain your balance, resulted in a stooped stance. One side of your body was very weak and seemed to progress even more slowly than the other. Despite all that, you knew that somehow, no matter how hopeless and difficult it seemed, you had to keep on facing each day and challenging your brain in order to relearn these skills. Giving up was just not an option. This wasn't some sort of difficult job or sporting challenge that you could just resign or walk away from. This was your life.

After writing the above paragraph, I ran it by Matt and, while he agreed that it was a fair summary of the situation, he then turned it completely on its head by pointing out that actually he was in a win-win situation. As he saw it, if he tried and tried and still couldn't do something, then people could only sympathise and admire his tenacity. However, if he should succeed, he was then treated as some sort of mini hero. Also, he was receiving a lot of really nice presents from visiting friends. Right there, you have an excellent example of the ultra-positive attitude that would serve to spur him on. He is one of the most optimistic and determined characters you will ever meet. His glass is permanently well over half-full. Believe me, though, when I say it really wasn't at all easy at the time, yet he seemed to relish it.

To get through this sort of situation, you do need the character of an Olympian going for gold.

An injury described as 'life-altering' sounds really scary. Most of us don't really want our lives altered by something out of our control – especially if you're young and having the time of your life. There was no question that Matt's life had drastically altered. The future that lay ahead of him was, at that moment, just a giant question mark. Over time, it would reveal itself, so for now he just had to take one step at a time – except he couldn't even do that – and see where he ended up. Hopefully, by the end of his stay in rehab, he would be taking those first few steps.

By the time Matt was about to go into Donald Wilson, we had worked out that we had a huge challenge ahead of us. We were determined that Matt would not be depressed or overwhelmed by what had happened. Easy enough for us to say, but had he been depressed, in reality we probably wouldn't have been able to wave a magic wand to make it go away. We had no real idea of what we were doing, but we knew that we had to keep him stimulated, but not overstimulated, as the brain needs plenty of rest in order to recover. We had to believe that he would recover and we knew that he would never give up. Above all, we had to remain cheerful. This last requirement proved to be relatively easy as Matt had so many bright and cheery friends who would visit and laugh with him. Boredom never became an issue. There was always someone visiting. I think the fact that, at the time, we were largely ignorant of the enormity of the task that lay ahead was probably an advantage. I think we were fully aware that it might not work out at all, but we decided to file that thought away, only to be brought out at a later date if needed. We were about to embark on an epic adventure, and little did we know how surprising it would turn out to be.

NINE

THE HARD WORK BEGINS

Monday, 31st January, 2011 arrived and Matt's rehabilitation adventure was about to begin. I had packed a bag for him with proper clothes in it, because in Donald Wilson House, patients were encouraged to be dressed during the day. There was to be no more lying around in PJs for Matt. I set off for Donald Wilson, only to find that Matt wasn't there when I arrived. He had had a dizzy spell that morning, so they were keeping him on the ward for observation for a while before letting him go. He was actually in excellent spirits, as his friend Pilot Pete was visiting and keeping him amused, but I have to admit to being in a bit of a panic. I knew how sought after beds in Donald Wilson were – a bit like being offered tickets to Wimbledon. If you weren't able to snap them up, they would have no trouble finding someone else to take your place. If he missed this opportunity, goodness knows how long he would have to wait until the next one became available. Fortunately, he was given the all-clear later that day and was wheeled across there accompanied by Pilot Pete – much to his delight.

*

Although I'd only been in St Richard's for a couple of weeks, because of my dodgy memory it was all I really knew. So when the day came to move to Donald Wilson, that was a very exciting time.

The first thing I noticed when I saw the building was that there was grass on the roof. If you've ever seen the kids' show 'Teletubbies', it's just like their house. Round roofs with grass on them!

I was told that I'd have daily physio, occupational therapy and speech and language training. I would also have to wear actual clothes (not hospital gowns) and I would eat in a dining room three times a day, so I'd have to kiss goodbye to my luxurious spoonfeeding of homemade meals.

My old roommate from Courchevel, Pete, was visiting the day I moved, so he actually pushed me in my wheelchair to my new 'home'. Me and Pete both worked in the same bar in Courchevel. I was twenty-one and fresh from dropping out of uni, whereas Pete was twenty-nine and had just retired from the Royal Air Force. In many ways, we were polar opposites, but we became great friends and shared a bunkbed in our flat. I was on the top bunk and he was on the bottom. Pete christened us 'Team Bunkbed'. I liked it that 'Pilot Pete' would take me to this new place. After all, he was a fighter pilot, so I'd be all right.

*

That evening, Nick and I went to visit him and we experienced that, by now, familiar feeling of unfamiliarity, as he was in yet another strange bed in another strange place. Once again, he looked very lost sitting all alone in the middle bed of a three-bed ward. He just wanted to come back home with us. We knew that he would soon be fine and would settle in, but it was very hard leaving him that night. I can't even begin to imagine how I would feel being in a strange place, with strange people, not really understanding how I had come to be there and knowing that I was completely powerless – not even being able to sit up in bed by myself, let alone walk anywhere. It was the first time he'd expressed any kind of homesickness, so I did the only thing I could think of, which was to go home and sort out a load of photos to put on the noticeboard beside his bed to try and make it feel more like home for him. It was so upsetting to think of him being lonely and unhappy, but it was unrealistic to think that he would always breeze along with no down moments. I know that I tended to panic at any suggestion of him being unhappy, always fearing that it could be the start of a downward spiral towards depression.

When Matt arrived at DWH, he was the most disabled patient there. All the other residents, and there were fourteen of them, were a lot older than him. They were mainly stroke victims over the age of forty, mostly over the age of fifty-five. They could all get themselves about somehow – either completely independently, with walking frames or in wheelchairs. Matt was totally dependent on help from the nurses for everything. To move him out of his bed to his wheelchair, they had a special hoist, which was like a crane for people. He actually quite enjoyed dangling from it. For the first few days, Matt was still confined to his bed, which meant that he was mainly in the ward on his own, as the other two occupants were usually out and about. Having said that, the other patients were all extremely kind to him. It was as if he had acquired fourteen extra mums and dads.

Matt was enrolled for three types of therapy: physiotherapy, speech and language therapy, and occupational therapy. Most of the therapists were young and fun, so he was looking forward to it all. He was clearly loving being back in the land of the living and lapping up all the attention he was getting from everyone. I don't think he fully realised how close he had come to not being here at all, but he seemed determined to make up for lost time and threw himself into everything. Despite all the dire warnings, he seemed to us to still be the same old Matt.

The physiotherapy was all about getting him back on his feet and walking. This was a very specific type of physio, namely neurophysio, carried out by specialist neurophysiotherapists who understand all the connections between the brain and everything we do. Initially, it was a challenge for them just to get him sitting up on his own. They would put him in the sitting position, but the second they let go of him, he would either flop backwards, forwards or sideways. He had no strength at all. It was seen as a huge achievement when he was first able to sit up by himself unsupported. However, after a couple of days, they had Matt standing, albeit with a lot of support from the physios. This still represented a huge milestone in his recovery. Any progress would be slow and tiny. We would have to adjust to setting our sights low, with every little improvement celebrated. There were not suddenly going to be any great leaps forward. I could now understand exactly why physiotherapy was necessary following a brain injury.

The occupational therapy was about being able to live independently. As with the physio, it started at a very basic level by teaching him to brush his teeth and wash and dress himself. Then he graduated on to more complex tasks, such as tying up his shoelaces and cutting up his food. They also had a little kitchen where the patients could learn such things as how to make a cup of tea, prepare a sandwich or make a simple breakfast. I remember one occasion when Matt prepared some lovely fresh strawberries dipped in melted chocolate – very yummy. A lot of the patients were very happy just to be able to do these simple things so that they could go back home, but it was not enough for Matt. He was intending to aim a lot higher than that – literally. Nothing less than being able to stand at the top of his favourite ski slope on les Grands Montets above Argentière in the Chamonix Valley would be acceptable for him.

The speech and language therapy is self-explanatory. Those therapists were teaching him to speak again. Apart from his brain damage, which caused Matt to slur his words, his speaking had also been affected by having his trachy tube in for so long. It had weakened his vocal chords and his voice was very quiet, and it was quite a strain to speak, so there was a lot of work to be done there.

We quickly began to understand what being disabled meant. On one occasion, Matt was quite upset because he had been in his wheelchair in the dayroom happily watching his favourite TV programme, *Top Gear*, when one of the nurses came in and just switched channels and left him there. As he was the only patient in there, it seemed a bit of an odd decision anyway. He was then helpless, having no choice other than to remain there, as he couldn't operate the wheelchair by himself. I have to say such thoughtlessness on the part of the staff was rare, but it does make you realise how vulnerable a severely disabled person is and how they depend utterly on the goodwill and intentions of others. The vast majority of the staff were extremely thoughtful and would always make time to stop and have a little chat with Matt when they were passing.

Only once did we encounter real thoughtlessness and that wasn't from a member of the regular staff, but from an agency nurse. I arrived one evening to visit Matt and he was very down, which was unusual for him.

"Hey, Matt, how are you tonight?"

"Not great," was the unexpected answer from my usually cheerful son.

"Why? What's happened?"

"There's a new nurse here this evening and she was asking what had happened to me. I told her about my accident and do you know what she said?" From the expression on his face, I was guessing it wasn't good.

"No, what did she say?"

"She said that in the space of a few seconds of stupidity, I'd ruined my life. You don't think I have, do you, Mum?" His eyes were begging me to put it right. I felt as if someone had punched me in the heart and I tried to reassure him.

"Oh, Matt, I am sure she didn't mean your whole life. I expect she meant that right now things have gone a bit wrong. She obviously doesn't know how hard you are working and how much progress you've already made!" I was hoping that, on this occasion, his wonky memory might serve him well and he would eradicate that conversation from his memory banks straight away.

When I told a member of the regular nursing staff about it, they were furious. That is definitely not how you should talk to a young man facing an uncertain future and working his socks off to recover from a serious injury.

On a lighter note, one highlight of his week was his weekly sports report. Our friend Rob was responsible for these. Like Matt, he is a Man United supporter and general all-round sports fan. He is also very funny. He took it upon himself to send Matt a weekly humorous sports update. As Matt had severe double vision, which made reading for himself impossible, it was my job to read it aloud to him, which we both enjoyed. It was another example of friends being keen to help and then doing something about it.

Within a few days, Matt was well into his new routine of therapies, resting and visits from friends. He was always in excellent humour and there was much laughter when he was with his pals. I think he was a firm favourite with the staff, as he was always smiling, laughing and very grateful for all that they did for him. That was another funny little change that we had noticed. Being a well-brought-up young man, he had always been fairly polite and good with his pleases and thank yous. However, now he had become super-polite! He would often say something like: 'Please, thank you very much for my lunch, thank you.' It was amazing how many pleases and thank yous he could fit into one sentence!

Everything Matt did seemed to be exaggerated at that time: BIG smiles, BIG frowns, BIG expressions of surprise. He also had certain phrases that he used continually: 'Ooooh, yeees!', 'Hopefully', 'Oh dear' and 'Pretty good'. His short-term memory was still awful and there was much repeating of everything, but we realised that this was just his fuddled brain not being able to think clearly yet. The fact that he could say anything at all was a miracle as far as we were concerned.

One of the first major goals in rehab was simply to be able to stand. Our bodies are not designed to be horizontal or even sitting all the time. Standing is important because it allows the organs and skeleton to be correctly aligned as nature intended. For Matt to be able to stand obviously required a lot of support, and usually it was the physios who supported him. However, one tool they have at their disposal is a machine known as a 'passive stander', which allows the patient to stand passively, i.e. without any input from the patient. It looks a bit like a torture device. Matt was placed in it against the supporting back area, which includes support for the neck and head. The fronts of the legs are also supported, and his hands were placed on a sort of lectern. He was then securely strapped in and looked like a cross between the filling in an electric toastie maker and a vicar imprisoned in his pulpit. On one of his first occasions doing this, the nurse wandered off, intending to release him after a little while, leaving my brother and me there to keep an eye on him. Unfortunately, after only a few minutes, he suddenly went deathly white and passed out. It was a sobering reminder of just how weak and disabled he was. Looking at him when he was sitting in his bed or chair, it was easy to imagine that he would just be able to get up and walk off, but of course he couldn't. Even just being upright was too much of a shock to his compromised system.

Again, I can't remember too much about these early stages, but it was pretty obvious that I was the youngest by some distance. The majority of the other patients were over fifty. Most of the nurses were nice and I soon got into the therapy routines.

One thing I liked was that one of my OTs, Brigitte, was French. This meant that I could practise my French, which was vital, because I think, at this point, I had decided that I was 100% French!

I thought physio progressed quite quickly, not sure it seemed that way for my friends and family. There were handy landmarks, such as progressing through the wheelchairs – from being pushed to pushing the wheels round myself. I think it was being in the wheelchairs that started my passion for breaking personal records. The physios used to time me going around the halls and back to the gym. I can't remember the times, but they weren't fast enough for the nurses to worry about me crashing into elderly patients!

There was a fancy-looking machine in the corner of the gym. I was told that you strap into it and it helps you stand when you don't really have the strength or balance to do that. I was desperate to get in it, but when that time came, I stood a tiny bit too long and the blood rushed from my head and I passed out.

That happened on the 14th of February 2011 and was the last thing recorded in Volume I of my diaries. As I began Volume II, I fervently hoped I wouldn't need to go on to Volume III, but I was going to continue until we reached somewhere significant in terms of recovery, not that I knew when or what that would be.

In mid-February, Matt progressed from his fancy all-supporting wheelchair (which he hated) to an ordinary one, and also his mattress was changed from an electronically controlled one, which could be put into all sorts of sitting/lying positions, to an ordinary one. These were significant changes as it meant that he no longer needed so much extra support. He could now sit up by himself. Only a few weeks previously, he had been completely floppy and unable to even hold his head up, so this represented real progress.

Having an ordinary wheelchair also meant that we could now take Matt on little outings. At first, these involved just going across the road to the main hospital building for a drink in their café. At that stage, this was quite an adventure for us all and was one more tiny step towards normal life.

Looking back on that time, it's surprising what passed for excitement. Forget hurtling down a ski slope or crashing through the waves in a sailing boat, we now got our adrenalin rushes from seeing our son stand for five seconds or being able to tie his own shoelaces.

Life in rehab followed a daily routine. There were strict rules about eating in the dining room and no visitors were allowed at mealtimes in order to avoid distractions, as a simple thing like eating was quite a challenge for a brain injury survivor or a stroke victim. Every little thing that most of us take for granted requires a huge amount of brainpower: using a knife and fork, brushing teeth, shaving, etc. In order for our hands to work properly to do these seemingly simple things, many messages have to be relayed from the brain to the hands, and when these messages are not going through properly, if at all, it can be quite a challenge. By the evening, you could pretty much guess what Matt had eaten during the day, as half of it would be splattered over his clothes.

We decided to upgrade Matt's little DVD player to a Freeview TV/DVD player to have by his bed, so that he could watch his own choice of programmes. According to Matt, the TV in the dayroom was mainly tuned into 'old people's' programmes. On his own little set, Matt could watch football, ski films or *Cool Runnings* (the Disney film about the Jamaican bobsled team). He watched *Cool Runnings* so many times that one of the occupational therapists was genuinely concerned about him. They were also worried that watching endless ski films might prove to be upsetting, as they would remind him of what he could no longer do. I don't think it did him any harm at all. On the contrary, it allowed him to escape into the world he loved. Also, he saw it as watching an activity that he would return to one day. For him, it was his future, and it was out there waiting for his return. It was so important to have goals for the future, and skiing was Matt's goal. What did it matter if the general consensus of opinion was against that ever happening? He had to have a future to look forward to, or what would be the point of all that hard work? After all – nothing ventured, nothing gained.

*

At the beginning of March, he was moved out of the three-bed ward into his own room. This was a good thing, but it also signified that he was going to be in there for a while yet. Only long-term patients got their own rooms. However, a major advantage was that his pals could all pile in there without disturbing the other patients. It was a wonderful room, full of light, with a door opening straight onto the outside terrace. I don't think he could have had a better room had he been in a private hospital. He didn't quite have his own en-suite, but the bathroom was just across the corridor.

That same day (4th March), he also took a few steps supported by a physio on either side. This was very exciting, although, as Matt explains, any physical effort was extremely tiring.

> My first steps were between some parallel bars in the gym. The first few times I did it, it was so tiring. It genuinely felt like I'd run a couple of miles, when in fact I'd only taken two steps. That's what I think people don't understand. I know I wouldn't have in their position, but it's not so much the physical fatigue that's the problem. I just felt completely knackered from thinking about every tiny part of the movement. I'd often have to have a little nap after physio. I miss those afternoon naps!

As he was doing more things, Matt was getting more and more positive about his recovery. He was in no doubt that he would make a full recovery, although no one was coming forward to support this view. As he put it, "Once I get this voice sorted out and start walking, I'll be fine."

At our first family meeting with the medical staff, they once again emphasised that it would be a long recovery: 18 months to 2 years. As it happened, even that turned out to be very optimistic. All we knew was that we'd just have to wait and see. Matt's brain would do exactly what it wanted to do when it decided to do it. We could try and encourage it in the right direction, but ultimately it was out of all of our hands.

When Tim made another flying visit from Switzerland, we arranged for him to take Matt to the cinema in Chichester. This involved booking a special wheelchair-friendly taxi and making sure that the cinema could accommodate wheelchairs. They went to see *Rango*, an animated film, but that wasn't actually the highlight of the excursion. For Matt, the best thing was the drive to and from the cinema. The 10th of March was to be his first sight of the outside world (other than the hospital grounds) since the 26th of November 2010. Just seeing roads, cars, a football pitch, car parks, town centre shops and buildings was incredibly exciting for Matt. They also went to the pub next to the cinema beforehand, where Matt had a large orange juice, and in the cinema, he had a jumbo hotdog. It was a fantastic occasion for him. Simple pleasures suddenly meant so much.

At about this time, he was also allowed the use of his own phone again, and use it he did! As far as I was concerned, this was both a blessing and a curse, as it was now out of my control. I think maybe the medical staff were unaware of quite how many pals Matt had. Once word got around, they were all constantly phoning, which was great, but you do have to be careful about brain overload. The patient mustn't be overstimulated, as the damaged brain continues to try to repair itself. As a parent, you don't want to be a killjoy and tell people not to phone quite so much, but nor do you want to allow anything to get in the way of the recovery. As we got further along the road, this was a dilemma that Nick and I would frequently find ourselves in. Matt was up for everything and anything, but sometimes we just had to say no. At the very least, we had had to put the brakes on to slow him down. In the early stages of recovery, good judgement on the part of the patient can't be relied upon. It wasn't pleasant to have to be the killjoy parents, but better that than leaving Matt to make some horrendous decision.

Now that Matt had his own room, we had great fun decorating it. We put photos all around the wall and copies of all the things that had been sent to him, including the Jacob Wester signed photo and a signed David Beckham shirt. I also had to take photos of his skis and put those up on the wall too. Even though I do say so myself, he definitely had the brightest, jolliest room in the place.

As time went on, various Lego models built by Matt were also put on display. I had heard that Richard Hammond from *Top Gear* had built Lego models as a form of therapy after his head injury, so we thought we should give that a go too. It turned out to be a very good idea and provided Matt with many hours of stimulating and useful challenges. Sadly, they only remained on display for a few weeks and then Health and Safety intervened. They were a dust hazard, so I had to take them home, where they continue to gather dust to this day.

One thing that Matt absolutely hated was the nightly injection in his stomach. This was a necessary procedure because he was so immobile that he needed it to protect him from developing deep vein thrombosis. He was delighted when, at the end of March, they announced that he was now moving around enough for these injections to be stopped. He was now able to stand for one whole minute unsupported, and his next achievement at the beginning of April was to kneel unsupported, which was regarded as massive by the physios, although I'm not sure why.

Also, towards the end of March, we were excitedly looking forward to a visit from the occupational therapists to see if Matt could start making home visits. Unfortunately, it turned out to be a less-than-positive experience. Two OTs turned up and one of them was very positive and upbeat, but the other one informed us that Matt didn't know who any of them were, and that he had no insight into his condition. We felt quite depressed until we realised that it just wasn't true. He did know everyone's names. As for the 'insight' bit, who knew what he was really thinking? He was so determined to be upbeat and positive that he just concentrated on getting better. He had his own golden rule, which he still has to this day – no negative thoughts! I personally support him 100% in this and I think that has got him a long way. I sometimes wonder if these people know the impact that their negativity has on people who are already under a huge amount of stress.

The following week, we had a lovely surprise arrive through the post. I had written to Matt's favourite ski company, Armada, to ask for a few stickers for his wall. They did better than that: we had stickers, a glass holder, a signed card from Tanner Hall (top freeskier) and a handwritten letter from someone called Tom in the Armada office, which finished with the words, *Stay strong and get well soon, buddy, we're thinking about you. Best, Tom and the rest of the Armada Family.* Once again, the skiing fraternity had come up trumps. Matt was thrilled or, as the skiers say, stoked.

Nick and I were bearing up pretty well, but there was one evening when it all got too much for me. I was driving home from an evening visit on my own with the car radio tuned into Radio 2. Suddenly a song came on that surely must have been written for Matt – *I Hope You Dance* by Lee Ann Womack. Normally, I might have dismissed it as a bit overly sentimental, but that night it really resonated with me. I'd managed to keep the tears to a minimum over those past few months, but as I listened to the words the dam burst and I wept floods of tears. All my thoughts were being expressed out loud in this song. When I got home, I found it on YouTube and listened to it again and again and again, and wept some more.

She sings about the ocean and the mountains, doors closing and others opening. She tells him to never settle for the path of least resistance and that living might mean taking chances, but they're worth taking. If he gets the chance to sit it out or dance, she hopes he'll dance.

I knew that he *would* dance, *kick* those doors open, *always* do it tough and *grab hold* of those chances. When she sings about never taking things for granted, I could already see that he would never do that. He had been given this second chance and he was going for it and savouring every second of it.

TEN

HOME LEAVE

The spring of 2011 was beautifully warm and sunny, which meant that the patients could take full advantage of the terrace. There were tables, chairs and sun-umbrellas out there for the patients, as well as raised flowerbeds for them to work on should they so desire. While Matt was up for just about anything, gardening proved to be one of the exceptions. At weekends, weather permitting, they would eat outside at lunchtime. Matt was often to be found out there, usually sat in his wheelchair with his feet up on another chair just soaking up the sun. We were so lucky that he was in such a great place for his rehab.

In early April, Nick was away on business, so I decided to challenge myself and take Matt into Chichester for a pizza. This was my first attempt at negotiating roads, pavements, people and getting into a restaurant with Matt and his wheelchair. I am happy to report that all went well. It was a Saturday night and the town was full of groups of young people all setting out on their Saturday night adventures. Matt enjoyed the experience, but I felt very sad for him. He too should have been off out with his mates, not being wheeled along on a Saturday night by his mum. He was just so happy to be out and about that he didn't seem to feel any resentment about his situation. When I wheeled him back into Donald Wilson later that evening, he was very excited to tell everyone about it.

Shortly after this excursion, he was brought home for an hour to see if he would be ready for an overnight stay. We had moved his bed downstairs to our TV room. We had been provided with a commode for the loo and ramps for the external doors. He had to prove that he (and we) could manage the various transfers from the wheelchair to the car, car back to the wheelchair, wheelchair to commode, wheelchair to bed, and so on. We also had to learn how to fold up the chair to put it in the car. We all passed with flying colours. The two occupational therapists then announced that he could come home for TWO whole nights. We were all so excited.

At midday on Friday 15th April, we picked him up and brought him home for two days. He overdosed on Sky Sports, which he now had the luxury of watching from his bed. The main challenge of the weekend was the loo. Funnily enough, Nick didn't leap forward to volunteer for that particular job. Fortunately, Matt made it very easy by joking and saying to me, "I don't suppose you'd ever imagined that you'd still be wiping my bum for me at the age of twenty-three!" I guess over the last few months he had been poked and prodded by so many different doctors, nurses and carers that he wasn't easily embarrassed about personal things anymore. All the same, I did rather hope that this was one aspect of life where he would quickly regain his independence.

At the end of a lovely, but exhausting, weekend, Matt was returned to DWH for another week of therapy.

We soon got into our new pattern of DWH during the week and back home for the weekend. Matt was still in his wheelchair, but he had also been given a four-wheeled walking frame to try. Every new breakthrough was hailed as a major event. On the 30th of April, for the first time, he laughed the big belly laugh that he always used to have, as opposed to a rather strange silent chuckle that he had been doing since waking up from his coma. At home, he moved around freely in his wheelchair, but he was also beginning to use his frame to walk very short distances from room to room. His memory was still awful, though, and his speech wasn't great, either.

Now that he was coming home every weekend, we tried to think of things to do that would take him out and about. The internet proved to be an invaluable source of information for us. I searched for wheelchair-friendly walks and found that there were quite a few in our area. This meant that we could go out with the dogs and Matt could come too in his chair. You soon realise that other people treat people differently if they are in a wheelchair. A lot of people just talk straight over the top of them as if they aren't there. I made a mental note to myself not to do this and to look people in wheelchairs straight in the eye as I would with a 'normal' person. Perhaps the strangest reaction we had was from an Irishman, who I suspect was a little bit tipsy. I was pushing the wheelchair along the Bognor Regis Promenade and he saw Matt and just kept saying over and over again, "I'm so sorry, I'm so sorry," and then started weeping. Perhaps he found the sight of a young man in a chair just too tragic to bear. Matt looked totally bemused and didn't quite know what to make of it. We were certainly seeing life from a whole new perspective.

At the beginning of May, Matt decided the time had come to try out his skis and ski boots.

Tim was at home and I was in the kitchen when I heard him calling me. "Mum, Mum, come into the TV room and have a look at this!"

I hurried in and there was Matt in his ski boots, clipped into his skis.

"Look at that, Mum," said Tim very proudly. "Matt's ready to go skiing now."

"The skis help my balance. I can stand up properly in them," exclaimed a very happy Matt.

And it was true; they obviously did help his balance. It was wonderful to see Matt and Tim both standing there with big grins, looking so proud of Matt's achievement. If Matt had been on an actual ski slope, I don't think he could have been any happier.

The next day, back at Donald Wilson, he had another first when he climbed the little set of stairs in the rehab gym.

He was so excited to tell me about it when I arrived to see him later on. "Mum, I walked up three stairs in the gym! It was much easier than just walking."

"Is it? Why's that then?"

"Well, when you walk, you have to decide where exactly you're going to put your feet and where you're heading. With stairs, you don't have much choice – you just have to put them on the step in front of you."

That's something that would never have occurred to me in a million years! Those of us without a brain injury don't normally consciously think about the processes involved in moving around. But in Matt's case, I suppose it does make sense, because there is less brainpower involved in the climbing stairs activity, and at that stage his brain was having to consciously figure out everything. It did seem as if things were really beginning to progress now, though.

Funnily enough, shortly after those two positive events, Nick and I slumped. That was to be the pattern: something good happened and up went the spirits, then nothing much would happen and they would go down again. All the time, there was an underlying feeling of anxiety and exhaustion. To see someone you love battling so hard to get back on their feet and never complaining or feeling sorry for themselves is, well, I don't know what it is really. You stand back and watch with awe and admiration, but also your heart is breaking at the slowness of it all.

The most harrowing thing I ever saw was when one of the physios made Matt stand in the middle of his room unsupported for the first time, with no one near him. He was absolutely terrified. It was as if he had been left outside on the window ledge of a New York skyscraper with the window closed behind him. It was so upsetting to see and brought home to me how his life had changed. What should have been a simple everyday occurrence (standing up) was for him now the equivalent of climbing Mount Everest. He was about 2 feet away from the edge of his bed, but it might as well have been a small pinnacle of rock 5,000 metres above the ground – that is how frightened he was. He pleaded with the physio to let him sit down. "Please, I can't do it. Please, let me sit down." The desperate look on his face was heartbreaking. As his mother, every part of me was wanting to intervene and let him sit down, but I knew that actually he had to do it. He had to overcome this fear. He probably only had to stand there for a few minutes, but it seemed like hours. It's another image that will be forever etched in my memory. Something as simple as just standing up unsupported now required a huge amount of courage.

Matt also remembers it vividly:

This is another thing that is impossible to understand unless you've had a head injury. But then again everyone says that every head injury is unique, so I don't even know if another head injury survivor would understand it. One day, I was having a physio session in my room, so that

we could use the bed for support. The physio asked me to
stand up and, with a bit of a hand-up from her, I could do
that with the back of my legs still leaning on the bed. I was
then asked to move literally 6 inches away from the bed, so
I was standing completely by myself. My mum always tells
me that I looked terrified. I was. I hated it. The only way
to describe it is for you to imagine if I got you to stand on
a doormat stuck on a 100ft pylon. Thankfully, it all started
to get easier from there.

*

One day, Matt told me about a young American skier called CR Johnson, who had also suffered a TBI and whose recovery pattern resembled his own. CR had been in a coma and took a while before he was skiing again. We adopted him as our role model and inspiration. As one of the best pro skiers of his generation, I was able to find out all about him online. After I had googled everything I could about him, I really did begin to feel that we weren't being unrealistic to hope for a good recovery. CR had done it, so surely Matt could too. Tragically, although CR recovered well from the TBI, he consequently died in a second serious ski accident. I cannot even begin to imagine how his family coped with that. In the future, CR would play more of a role in Matt's recovery than we could ever have guessed at that stage. For now, though, we looked at his ski movies and read all the reports of his accident and his subsequent recovery. He was an extremely inspiring young man and gave me real cause for optimism.

CR got back to fitness by working extremely hard at all of his physical therapies, including sewing. One of the challenges he was set was to sew a pleated skirt. Whatever it takes! Working hard was what Matt needed to do too, and he was more than ready to do whatever was asked of him.

By the beginning of June, Matt was really fighting back. He had come so close to losing his life that now there was no way he was not going to get it back. He was constantly laughing and joking with the nurses and therapists. He loved all of his therapy sessions and worked hard. Visits from friends kept him in touch with the outside world and gave him a further boost.

I remember visiting him one day and finding him in his room busy doing his exercises for his still-weak left shoulder. He then asked me to accompany him on a complete circuit of the outside of the building using his walking frame. When I returned in the evening, we went to the gym for him to take basketball shots, then two more circuits with his frame, followed by another set of shoulder exercises. There was a static exercise bike in the gym, which no one apart from Matt ever used, so the physios had moved it into his room. He then proceeded to do 20 minutes on that, followed by a final circuit. I left for home that night with a spring in my step, feeling so proud of my son with his Herculean determination and optimism. Go for it, Matt!

On the 10th of June, we had a family meeting with the consultant and the various therapists and we were given a final discharge date. As always, the neurologist, Dr Bradley, urged caution, but he did say that he thought that Matt might eventually be able to ski again and even teach sailing. He also warned us against getting obsessed with physiotherapy and exercise. Matt must also be encouraged to do normal things, such as going out with friends. Well, that wouldn't be a problem. They were already planning all sorts of things for him.

Before he came home, we had a second bannister installed, courtesy of the NHS. We now had all sorts of stuff at home, including ramps, a commode, a stool in the shower and grab rails. Nick and I will be fine in our old age – the house is already fully equipped for it.

The 21st of June was Matt's twenty-fourth birthday. I took in a cake for everybody in Donald Wilson, but the real celebration would be the following Sunday at home, after he had been discharged.

On the 23rd of June, Matt finally left the hospital. Yet again we were saying goodbye to an amazing group of people who had cared for him so well over the past 6 months. Donald Wilson House had proved to be a very happy place, full of positivity and, as always, you felt that the staff genuinely wanted their patients to do well. That is the thing that stood out for me. Wherever we had been – the two wards in the Royal London, the first ward in St Richard's and the rehab unit – the staff were all genuinely thrilled to see their patients progress. They weren't just going through the motions; they really meant it. This time, Matt had actually got to know them all too, as he was well and truly awake. He wasn't saying a permanent goodbye just yet, as he would be going back twice a week as a day patient for therapy. That night, for the first time since November, he actually went upstairs to his own room to sleep. I was just about to tell him to wait for me to help him up the stairs, but when I looked round, he was already gone! He just couldn't wait any longer to see his room again and he made good use of the new second bannister to haul himself up those stairs. It had been seven months since he had been upstairs in our house.

As my therapy progressed, I became more and more impatient. I wanted to get out of hospital. I'd ask the physios, nurses and doctors almost daily, "When can I go home?" It started with weekend home visits before I was fully discharged. When the time finally came, I was a tiny bit sad to leave the nurses and therapists, but I was excited to get back to normal. Ha ha! I say 'normal', but my balance still wasn't good enough to wipe my own bum!

So it wouldn't be a sudden "Okay, I'm home, completely back to normal." Still, it was nice to be with everyone, especially Bobby and Benji.

ELEVEN

IT'S UP TO US NOW

This was it then. On the 23rd of June 2011, after seven months of hospitals, Matt was back home and now it was up to us to provide him with everything he needed in order to give him the best chance of recovery. He had arrived home with a wheelchair, a walking frame and a whole load of self-motivation, and he was determined not to waste a second in going after his goals.

The next day, his friend Tim arrived from Australia. He was on his way to the Scilly Isles to teach sailing and, ordinarily, Matt would have been going with him. Not this year, though. As this was Matt's first full day back home and Tim was suffering from jet lag, I thought they could just have a quiet day. Matt had other ideas. "I think you two could come on a walk with me. I need to keep exercising and going for walks if I'm going to get better. What about a circuit of Chichester Marina?" He was clearly setting down a marker for his future recovery programme. If I thought I was going to be able to sit around and relax now that he was back home, I was wrong. Matt clearly had other plans.

However, a circuit of the marina was not a bad idea, actually. The marina had a smooth tarmac path that ran right around it, so it would be ideal for pushing a walking frame. We bundled the walking frame, along with the dogs, into the boot of the car and off we went.

Matt had set himself quite a task, as this was going to be the longest walk he had taken in over 7 months. It was a lot further than the circuits of the building he had been doing around Donald Wilson House. Normally, this walk would take about 20 minutes at a brisk pace. That day, it took Matt one and a half hours. He had set himself the target of walking the whole way round, and he only allowed himself to sit and rest on two occasions and then, only briefly. As far as we were concerned, it was brilliant, and we now had a yardstick by which to measure his progress. Chichester Marina would play a big role in Matt's recovery as he sought to get that time down to at least half an hour.

After the walk, we needed to turn our attention to the big party we were planning. We had two reasons to celebrate: Matt's twenty-fourth birthday and the fact that he was still here. We also wanted to thank all of his friends who had contributed so much of their time and efforts to getting him this far. Nick and I were planning on providing quite a feast for them.

Sunday the 26th of June was party day and friends came from far and wide. As well as his friend Tim, his other Aussie pal, James, had arrived in the UK at the start of his European tour, and Greg came over from France. Many of his old friends from school and university were there, as were his Courchevel ski buddies. Only his Scilly Isles pals were missing, as they were already into their busy holiday season. I had been looking forward to throwing a wonderful summer party by the beach but, much to my dismay, that morning our garden was engulfed with a thick sea mist. On a quick visit to the shops, I discovered that a few hundred metres inland, the sun was shining and it was boiling hot. The party was due to start at 3pm and, as if by magic, at 2.50pm, the mist finally lifted and the sun shone. That *definitely* counted as a good omen. It was just a lovely, lovely afternoon – full of smiles and laughter. Matt lapped up all the attention and any thoughts of the future were forgotten as we all just savoured a very special day.

I think the abiding memory I will have of that day is the amount of affection that those wonderful young people obviously had for Matt. They had all stuck by him and played their part in his recovery. During his time in Donald Wilson, many of the staff had commented to me how unusual it was to see how many friends kept on coming in to visit Matt. Sadly, with young men, the usual pattern is that friends all come in during the first few weeks but then tail off. Their brain-injured friend can't come to the pub with them or play in the football team, so as time goes on, they just continue doing all these things without him. It's not intentional or mean-spirited, it just happens. Often the brain-injury survivor gets very angry and aggressive and depressed about the whole situation they find themselves in, which is not at all surprising. They realise that their life has changed and see the future as just completely bleak. That is why I firmly believe that from the get-go, you must surround the patient with positivity and hope. On the 26th of June 2011, we had much cause for hope.

While most people left for home at about 8.30pm, we still had quite a houseful in the form of Aussie Tim, our Tim, James, Greg and Matt himself. That night as I went to bed, I looked out of the window and could see them all sitting down by the beach in the flickering candlelight and, more importantly, every few minutes or so I could hear great explosions of laughter. No one was laughing louder than Matt.

By Monday evening, James was the only houseguest left, but he was an ideal companion to help ease Matt back into the real world. Matt was now having to deal with the reality of his situation outside of the protective hospital environment, and during that first week, he had a couple of down moments. At his party, his friends had been on the beach jumping in and out of the sea, and I could see Matt looking a little bit sad, as he couldn't join in. A couple of days later, we went on an outing with James to Portsmouth to visit the Spinnaker Tower, which is a tall structure providing views of the surrounding area. It was full of children running and leaping around. Matt was in his wheelchair and it was obvious that he was a little upset by this too. Considering it was his first real exposure to 'normal' life in such a long time, he coped remarkably well with both situations and didn't stay down for very long. In Donald Wilson House, he had been the same as everyone else – no one there was leaping around. Now that he had left that unique environment, we couldn't protect him from reality forever. Life does go on around us and we had to just deal with it as best we could.

After a few days, it was time for James's departure as he continued on his European adventures. We would be seeing him again in a few months' time, so it wasn't goodbye, merely *au revoir*. All being well, he was planning to join us in Chamonix over the winter.

We were so lucky that Matt had all these wonderful friends. Their support has been hugely important to us all. It is often impossible for the TBI survivor to plan things, let alone remember them, even if they do succeed in actually making an appointment. This is what really makes a brain injury so different from any other. Not only do different bits not work physically, but the ability to think in order to try and plan a recovery is impaired. One of the 'hats' that I wore during Matt's rehab was that of his PA. I scheduled and kept a diary of his various physio and training appointments. His friends knew to phone me to check when would be the best time to schedule a visit and also to confirm that he would be capable of doing whatever it was they had planned.

That last point was very important. His friends were so enthusiastic and keen to help, but sometimes they promised him things that he just couldn't do and then he would end up feeling very disappointed, which was the opposite of what they had been hoping to achieve. This was especially true when he was still in a wheelchair. Getting someone in a wheelchair to and from a destination can be a logistical nightmare!

Not only is this support network vital for the patient, it is also a lifeline for those most closely involved with their care. A problem shared really is a problem halved – not that I like describing Matt as a problem; he really wasn't. However, knowing that Matt was off doing something fun and, most importantly, in safe hands, provided Nick and I with some real respite and time to catch up on everyday chores or even just provide the opportunity to relax with a good book.

At the end of the day, for Matt himself, it was essential to get the right mix between physio, exercises and having fun with his pals. We were so lucky that everyone connected with Matt, either in a professional or personal capacity, seemed to be upbeat and fun. This meant that he always looked forward to every single day and what it might hold for him. If every day had been empty with nothing to do, I fear the eventual outcome would have been very different. For those without such a network, I would strongly recommend contacting a local support group through an organisation such as Headway, which provides a real lifeline for people struggling to come to terms with their newfound circumstances. Their website is an invaluable source of information.

*

Now that Matt was home, we embarked on a new routine consisting of twice-weekly visits to Donald Wilson for therapy, exercising and walking at home, and generally trying to think of ways to make Matt's life more interesting and stimulating for him. His Lego therapy was ongoing. We had also been very fortunate in finding an excellent personal trainer for him, who visited Matt at home to train with him. Paul is an ex-Army instructor and perfect for Matt. I don't think he had ever had a brain-injured client in a wheelchair before, but he was clearly up for it and full of ideas. Matt was delighted at the prospect of hard training and couldn't wait to get going.

In addition, we had also managed to enlist the help of a lovely neuro physiotherapist who had been at DWH. Lisa had left there at the same time as Matt, and we were so lucky that she agreed to come and work with Matt at home. She is very bright and bubbly and was just what Matt needed. We now had the dream team!

Lisa explained to Matt, in simple terms, using a couple of metaphors, what had happened to his brain. One example she gave compared Matt's brain to a busy motorway that has suddenly closed, causing chaos in the surrounding areas, and now he has to seek out new B-roads to travel on in order to reach his destination. Alternatively, it's as if some disaster has befallen him at home and he needs to ask his neighbours for help. He needs to bang hard on their doors, as they are lazy couch potatoes and will take a lot of rousing. In other words, he needs to find and use the spare capacity in his brain. Fortunately, there is plenty of spare capacity in the average brain, although it is in part dependent on what bit is damaged. As I understand it, some parts are easier to reroute than others. Obviously, if certain vital areas of the brain are destroyed completely then the outlook can be very bleak.

Our roller-coaster ride continued and our emotions were all over the place. Now that Matt was back living at home, we were much more aware of how limited he was in what he could do. For the last seven months, the professionals had taken care of him and we had been daily visitors to his life, with very little responsibility. Now he was entirely our responsibility. I know that Tim found it very difficult. He just wanted his brother back as he used to be and was very frustrated that it was all so slow. "Do you really think he's ever going to be able to walk by himself again, Mum? He's not, is he? I think you need to be tougher on him. Force him to do stuff."

"We can't force anything. He is working so hard already, but it's down to his brain to reroute in its own time. It'll either make the connections or it won't. There are no instant fixes." I felt for Tim as I tried to explain that we had to be patient. Patience was not something that he was familiar with.

All I wanted was a crystal ball in order to be able to see the future, but I couldn't find one. The person coping best with it all was Matt himself. He was, and is, quite amazing; always positive and cheerful. As far as he was concerned, what had happened had happened, and the only thing to do was to work as hard as possible towards the best recovery possible. He planned to be skiing by January 2012 and couldn't foresee any obstacles in his way.

While our main focus of attention was our son, life went on around us with its everyday problems and challenges. I had to keep reminding myself of the Chinese lady I had met in London who had told me I had been chosen to fight and that I would win. When things get bad, to this day, I still remind myself of her words and declare to myself, *I WILL WIN!*

During the summer, we received a letter from BMW asking if we knew of someone inspirational whom we might like to nominate as a torchbearer in the forthcoming 2012 Olympic Torch Relay. Of course we knew someone inspirational – Matt. I wrote my little paragraph explaining why I considered him to be inspirational and submitted it. We would be told in December if the nomination was successful or not. I didn't hold out too much hope, as they had seventy places to fill and I was sure there would be all sorts of worthy people who had conquered even greater adversity and raised huge sums of money for charity, or saved their local school, hospital or whatever. I was simply nominating Matt for his great spirit, determination and positivity. If, by some miracle, the nomination was successful, it would be a great thing to look forward to and something to give a real purpose to Matt's training.

We were already looking forward to the Olympics being in the UK, and Matt and I adopted the Olympic motto 'Higher, Faster, Stronger' as our own. Matt was now going for his personal gold medal in life. Just for him to be able to walk properly would be equivalent to anything Sir Steve Redgrave had achieved as far as we were concerned, and it would take just as much training, if not more.

*

As summer headed towards autumn, I began to realise that this recovery process was going to take a very, very long time. Matt's brain was slowly rerouting, but his inner core muscles that had wasted away during his long period of inactivity would takes months and months to rebuild. He needed a combination of correct brain messages and strong core muscles in order to regain the necessary stability to be able to walk and move correctly. We had imagined that once he started walking on his frame, he would advance rapidly and be off. It doesn't work out like that, though. We had to learn to live in the present and not look to the future; nor was it much use looking back to how things used to be. Living each day as it came and learning to appreciate whatever happened on that day was the best way to move forward. As long as we could see the tiniest bit of progress, we were okay. As someone would later say to me, "The day-to-day progress is tiny, but over a timespan of five years, it will be huge." Would we really have to wait for five years?

Our house was gradually turning into a gymnasium. Over the first two years, we would acquire an exercise bicycle, a treadmill, a cross trainer, weights, gym balls and exercise bands. Matt worked like a demon to try and build up those muscles. I have never seen such determination. To see him cheerfully battling day after day to overcome huge obstacles made you realise that all our everyday moans and niggles aren't really that bad after all.

It's funny the things that become important. On the 31st of August 2011, I recorded in my diary that Matt did his first standing-up wee! Apparently, that is quite a big step forward and, as such, it should be noted as a significant event, but I have no idea why. Something to do with balance, I suspect.

•

At the beginning of September, Nick and I took Matt to visit his friends on the Scilly Isles. They gave him a hero's welcome and took him straight off to the pub; not that Matt has touched a drop of alcohol since his accident. Alcohol and brain injuries definitely do not mix. Indeed, I had read some Buddhist saying, referring to alcohol, that said something like, 'You should not invite a thief into your mouth to steal your brain cells'. Matt loved that little quote and supplemented it with his own words of wisdom: "Brain cells quite simply do not grow on trees." He certainly needed all of his remaining brain cells, as the ones that were gone were gone forever, and he must have been using up a fair bit of his spare capacity.

On the island of St Mary's, we rented an apartment and we had also hired a wheelchair, which Matt refused to use. He was determined to get around using only his walking frame – no mean feat in a place with very uneven paving stones and many little hills.

The highlight of our trip was Matt windsurfing. He had been determined to give it a go, and his friends Rich and Joe were on hand to help. Amazingly, he managed to climb up on the board and, even more amazingly, he succeeded in pulling up the sail. How on earth someone with so little balance could stand up on a wobbly board in the sea is beyond me, but he did. He actually got it moving for a little while too. Not quite up to Olympic standard, but quite something for someone who could hardly walk. Fortunately, there was not much wind, so there was no danger of him being swept out into the Atlantic Ocean. The best thing of all was hearing the laughter that accompanied Matt's efforts. We were all taking pictures to send off to various friends. We were gradually beginning to realise that when he sets himself a goal, he will move heaven and earth to achieve it. Nothing is impossible as far as he is concerned. Two words that never enter his vocabulary together are 'give' and 'up'.

One night, he went to the legendary St Mary's Friday night disco, which became a bit of a Health and Safety issue because he had to take his frame down into the basement. His friends had to convince the doorman that they would look after him in the event of a fire. It's not easy being disabled. Apart from the fact that you are disabled, there are all these other things to deal with, such as access to public places. We were really having our eyes opened to it all.

Probably the strangest thing that happened was Matt getting apprehended by the local policeman. Seeing Matt wobbling around with a walking frame, he immediately jumped to the conclusion that he was witnessing a drunken prank. He obviously assumed that some little old lady or man was now minus their walking frame. We see what we expect to see and rarely question whether or not we might actually be seeing something quite different. Matt saw the funny side of it, but his friends were furious about it on his behalf. I guess there was just not enough real crime on the Scilly Isles to keep the policeman busy.

As walking is the easiest way of getting around on the Scillies, Matt did more walking than he had ever done since his accident and it seemed to do him good. He was then determined to walk without using any sort of aid, which was quite scary, as he could only do it by lurching between things that he could grab on to. These could be anything from a wall to a piece of furniture or maybe someone's arm. He was very, very wobbly, but his confidence was growing. It was as if he had a point to prove to all his old friends: "Don't worry about me. I might be wobbly now, but I'll soon be better."

Once back home again on the mainland, he continued to try 'new' old experiences. These included helming our boat for a little while, playing crazy golf and riding a bike, all with varying degrees of success. He was quite the sight to behold on his bike, as he kitted himself out for the ride by donning his ski helmet, ski goggles and ski gloves. He was escorted on his ride by Tim and Lisa, who ran along on either side of him, prepared to catch him if necessary. Lisa was constantly trying new things with him, including hydrotherapy in the local swimming pool. Between her sessions, Paul's training and the twice-weekly visits to Donald Wilson, he was keeping very busy, which was our aim.

We were so grateful to have the same old Matt back. Maybe slightly more eccentric than before and definitely a lot more wobbly, but basically the same. He always had been a bit of a one-off and I frequently found myself saying to the neuro professionals, "Don't worry, he would have done this before" (whatever 'this' might be). Despite all his problems, he knew exactly where he was going and what he needed to do to get there and, for us, that was the main thing.

TWELVE

HEADING FOR
THE WINTER

In London, there used to be an annual event called The Freeze. This involved the defunct Battersea Power Station being turned into a snow park for a weekend in October and inviting some of the top pro skiers and snowboarders to come over and compete. Matt knew that Jacob Wester would be there and, unbeknown to us, he had written to the organisers to say that he would like the opportunity to meet Jacob and thank him for the message he had received from him in hospital. He received a reply from them saying that Jacob would be happy to meet him on the Friday night. Matt had arranged to go up to London with his friend Rich from the Scillies. Not the boss Rich, but another one of the instructors, and it was this Rich who had organised the photo in the first place. Despite knowing that Rich would look after him, Nick and I felt very nervous. This would be the first time that Matt had gone away without us since the accident, and he would be navigating his way around London with his walking frame.

It actually went brilliantly and he came back with some great photos of him with Jacob. Once again, it struck me how very special the skiing community is and how they look after each other. How many other top sportsmen would take time out in the middle of a competition to meet one of their fans and spend time with them? When Matt wrote to the organiser after the event to thank him, he got the following reply: *Dude, it was my and his pleasure. The only way you can repay us is to focus on getting up the mountains and having it to the max. What you have achieved so far is incredible. Keep going, man! Inspirational. People moan about their issues. They know nothing. You rule, dude!* Well, getting up the mountains was exactly what Matt intended to do.

While Matt was heading for his mountains, Nick and I were still plodding up our own mountains, metaphorically speaking. We naturally wanted the best outcome for Matt, so we had to keep putting all our efforts into helping him, and it was exhausting. It was a bit like hacking your way out of a dense jungle. There is simply no alternative; to stay trapped in the jungle would be unthinkable. You know that somewhere beyond the dark, dank vegetation is the outside world, so you keep going. One day, you will be in a good place and then you'll be able to rest, but until then you can't stop. Normal life has to be put on hold and you accept that. Any parent would do the same.

Of course, Nick had the additional burden of having to continue to earn a living in order to pay for all of Matt's therapy, which doesn't come cheap. As a self-employed business consultant, his income depended on him continuing to come up with bright and original ideas. His work also involved quite a bit of travelling, which is tiring in itself. If you add to that his worries about Matt, it's a minor miracle that he managed to keep going.

*

After the excitement of The Freeze, the first anniversary of the accident was now looming. We all felt that this should be marked in a fun and positive way. There would be no point in sitting around remembering the awfulness of the 27th of November 2010, so the 27th of November 2011 would have to be completely different. Lisa and I decided it should be the day when Matt skied again. Lisa was getting to know Matt really well by now and she realised that, come hell or high water, Matt was going to get back on his skis, so at least we could ensure it was done safely. She knew someone who was married to a ski instructor and arranged for us to meet him at the Milton Keynes Snozone. Not quite the Alps, but at least it was fairly local.

So, on Monday 28th November (only a day late), the three of us set off for Milton Keynes to meet Gav. The Snozone is essentially a giant fridge full of artificial snow. The snow is, I imagine, produced in much the same way as snow from the canons that are brought into action in the mountains during times of low real snowfall. It has a huge pile of snow going up the back wall to make the slope, with a couple of drag lifts to get skiers up to the top of the slope. It is an ideal place to give skiing a go before committing a lot of money to a full-blown ski holiday, or simply to practise and get your ski legs back before that holiday. It is also the perfect place for a young brain-injury survivor, hell-bent on skiing again, to safely test out his ski legs and see if they are still functioning or not.

Matt started off quite tentatively, with Gav's help, going a little way up the slope and down again, but as the hour progressed, he went a little further each time until he was going up on the longest button lift, right to the top, and skiing down again. He did it for just over an hour. He was so thrilled, and delighted in telling us that he had always known that skiing would be easier than walking. Gav had come all the way from Brighton and refused to accept any money for his time. Once again, we were experiencing just how kind people are. We were complete strangers to him, but he wanted to help Matt. He was busy running his own training company, *Definition*, organising ski and snowboard camps. I am sure he had a lot of stuff to do, but he gave up a day for us, as did Lisa. There really are a lot of great human beings out there. It was a fantastic day, and as for those slopes in Chamonix – bring 'em on!

A week later, there was yet more good news – Matt had been selected by BMW as one of their Olympic Torchbearers. He was going to do his bit on the 22nd of July 2012 in London, and received a certificate stating that he had been chosen as *One of the most inspirational people in Britain*. Needless to say, he loved that, and from then on he kept reminding people of that fact. Now all he needed to do was learn to walk 300m holding up a torch.

Christmas 2011 passed uneventfully, except for Nick scoring the equivalent to a hole-in-one for his presents. He and I are always a bit competitive on the present-buying side for the boys, but that year Nick excelled himself. One of the genuinely devastating aspects of Matt's accident, as far as he was concerned, was the fact that the emergency doctors had cut off all of his bangles and beads. Matt looks like a typical ski/surf bum with long dark hair and many beads round his neck, wrists and ankles. They had been collected over the years on his travels and all had a special significance. He was slowly managing to build them up again, but one piece had been a complete one-off. It consisted of the chain from a bath plug onto which he had attached a paper clip and then worn it as a necklace. Nick had been to a local silversmith and had the piece recreated in silver. He had one each for both Tim and Matt and had kept his idea a secret until the moment he presented them on Christmas morning, looking exceptionally pleased with himself, as well he might be. Nothing could have topped that.

Above all, though, it was just so good to have Matt there and wide awake. It was such a contrast to Christmas 2010. That was now well behind us. As a reminder of how far he had come, his walking frame remained out in the hallway decorated with Christmas tinsel. It was now redundant and would soon be returned to the NHS supplier.

THIRTEEN

BACK ON REAL SNOW

On the 27th of December, Nick, Matt and I, plus the dogs, set off for Le Tour and skiing. We have owned our place in France since 1997, but never before had we looked forward to going there as much as we did this time.

The 2011-2012 season was shaping up to be a snowy one. By the 27th of December, they had already had more snowfall than over the whole of the previous year. The only slightly worrying thing was that I had read somewhere that the world was forecast to end in 2012, which would have been really annoying after all the effort that Matt had already put into his recovery.

Wednesday, the 28th of December, 2011 was to be Matt's first attempt at skiing on real snow since his accident. I had arranged to meet Magali, our friend and ski instructor who had taught us all to ski back in 1997. She commented on how strange it would be to reteach Matt, as she had first taught him to ski when he was a little lad aged nine and had seen him develop into an amazing skier over the years. I really don't think anyone

OCTOBER 2011, LE TOUR – DREAMING OF BETTER DAYS, WHEN THE
WALKING FRAME IS REPLACED BY A PAIR OF SKIS.

DECEMBER 2011 – DREAMS
DO COME TRUE, BACK ON
SKIS WITH MAGALI.

LONDON 2012 OLYMPIC TORCH RELAY –
ABSOLUTE CONCENTRATION IS REQUIRED.

APRIL 2013, LES GRANDS
MONTETS – DEANO AND
FABIEN CARRYING MATT
DOWN THE METAL STAIRS
TO MAKE ANOTHER
DREAM COME TRUE.

MATT AT THE TOP OF HIS MOUNTAIN IN HIS MAGIC CR JACKET.

PAUSING TO TAKE IN THE VIEW WITH FAB AND STEPH.

MARCH 2014 – MATT AND ANNE, APRES–SKI, OVERLOOKING LAKE TAHOE, CA.

MATT WITH HIS CR JOHNSON SKIS IN FRONT OF THE CR MURAL,
WITH KAHLIL, STEVE AND ADAM.

SUMMER 2014 – HIGH ALTITUDE MARATHON TRAINING ON THE
SUMMER SLOPES ABOVE LE TOUR.

OCTOBER 2014, AMSTERDAM MARATHON –
TIM AND GREG ON 'ARM DUTY', ACCOMPANIED
BY THE REST OF TEAM MATT.

SUMMER 2017 – MATT AND ROY RIPPING IT UP AT NASCAR, SONOMA, CA.

JANUARY 2018 – ON THE LIFT WITH JACOB WESTER
AND CAMERAMAN, TOBY BRADLEY, ON THE WAY UP TO
SHOOT THE VIDEO.

MATT HALFWAY THROUGH THAT BACKFLIP.

REHAB EXERCISE, MATT-STYLE.

JANUARY 2019 - AT THE JUNIOR FWT WITH 3 TIMES FREERIDE WORLD TOUR CHAMPION, ARIANNA TRICOMI.

SPRING 2019 - MATT INTERVIEWING THE MOST SUCCESSFUL X GAMES SKIER, HENRIK HARLAUT.

else would have taken it on. Can you imagine going up to a ski school and saying, "Can I please book an instructor for my son who has a severe brain injury and can't walk properly? Also, he doesn't want adaptive equipment. He will only ski on normal skis." I think I might have been locked up.

Off we went to La Vormaine to meet up with Magali. This is a large area of very gentle slopes specifically for beginners, and it has the great advantage of being only about 150 metres from our chalet. For that season, they had made a new area for absolute beginners with a little tiny, short drag lift designed for children. You accessed the slope through a small, brightly coloured archway with a yellow sun on it, and dotted around the piste were little wooden teddy bears and flowers – a real baby slope. Also, it was absolutely free to use, which is something of a rarity in ski resorts. Some 24-year-olds might have been reluctant to be seen on such a slope, but our 24-year-old could not have been more thrilled to be there. He went up and down on the baby drag lift with great confidence and the joy shone out of him. The only time he crashed was when I took a photo. He flashed me a huge grin and promptly ploughed into the side netting and got completely tangled up. It took me and Magali a good 5 minutes to untangle him. He emerged completely unfazed, still grinning and raring to go again. With a brain injury, it is difficult to do more than one thing at a time – skiing and posing for photos at the same time was obviously an impossibility. Once again, I felt so proud of Matt and wiped away a few emotional tears. It was just so wonderful to see him back doing the thing he loved best in the world.

As much as I had loved skiing in Milton Keynes (and it was genuinely the most satisfying skiing I had ever done at that point), this was what I was really waiting for. In December 2011, I finally clicked into my skis on actual snow in Le Tour.

I may have been on the little kids' slope of the beginners' slope, but it might as well have been heli-skiing in Alaska. I loved it! Magali, the instructor who first taught me to ski all those years ago, had agreed to teach me for the second time. I didn't mind at all that I was with an instructor surrounded by kids on the beginners' slope.

That's the beauty of skiing. It really doesn't matter if you are skiing in waist-high powder, jumping off 50-foot cliffs or snowploughing on a kids' slope. I think it's just awesome being on skis. Maybe I would have thought differently before the whole coma and stuff, but now I was just loving being back on my skis. With Armada skis on my feet, I felt pretty cool anyway!

Unfortunately, the next day, we were completely snowed in. Everything was shut, so no more skiing. Avalanche warnings were issued and the village was cut off for a few days. This is not an uncommon occurrence during the winter months in Le Tour, but it meant that we weren't allowed to leave the village. Our New Year's Eve feast was pasta and salad, as we hadn't managed to do a proper shop before all the snow fell. We had failed to obey the number one rule of the mountains – be prepared. Normally, we were pretty quick to stock up on snow rations in case of such eventualities, but that year we had completely forgotten. We had been far too excited about the prospect of getting Matt back on the snow. We didn't really mind being stuck inside watching the snow fall. We were in our favourite place, with a log fire burning brightly to keep us cosy, and our son was back on his very wobbly feet and improving slowly but surely all the time. We couldn't have asked for anything more, bearing in mind that at that time the previous year Matt was in a deep coma and we didn't know if he'd ever be back with us. Well, he was certainly back now with a vengeance.

On New Year's Day 2012, normal service was resumed. Our only problem then was getting Matt back up to the slopes. It had been hard enough before, but now there was a great mound of fresh snow at the end of our road to be negotiated. Needless to say, nothing was going to stop him, so Nick and I hauled him up over the heap of snow and then on up to the baby slope. Actually getting him to the skiing was always going to be the hardest part of the enterprise, even without the huge amount of deep snow with which we were now presented. As anyone will tell you, walking in ski boots and carrying all the gear is hard work at the best of times. There was no way Matt wasn't going to get there, though. He would have crawled up there if necessary.

As well as the skiing, which he did most days for an hour or so, we had also brought out with us sheets of physio exercises for him to do. We tried to spend an hour a day doing these. The only way to recover from a brain injury is through practice, practice, practice until the brain rewires and things like walking once again become automatic, instead of something requiring a huge amount of thought and figuring out. That's the theory anyway. Of course, it doesn't always manage to rewire and some people will never walk again. As long as progress is being made, though, there's hope, and there was no way that we were planning on giving up anytime soon.

On the 4th of January, Nick returned to England, and the next day Aussie James and his lovely girlfriend, Grace, arrived to stay with us for three weeks. We settled into a routine of hauling Matt up to the beginners' slope for his lessons, skiing, walking the dogs, shopping, cooking, physio and eating. James and Grace were fantastic with Matt. They were very patient and they even took over the evening physio sessions. James also came up with the idea of digging steps into the heap of snow at the end of the road, which made getting Matt up there slightly easier. It still wasn't exactly a doddle as it required at least one person holding Matt up and another person carrying his skis. Once we were up James's stairs, we had a short walk along a flat piece of land, before clambering up the final little slope to the ski area – it was quite a task.

On the 16th of January, Matt graduated up onto the main ski runs and did the last part of a red run. For anyone who doesn't know the grading systems of ski slopes, in ascending order starting with the easiest they are: Green, Blue, Red, Black. So for him to progress to a red after a couple of weeks was pretty good. I had been very nervous about the prospect of him getting on and off the ski lifts but, as always, he surprised us by taking it in his stride and getting off the chairlift with no problems. The lift operators in Le Tour were to become our very best friends. To access the ski area, there is a system of small six-person cabins, which run on a continuous circuit, just slowing down enough for people to get on and off. For Matt, they would actually stop the cabins to allow him plenty of time to get in and out of them. We then had to transfer to a chairlift to get further up the mountain and the chairlift operators too would slow that down and help him. By the end of the season, they all knew Matt and followed his progress keenly. All the ski instructors also knew him and what Magali was doing for him. When they saw Magali and Matt coming, the other instructors would stop their classes and pull their students to one side to allow Matt to pass. He was becoming a mountain VIP!

Now that he had graduated onto the main slopes, we had the added obstacle of getting him up the steep car park to the even steeper flight of steps to access the ski lift before we even started all the getting-on-and-off business. It took three of us to get him up to the lifts, but as soon as he put his skis on, he suddenly became independent and skied off. It was exhausting for his helpers and I was always very grateful to collapse onto the seat of the cabin for a very short rest before we reached the top. His skiing was, of course, nowhere near what it had been, but he could truthfully boast (as he frequently did) that he could ski better than he could walk. He genuinely found it easier than walking. Should we move to Alaska?

Meanwhile, the snow just kept on coming. One memorable night, it completely filled the little road outside the chalet. I had to enlist Grace's help to take the dogs out on their pre-bedtime walk as the snow was now way over their heads. Grace and I had to shuffle through it in order to make a passage for the dogs to walk through behind us. The snow was actually up to the level of the ground-floor windowsills. It was a magical scene with the street lights dripping with icicles and thick blankets of snow covering every surface. It had been many years since even the locals had seen so much snow. When they are all out taking photos, you know it must be something extraordinary. Just locating our car out in the car park was going to be quite a challenge, as the whole area looked as if someone had scattered a whole load of giant fluffy white pillows around. Not a sign of any car was detectable, but they were under there somewhere.

Whenever there was a pause in the constant snowfall, I would get the bus down to Argentière to stock up on supplies, as there are no shops in Le Tour. We had a properly equipped 4x4, which was well able to cope with snowy roads, but it was all the other cars slewed across the road and stuck in all sorts of awkward positions that I didn't fancy dealing with.

January proceeded with a cycle of skiing, then being snowed in for a day or so due to the volume of snow falling, then back out skiing. I don't think our Australian friends had ever expected to see so much snow. On the 27th of January, it was time for James and Grace to leave us and continue with their European travels. After they left, I got a bit down. I just couldn't understand why, with all the hard work that Matt was putting in, it was taking so long to recover. Even though we had been warned it would take a few years, it still seemed impossibly slow to me. It was great that he was doing so well with his skiing, but why was the walking not improving at the same rate?

Due to the fact that I was feeling a bit low, I allowed a silly incident with a Frenchman to get to me. After Matt's ski lesson with Magali, I used to drive up the car park to get as near as possible to the lifts. The policemen who controlled the traffic up there knew me and allowed me to drive further up the car park than was strictly allowed. Matt would always be exhausted at the end of his lesson, and walking down the steep car park from the lift was very difficult for him, even with help. On this particular occasion, a group of middle-aged, perfectly fit-looking French people had arranged for someone to drive up in their car and be waiting for them in order to save them the trouble of walking down the car park with their skis. Fair enough, but their car wasn't even there yet. I pulled up to my usual place and one of the men banged on my window.

"You have to move your car. A friend of ours is coming here now to pick us up." He was quite adamant.

"I'm sorry, but I'm collecting my son. He's on his way down from skiing and can't walk from the lift down to here without my help. Even with help, this is the furthest he can walk, so I need to leave the car here." I was speaking in French and hoped that I sounded very reasonable and that would be the end of it, but no, he just laughed at me.

"Of course your son can walk that far!" He sounded quite incredulous, yet he knew nothing at all about Matt.

I immediately burst into tears and was still crying when Magali arrived with Matt. Magali has a son who is disabled and she understood perfectly how I felt, so she stormed up to the man and gave him what for. I never saw him again but, if I had, I don't think he would have dared challenge me for the parking spot the next time. The vast majority of people are so kind and helpful, but it only takes one idiot to bring you crashing down.

The other thing that used to upset me was when I saw other young men speeding down the slope as Matt used to do. I would think to myself that it should be Matt out there doing that and how unfair it all was. He himself didn't seem to feel at all resentful; he just loved being out there. I would pull myself together rapidly and remember my Chinese lady and get back to fighting!

*

At the beginning of February, we returned to the UK for a bit. Matt was thrilled to have achieved his goal of skiing and couldn't wait to tell all the doubters about it. I returned exhausted, which is why I think I slumped and began to doubt the prospect of a good recovery. Both Nick and I were completely stressed and worrying about Matt's brain. His thinking seemed to have become completely loopy and sometimes he would talk complete nonsense. He did tell me that he just enjoyed winding me up, but was that really it? People would look at him as if he really was mad. He would frequently ask me, "Who would you choose between Tim and me if you could only have one of us?" or "If you had to drown either Bobby or Benji, which one would it be?" I always refused to answer on the grounds that I would never have to do that, but he still persisted and persisted. His poor physios also suffered from his barrage of questions. With them, it was also often the same questions endlessly repeated: "What is your favourite film?" 'What's your favourite colour?" "What team do you support?" "Who is the most famous person you've ever treated?" Sometimes he would go completely off the wall and ask, "What would you do if I chopped your leg off?" (and numerous variations on that theme) Luckily, Matt is one of the least threatening people you could ever meet, so they were never unduly alarmed by these strange and sometimes gruesome questions.

Even my mother was worried about him after he had completely confused her one day by telling her that he sung in a choir with Gareth Malone (from a TV programme) three times a week and he calls him Steve. He then informed her that he also goes street dancing. None of it made any sense.

I did wonder what on earth was going on in that battered brain of his. I suppose it was just settling down and rewiring and, in the process, short-circuiting on occasions. I did take some comfort from Richard Hammond, one of the *Top Gear* TV presenters, admitting that he had been 'as mad as a box of frogs' after his brain injury. It was perhaps a little selfish of me not to be satisfied. Already, he had far exceeded all expectations. The trouble was, all Matt's ambitions and goals were big. He really was aiming high and I so wanted him to get there.

Another odd thing was Matt becoming obsessed with buying things. He was constantly buying beanie hats over the internet. He would have had to grow several more heads in order to wear them all during the year. He justified this by saying that he didn't smoke or drink, so where was the harm in buying hats? Put like that, I guess it wasn't too harmful. The strange thing is that before the accident, he used to wear hats all the time, but after the accident, he hardly ever wore them. Why buy them then? After hats, he went on to sunglasses! It seems this is a fairly normal occurrence following a brain injury. People do seem to go through spending sprees and become obsessed by particular things. Matt's obsessions weren't too terrible, but I have read of people getting themselves into serious financial trouble because of their non-stop purchases. One young man kept ordering motorbike parts and, as I recall, he didn't even have a motorbike. His house became full with all the bits of machinery, not to mention the damage it did to him financially. Thankfully, in

Matt's case, this did gradually settle down. It all reminded me of one of those humanoid robots in a Disney film when they short-circuit and go beserk and start doing crazy things. The brain is such a complicated thing that when it gets damaged, it can malfunction in the strangest of ways. I am just so grateful that we have never had to experience any serious malfunctions, but I know they can happen. Although we were somewhat fazed by these strange periods, we knew it was just his brain rewiring and occasionally misfiring. We were only too aware that it was going to take a while to sort itself out. It was a bit like being on a boat at sea during a storm. You just have to ride it out.

*

The main reason why we had succeeded in enticing Matt back from the snow of Chamonix was that he needed to attend a BMW Torch Relay Day to learn about what would happen on the big day itself. We went up to London on 13th February 2012. I had expected to leave him there, but the lady on the door said that I would be welcome to stay – much to my delight. It turned out to be quite an emotional day. We were shown an example of the torch that they would be carrying and then watched an inspiring film about the relay, with Take That's song *Greatest Day* playing as part of the soundtrack. It was all very uplifting and emotional and reduced most of the female section of the audience to tears.

We had the opportunity to meet many of the other seventy BMW torchbearers. They all had tales to tell, some very tragic. A couple of them had lost children to accidents or illness and then gone on to raise thousands of pounds for charity. Others had overcome various obstacles, and it was very awe inspiring to realise how many good people there are in the world who will take whatever bad thing life throws at them and then just throw it right back and do some good with it. I didn't know where we were heading, but I was determined some good would eventually come of it.

We also met the gold-medal-winning athlete, Steve Cram, who was one of the BMW ambassadors. He spent some time chatting with Matt and had his photo taken with him. There were many photos taken for posterity and we began to feel very excited about the 22nd of July. It was definitely a huge honour to have been selected, and I hoped that Matt would prove himself worthy of it. His wasn't a very noble sort of accident, but I truly believe that since then he has been an inspiration to others. At the very least, he makes people smile and laugh. He is full of that mysterious 'feel good' factor. If only we could bottle it, we could be very wealthy!

●

On the 9th of March, Matt and I returned to Le Tour for our last round of skiing. It was the same routine as last time: drive Matt the short distance up the car park to the ski lifts, meet Magali, get him up the stairs, stop the lift, get him on, stop the lift, get him off, carefully make our way over to the chairlift, slow it down, help him on, get off at the top and ski off. No problem!

The weather this time was wonderful with lots of sunshine. Matt could now manage 2 hours of skiing every day. The lift operators were fantastic. They all knew him by now and he was treated like royalty. Once again, Matt had brought out the best in people. The funniest fellow was Jean-Luc, who would quite happily hold up the whole queue behind Matt while he chatted to him about Manchester United. He is quite a character and couldn't really give a toss about what people think about him. For some reason, he took a great liking to Matt, and when people behind us in the queue started tutting about the delay, he simply gave them a dirty look and continued with his conversation.

One day, he spotted me hauling Matt and his skis up the car park. "Hey! You need to park in the disabled space. That would be so much easier for you."

"I know. I can't, though, as you are supposed to have a special badge to park there and I don't have one," but I appreciated his concern.

He didn't see that as a problem, "*Pfouf!* You just park there and if the policeman says anything to you, you know what to say to him."

"Do I?"

"Yes, you say, 'F—k you!'" I decided not to take his well-meant advice on this occasion.

Matt was even rescued by Superman one day; at least I think that is who it must have been. We were crossing the road down in Chamonix from a particularly icy pavement and Matt wobbled and started to fall. From out of nowhere, a Frenchman leapt forward and scooped him up, just like Superman! With the exception of Mr Nasty in the car park, in Chamonix, we encountered nothing but kindness and helpfulness. Doors were held open for Matt and complete strangers stopped to help him up steps. They couldn't have been nicer and they were duly rewarded with one of Matt's dazzling smiles. *Vive la France!*

During that winter, Matt decided that he actually was French. This wasn't a new thing. He had often said it before. We left England when he was six and Tim was nine to live in France for Nick's job, followed by moves to Germany and Switzerland. England hadn't really played a huge part in their upbringing. He usually skied with either Magali or her friend Carole, and they spoke only French to him, which was great and, much to my relief, his French language was all still there in that brain of his. Obviously, the 'speaking a foreign language' bit was undamaged.

On the 9th of April, we had to say goodbye to all our French friends and come back home – although not Matt's home, of course; that was Le Tour. It felt like quite an anti-climax to be back in England after all the fun of Le Tour. It was obvious that all the skiing had done Matt so much good. During March, we had been able to notice an improvement in Matt's walking, and even his speech was getting a little better. We were very fortunate to have been able to do it. It was an important part of the big plan we had worked out to keep Matt as stimulated as possible.

So far, it was all going very well.

FOURTEEN

SOME SERIOUS TRAINING FOR SOME SERIOUS TORCHBEARING

On his return to the UK, Matt was like a man possessed. He was more determined than ever to make a full recovery as quickly as possible. He was obsessed with press-ups or, as he preferred to call them in his native French, '*les pompes*'. He was doing 111 a day, divided up into smaller sections throughout the day.

He had been using a treadmill at home for his walking, as he could walk quite fast on it while holding onto the bars. It was great until he dropped his water bottle on it one day and it blew up in spectacular fashion with a great many flashes and bangs! We were also trying to go for a real walk outside every day. His walking was definitely slowly improving, with the emphasis being on *slowly*. We made frequent visits to nearby West

Wittering Beach, which provided a flat, firm surface to walk on if we kept to the wet sand. Lisa had also upped the game and had him doing some quite tough exercises. Paul was now including swimming in his weekly training sessions. That proved harder for Matt than I thought it would, as his weak core meant that he couldn't keep his legs up very easily. He was certainly keeping very busy.

He had also started to move more freely around the house. Rather than sitting around waiting for us to take him things, he was pootling around by himself. He was still very wobbly, but we were beginning to see a light at the end of the tunnel. Even as we began to see the faintest glimmer of light, we knew that we couldn't allow ourselves to get too excited, because the end was still very far away. I think recovery from this particular brain injury could be compared to a tortoise circumventing the globe. Fortunately, our tortoise was having plenty of fun and meeting lots of interesting new people along the way.

Matt's next post-injury first was to be dinghy sailing. As he had been a sailing instructor before his injury, we thought he should give it a go, although he was convinced he couldn't remember any of it. He went off to a local sailing centre to see what would happen. As always, the actual walking to the dinghy was difficult, but once he was on board, he was away! He hadn't forgotten how to sail after all. That was another thing that was still hardwired into his brain. It wasn't something that he could do unaided, though, as moving around a little boat was too difficult. He didn't really have the same passion for sailing as he did for skiing, so it wasn't something he pursued any further. It was just good to know that it was another bit of his brain that had retained the knowledge.

Within 18 months of an awful accident, he had tried windsurfing, skiing, sailing and cycling with varying degrees of success, but it didn't matter if it wasn't perfect. What mattered was the trying. What could be better than taking a leaf out of the SAS's book and adopting their motto of 'Who Dares Wins'? Back in October, he had also driven an RIB (rigid inflatable boat), which was a huge achievement for someone with balance problems. Bouncing around on a rough sea is hard enough for anyone, let alone someone with Matt's problems. He had tackled all these challenges with confidence and determination. That's why to me it seemed so unfair that the walking was not progressing faster. It *was* still progressing, though, and we had to be grateful for that.

I was reading a lot about the brain and had a light-bulb moment when I read about the cerebellum. This is located behind the top part of the brain stem, where the spinal cord meets the brain. It controls voluntary movements such as posture, balance, co-ordination and speech. We had waited to see which bits were damaged, and now I had worked it out. I felt very proud of myself. "Matt, I know which bit of your brain was damaged. It's called the cerebellum."

He gave me a puzzled look. "How did you not know that? The doctors and neuro physios have always said that."

"Oh, I must have missed that conversation. At least I got it right, though!"

Between his return to the UK and the end of July, Matt was in serious training for his torch relay. He was going to have to walk 300 metres carrying quite a heavy torch and he was determined to do it on his own, without even the support of a stick. We spent many hours walking up and down our road. I spoke to people I had never spoken to before, as they would come out to say how well Matt was doing or, if I was on my own, they would enquire as to his progress. Without exception, they were all impressed by the way he kept at it. His performance was always affected by his level of tiredness. If he was tired, everything would go – his speech, his balance, his ability to walk. It was hard to persuade him to get the balance between exercise and rest in proportion. He saw exercise as his route to recovery, which it was, of course. In order for the rerouting to take place in his brain, it was necessary to keep repeating things until his brain had got the message. However, his brain also needed time to rest. A bit like an army resting and regrouping. It was all such an alien world for us and we didn't really have any professional advice on the overall plan. We did have our excellent team of Lisa and Paul, thank goodness, who worked him hard and were as determined as we were that he would progress.

By the end of July, Matt had actually put on a bit of weight. He was up to 67kg, still not the 75kg that he had been pre-accident, but better. The trouble was, he was burning up an incredible amount of calories with all his exercising. Apparently, the amount of effort it takes a brain-injured person to exercise is a lot more than an average person. We can all walk, talk or run without too much thinking. It just happens. With a brain injury, it doesn't just happen. A huge amount of thought and planning has to go into it. Matt often said that he was not so much physically tired as mentally tired, because of the amount of concentration he had to put into everything he did. During his first year of recovery, it was practically impossible for him to walk and talk at the same time. He could do one or the other, not both. It was just too difficult.

Nick and I were still finding that our emotions were all over the place. The slightest little thing would give us cause for celebration, but then something else would plunge us into despondency. We constantly worried as to what the future would hold for Matt, despite our best efforts to try not to. He had always been such an active and adventurous young man. I just couldn't imagine him ending up doing some static job. I revised my estimated recovery period to 5 years in the hope that would give him further scope for a good recovery. The trouble was that Matt was already hell-bent on doing a ski instructor's course the next winter. Even at my most optimistic and positive, I knew that was totally unrealistic. We all needed something special to lift our spirits. Fortunately for us, maybe that was about to happen.

FIFTEEN

MATT'S FEELING VERY OLYMPIC TODAY!

Finally, the big day arrived – Sunday 22nd July 2012. All Matt's walking practice was about to be shown off to the world, or at least to the residents of Barking and Dagenham and anyone watching on the internet. Torch Day had arrived. With the London 2012 Olympics about to start on Friday 27th July, there was much excitement as the Torch Relay went back into London to start its final leg of the journey towards the Olympic Stadium, and Matt was to be a part of it.

We went up to London the night before to stay in Highgate with John and Sally. How lovely it was to be back there again, but this time with Matt. All four of us were there: Matt, Tim, Nick and I. Bobby and Benji missed out this time, but I am sure that they were happy to be back with Fiona in Pagham for the weekend.

That evening, we did a little recce of the area to see where Matt would be walking. He panicked a bit when he saw that it was all downhill. Downhill is the hardest thing for him to do, but we reassured him that he would manage it. After all, hadn't he always achieved his goals so far?

The 22nd of July dawned bright and sunny, which was quite a miracle in itself. We had been having dreadful weather that year with incessant rain. The vast majority of people seemed to have been carrying their torches in torrential rain under leaden skies, but this was a beautiful day. At 9.30am, a white BMW pulled up outside the house to take him on his adventure. The car was driven by a man called Chris, and he was accompanied by Olivia, who represented BMW and would be looking after Matt all day. Matt was very impressed to discover that Chris was a police driver trained in getaway techniques. He had also driven many celebrities, including Sir Alex Ferguson, the legendary Manchester United manager. That was certainly good enough for Matt. We were very confident that he and Olivia would take excellent care of Matt. Most of the torchbearers would have to find their own way there and back, but being a BMW torchbearer meant that everything was taken care of. We wouldn't have to stress about anything.

We spent some time taking photos of us all beside the car before Matt was driven off in style to Dagenham Civic Hall, where he was given his white torchbearer's uniform and his torch. He also received his instructions regarding his torchbearing duties, together with all the other torchbearers who would be with him on the Olympic coach delivering them to their respective points on the route.

Meanwhile, the rest of us made our way to Whalebone Road North in Dagenham to await Matt's arrival. Lisa had driven up to join us and she was as excited as I was. As she said, "When I think back to when I first met Matt in hospital last year, he could hardly do anything. Now here he is about to carry the Olympic Torch – it's just amazing." Also joining us there were several of his friends who had come along to cheer him on.

Matt was due to start his stint at 13.08 and shortly before that, it all began to happen. The procession approached, escorted by police outriders on motorbikes. A gold car, followed by the gold-coloured LOCOG coach (London Organising Committee of the Olympic Games), headed the procession, and they in turn were followed by three double-decker buses, in red, blue and green respectively, relating to the colours of the three sponsors. The LOCOG coach carried the torchbearers, while the sponsors' buses had music blaring out and were festooned with balloons. They contained groups of very enthusiastic young people leaping and dancing around, creating a carnival atmosphere.

Matt's bus stop was number 77 to match up with the number on his uniform. He got off the bus carrying the torch with just the biggest grin on his face and I promptly burst into happy tears! One of his friends gave me a lovely hug and said, "It's okay, Anne, you're allowed to do that after all you've been through." Eighteen months previously, I would never have dared to dream of Matt being part of something like this. Chris and Olivia were there to greet him and make sure that he ended up in the right place.

The torch itself was a splendid bright gold colour and a triangular shape, with a small badge of the 2012 logo on one side. The triangular shape had a specific purpose. The three sides represented London's third Games. It was also inspired by the three-word Olympic motto – *Citius, Altius, Fortius* (Faster, Higher, Stronger). The third inspiration behind the design was the trio of conditions the flame would have to contend with to stay alight on its journey: wind, fluctuating temperatures and rain. It was perforated with 8,000 small holes – one for each of the participating torchbearers. By the end of the 70 days it would take to complete the relay, it would have covered some 8,000 miles. And now there was our Matt proudly holding one of these torches in his hand.

One of the young men from the sponsors' bus came bouncing up to Matt to give him a hearty 'high five' and nearly pushed him off his feet. Luckily, there were plenty of people around to catch him or his day could have been over before it had begun. He was able to come over and see us and have yet more photos taken before getting into position to wait for the flame to be passed on to him. His forerunner was a Frenchman (how appropriate) called Baptiste who had run his leg, as opposed to walking it as Matt would have to do. The torches 'kissed' to light Matt's torch and off he set.

He was accompanied by a policeman and policewoman – one on each side of him. I had seen the policewoman asking him if he was absolutely sure that he wouldn't need to hold on to someone's arm. No, thanks! He was adamant that he was going to do this on his own – he hadn't been practising all those weeks for nothing. That practice paid off, as his walking was brilliant. He had such a look of sheer determination and concentration on his face as he went down that hill. There was no way he wasn't going to complete his 300m successfully. All around him, people were cheering and clapping. Perhaps the very best thing as far as I was concerned was the sheer delight and joy on the faces of his friends as they roared him on from the side of the road. I think a few of them hadn't ever expected to see their friend up and about again. Now there he was wobbling his way along the road in front of hundreds of cheering people. Complete strangers were willing him on and taking pictures of him. Nick, Tim and I were so proud of him.

We had been told back in February at the BMW meeting that it would be a day to remember, a once-in-a-lifetime event. However, I have to say that it far, far surpassed all our expectations. As Tim said to me immediately afterwards, "That was awesome, wasn't it, Mum?" It was indeed awesome, fantastic, amazing – all the superlatives you could ever think of. It was just such a happy day and one that we would never have experienced if Matt hadn't fallen on his head. Not that I am advocating falling on your head in order to find happiness! It's just that we seemed to have been having so many uplifting experiences recently and had learnt to appreciate every good thing that came our way. The crowd knew that in order to have been chosen to carry the torch, all these people had done something special, and they were going out of their way to make them feel even more special by their hugely supportive cheering and clapping.

It took Matt just 5 minutes to walk his 300m, and then he passed his flame on to a Russian girl, and he was once again whisked off by Chris and Olivia to the coach to return to base, where the torch was decommissioned. They removed the gas mechanism and returned the torch to Matt in a nice bag. A wonderful gift, courtesy of BMW. It is such a fantastic thing to have and it takes pride of place in his 'museum' (aka his bedroom), together with all the other special things he has acquired since his accident.

The rest of us returned to Highgate, where Sally had invited everyone to a barbecue. The sun was still shining brightly and it was the perfect end to the perfect day. Matt was safely returned to us a couple of hours later by Chris and Olivia and a good time was had by all. There was, as always, much laughter and an exhausted Matt lapped up all the attention. Yet again, I was struck by the love and support of his friends who have been with him every step of the way. Over the next few days, his friends and Olivia from BMW were to send me loads of photos, which I later put into a special album, which provides the perfect souvenir of the day. It had been 'Matt's moment to shine'.

At about 8.30 pm, we headed for home. On the journey, Matt was getting text messages from people who hadn't been able to make it to London but who had seen it on the internet. There was a great message from Greg and his family in France.

I could just imagine them all crowded around their computer cheering Matt on. It really had been the very best of days.

The next day, someone put a clip of Matt's bit on YouTube. It only lasted about 30 seconds, but it really captured the atmosphere. Needless to say, I watched that more than once. Immediately following the event, more than 1,500 people had looked at it. I often wonder who those 1,500 people are – even Matt doesn't have quite that many friends.

I think he agrees with me that it was a truly awesome day.

*

The Olympics are a pretty big thing. My first memories of the summer games are from Sydney 2000. I now had the chance to be a (tiny) part of them.

BMW sent a car to take me from Highgate to Dagenham. Being chauffeur-driven meant that I now felt very important. Then the driver told me he used to drive Manchester United players and coaches, so the journey to Dagenham was dominated by me asking him if he'd ever driven certain players (I had quite a long list).

I got given my torchbearer's uniform and first look at the torch. I had held one at the meeting a few months before, but they now had a gas canister in them. I had been a tiny bit worried that this canister would be really heavy; it wasn't. I slipped into my white tracksuit and I was ready for some serious torchbearing.

We were dropped off at our various starting points by bus. Obviously, the big crowds were there to see the Olympic Flame, but it did feel pretty cool with everyone cheering. When I got off the bus, I instantly saw my friends and family in the crowd. They were waiting exactly where I'd start my 300m. Many 'hilarious' jokes were made about me dropping the torch or setting myself on fire, but it was all amazing fun and felt like a big carnival.

If I'm brutally honest, it did all go by in a bit of a blur, but it was another bit of luck that I could use such a huge event to mark my progress. From those first few steps in the parallel bars to carrying the Olympic Torch. That's pretty cool by anyone's standards!

SIXTEEN

SLOW AND STEADY

After all the excitement of the Torch Relay, we were ready for another major event – Matt returning to work on the Scilly Isles where he had already spent four summers teaching watersports. He loved it there and fitted right in with the laid-back pace of life on the island. There were two sailing centres – one on the island of St Mary's and one on Tresco. Had his life worked out differently, he might well have been running the Tresco centre, as Rich, the owner, held him in high regard and looked on him as his right-hand man.

That year, although we knew he couldn't teach, he was hoping to be of some use doing either basic maintenance work, taking bookings or doing any other odd jobs that might be around. Unfortunately, things hadn't been thought out and everything was just wrong. His accommodation was up steep stairs with no bannister. He was based far away from the centre and had a long, difficult walk in order to get there. Suddenly, from being a hero in the Torch Relay, he found himself completely floundering around. He desperately wanted to work, but no one had really thought in advance what he might be able to do. I initially felt very angry, but then realised how difficult it must have been for his employers. They hadn't seen him for over a year and had no idea as to his abilities. In fact, no one could really have predicted what he might or might not be able to do. So after only two weeks, Matt returned home, admitting that it had been "a bit rubbish."

I think we were all guilty of being over-optimistic with regard to his abilities. It's hard to discourage someone who so obviously wants to succeed. It's back to the dilemma that Nick and I so often had – when to say no and when to let it go. I still think we would have done more harm on this occasion had we refused to let him go in the first place. We couldn't have kept him wrapped in cotton wool forever. He had to come to terms with what he could and couldn't do, even if it would be painful at times. Maybe a reality check was a good thing, although I didn't see it that way at the time. We had put so much work into making sure that Matt remained positive and, once again, I was really scared that this experience would plunge him down into depression. Fortunately, he once again proved his resilience by putting it behind him and pushing on. Lisa and Paul were still on board back home, and he had even been invited back to DWH for the occasional physio session there. So it was back to business as usual.

Paul was proving to be quite a find. He was perfect for Matt, as he is very, very funny. They both shared the same sort of whacky humour. He had rapidly become as much of a friend as a trainer. He seemed to have done all activities known to man, including skiing, kite-surfing, roller-blading and slack-lining – to name but a few. In August, he took Matt kayaking along the shoreline in his two-man kayak. They were gone for an hour and it was something different for Matt, which he really enjoyed.

They say that variety is the spice of life. If that's the case, Matt was certainly leading an increasingly spicy life.

Apart from the huge reality check, the Scilly Isles experience had also given us food for thought. During the critical phase, everything is taken care of for you, and the NHS is brilliant, but then you're discharged and left to fend for yourselves. Nick and I have done everything in our power to help Matt, but it was very difficult with no guidance. What should we have been concentrating on? Matt loved his physical exercise and therapy and saw those as key to his recovery, but what about speech therapy and cognitive therapy? Just the mention of those upset him. I was still adopting the ostrich approach – stick your head in the sand and wait for it all to sort itself out. I just had this complete faith that it would all be okay in the end somehow.

The disappointment of the Scilly Isles was followed quite quickly by disappointment number two. We decided the time had come to see about Matt getting back to driving. We had been told about the Queen Elizabeth Foundation at Carshalton where they do assessments for disabled people. They test various aspects, such as decision-making, speed of reactions, co-ordination and cognitive thinking. We made an appointment for an assessment and off we went.

They have a tiny little driving circuit, with a small car, to test the practical side of driving. That didn't go very well, as Matt had difficulty with turning the steering wheel quickly enough, and also he kept getting his foot stuck on the pedal. Then came the interview. We were in a little office at the QEF with me sat quietly in the corner while Matt answered various questions. He kept making little quips and was already getting funny looks from the man asking the questions. I was just about managing to keep a straight face and then the man asked Matt, "Have you ever had any spasms, pins and needles or involuntary movements?"

"No," replied Matt as he shot his arm rapidly up above his head and down again and gave the man a delighted smile, very pleased with his great joke.

I'm afraid I dissolved into fits of laughter. The poor man gave a rather nervous chuckle. I think that from that moment on, Matt was doomed. The man obviously thought he was completely loopy and that he should leave the driving for a few months yet. So that was that. I have to say, though, that he did pass the cognitive test with flying colours, so that, at least, was a very good result.

This just served to make him fuel all his energy into reaching his goal of doing his ski instructor's course in January 2013. That was not going to happen, either, but how do you explain that to someone who has put so much effort into pursuing their dream without destroying them? After two years of fighting all the way for his recovery, he just wanted his life back. All credit to him for aiming for the moon and beyond and accepting nothing less. As he used to tell all his various therapists, "I don't expect to be as good as before the accident, I expect to be better." He was determined to do the instructor's course, but his walking was still far too wobbly. He couldn't even carry his own skis, so how could he expect to be able to teach others?

We had now reached the stage of rehab that we had been warned about. Patients can see the finish line in the distance and try to rush to get there and subsequently come crashing down. I could see why Matt would be impatient, but slow and steady is the best way to reach the finishing line in this race.

In mid-October, Matt and I had a little visit to Le Tour. One of our challenges while we were there was to walk from the next village down, Argentière, back up to Le Tour. This was a distance of roughly 4km straight up the mountain. We did it in about an hour, which was excellent. It would normally take a fully fit person about 40 or 45 minutes. Matt refused to stop or take a break (or give in and catch the bus as I suggested). He just put his head down and trudged on until we reached our chalet. I should have known that he would never give up.

We brought Matt's skis back to the UK with us in anticipation of his trial ski for the instructor's course. He had emailed a ski school called New Generation and arranged the whole thing by himself, so we figured we should go along with it. So one Wednesday in October, off we went again to the Snozone in Milton Keynes. There we met a young man called Tom from New Gen, who put Matt through his paces for about an hour. He did very well and even managed to ski on one leg for a while. However, at the end of the session, he sat down with Tom, who very diplomatically suggested that it might be an idea to wait until next year when he would get more out of it. As we walked out, Matt turned to me and very matter-of-factly said, "Oh, well, I expected that." And that was that.

Meanwhile, he continued seeing friends and having a fine time and funny experiences. On one occasion, he went up to London to see his friend Sam and various other pals. On the Saturday night, they went to some basement bar. He wobbled his way down the stairs as best he could and was refused admission on the grounds of his being too drunk. His friends soon put the doormen straight and explained what had happened to him. The red-faced doormen immediately let him in and offered him a drink on the house. At that stage, they would have been subjected to his lecture about alcohol and brain cells not growing on trees. This was not the first time this had happened. After a stumble in the main street of St Mary's on the Scilly Isles, he had also been asked by a helpful gentleman if perhaps he had had one too many. Fortunately, he always sees the funny side and is rarely offended. He takes great delight in telling them all about his fall and his coma. I have also now learnt that if I see someone stumbling around all over the place not to immediately assume they are drunk – they could be suffering from a brain injury. As Matt would say, "Never assume, assume makes an ass out of u and me."

We regularly went over to Brighton to see Nikki, yet another excellent neuro physio. We had met her while Matt was in rehab. She had come to give a talk to the neuro physios and Matt had been volunteered as the guinea pig for her demonstration. On one of our visits, she explained that as Matt recovers, his body will try to find other ways around the muscles that aren't working. It develops coping strategies, which are not perfect, for example, stooping forward while walking, in search of the lowest point of gravity to aid with balance. To use the drunk analogy, you only have to look at how a drunk lurches forward in order to try and stay on their feet. He therefore has to keep constantly reminding his body to go back to using the muscles it originally used and should still be using. That is why it is so important to keep on doing the physio and doing it correctly, so that bad habits are not formed. She suggested that for the next year we should make rehab exercises our absolute priority – as if we didn't already! Matt never stopped doing his exercises. During the course of an evening, he would do at least three sets of different exercises. As for me, after a couple of years of helping with the supervision of exercises, I think I could set up my own clinic now.

*

On 6th November 2012, Matt flew to Australia to visit his friends James and Grace in Sydney. We had booked the trip for him several months previously and, at the time, it had seemed like a wonderful idea. It didn't feel quite so wonderful now – as I drove him up to Heathrow, I felt quite terrified. We had asked the airline for assistance, but even so, it seemed crazy to put him on a flight to the other side of the world. My fears remained as he checked in. The 'assistance' seemed a little haphazard and they didn't seem to grasp what help he would require.

However, after two years, we felt that it was important for him to have some independence and live as far as possible the life that a normal 25-year-old might live. So I took a deep breath, walked away to the car park and drove home asking myself, *What on earth were we ever thinking to do this? He could end up anywhere.* Although his brain functioned quite well now, he did still get confused and sometimes doubted his own memory as regards times and dates. Also, there was the issue of his wobbliness and slurred speech, leading to him being mistaken for a drunk – what if they threw him off the plane? After a very anxious 24 hours, an email pinged through and, when I opened it, there was a picture of a grinning Matt standing on James's balcony in Sydney. He'd made it there. Now he only had to get back.

On Tuesday 27th November, coincidentally the second anniversary of the accident, he managed the return journey too, arriving back at Heathrow Airport in one piece. I was so excited about collecting him from the airport. He had been my constant companion for so many months and it had been very strange without him around. He took a very, very long time to appear in the Arrivals Hall, but then I saw that broad smile coming towards me. I have since learnt that Matt will now always be the last person off a train, plane or bus. He prefers to let the other passengers rush off, so that he can do things in his own time. His walking seemed to have improved after his holiday. He was still limping, but less stooped forward. He was full of tales about his trip, where he had obviously been thoroughly spoiled and fussed over by everyone.

*

So now we had passed the second anniversary of the accident and were into the third year of recovery. Things were changing on the therapy front. Richard, his NHS physio, who he still saw on an occasional basis, seemed to think that normal movement and posture were retrievable for Matt. He suggested that the time had come to seek out a musculoskeletal physiotherapist. The neuro physios had been essential to Matt's recovery, as they were the experts in problems of the central nervous system, whether these were due to brain or spinal cord injury. They understood the recovery process from a brain injury and how to help the brain rewire and open up neural pathways. They knew that Matt's muscles weren't broken in any way; it was simply that the messages couldn't get through to tell them what to do, although there wasn't much about it that was simple really. They knew that Matt had to repeat tiny little movements with great precision in order to get himself going. However, now that his brain function was improving, he could benefit from some musculoskeletal input to give him greater strength and his movement patterns could be investigated to further help with his recovery. We could keep the neuro going but introduce some musculoskeletal alongside it. Sounded like a plan to me.

Once again, we were due to spend a lot of time in Chamonix during the winter, so we needed to find a physio over there. After a bit of googling, we found La Clinique du Sport who said that they would be happy to help. This was great news. The winter held much promise of progress now that we could combine the skiing with seeing a professional physiotherapist, not just me, as had been the case the previous year.

SEVENTEEN

SURELY THE BEST SKI SEASON EVER

We were all looking forward to a great winter season in 2012/13 and hoping for yet more progress with Matt. The previous year, he had only been able to walk around with the support of a friendly arm, after having just parted company with his walking frame. Thinking about that brought home to me just how far he had come over the past year. How much further might he be able to progress during this coming year?

For Christmas, we had bought him a new ski outfit. Armada, Matt's favourite ski company, had brought out a special ski jacket in memory of CR Johnson, the young skier who had also suffered a serious traumatic brain injury and who had been our main inspiration throughout Matt's recovery. It was green with a big yellow lion on the back, so we had also bought him matching bright yellow ski pants. He would now be really easy to spot from a distance on the slopes. Profits from the jacket went towards the CR Johnson Healing Center (sic) in Truckee, California, which made it even more special. Needless to say, Matt couldn't wait to get out onto the slopes in his very cool new gear.

He spent his first day back on the slopes with a young instructor called Maeva. She is a very vivacious young lady and I had a feeling that she and Matt would have fun. When I strolled up the car park to meet him at the bottom of the piste at the end of his lesson, much to my surprise, he wasn't there. I was then informed by various excited instructors that he was on his way back down the front. 'The front' is the red slope leading from the top ski area back down to the village, and he certainly hadn't been capable of skiing down that the previous year. The other instructors were all just as excited and pleased for him as I was. They were all aware of what had happened to him and how hard he had worked to get back on his skis. With his distinctive outfit, I was soon able to spot him and follow his progress down, and it was quite remarkable. He was winding his way down the front of the mountain, putting in some good turns, and he was obviously so much stronger than last year. On his arrival at the bottom, it was hard to tell who had the biggest grin – Matt, Maeva, me, or the assembled watching ski instructors!

Going back to Le Tour was like coming home for us. Matt was given a huge welcome by all the lift operators and instructors. There was much patting on the back, high fives and handshakes – even a few kisses from the lady lift operators. They all remembered him by name and were genuinely pleased to see his improvements. It was all beginning to look rather good.

There was further cause for optimism when La Clinique du Sport proved to be every bit as good as we had hoped. Neil, the physio in charge, had some great ideas and was confident that he could do a lot for Matt. He had decided to treat Matt as if for a ski injury and gear all his therapy towards skiing, which would in turn help his walking and everything else. On his arrival at the clinic, Matt soon spotted the photographs on the wall, which featured Neil standing with various sports professionals, including a few Olympians. He figured that if Neil was good enough for them, then he would probably be good enough for him too. At the end of the season, Matt was very honoured to join those professionals on the wall, as Neil had requested a picture of him carrying the Olympic Torch.

On 3rd January, we had another first for Matt. He was skiing with Magali and she took him right round to the back of Le Tour – the whole circuit. It is a lovely run and takes you on a road through a pine forest and then you take a chairlift right up to the highest point of the resort, before returning to the first chairlift. There are some great views down the valley on the Chamonix side and then across to the Swiss Alps on the other side. It is actually right on the Swiss border and you can stand with one foot in France and the other in Switzerland. Matt must have felt that he had well and truly got his skiing mojo back on that day. This was a place he hadn't been for four whole years, due to a combination of his accident and working away prior to it. Doing the circuit represented HUGE progress!

My feelings were all over the place. I veered between great optimism and excitement and then worry in case he didn't keep progressing. I still resented seeing other young men on the slopes whizzing past doing tricks and flicks, although Matt didn't seem to begrudge them their fun at all. We had been constantly told from Day 1 that no one ever fully recovers from such an injury, but what does 'fully recover' mean? I would happily take 99%. Basically, it was hard to know what anyone was talking about – they all seemed so vague and uncertain, which is why I chose to largely ignore them.

In January 2013, a new character entered our lives: Mr Roy Tuscany, and what a character he proved to be! We didn't realise it at the time, but Matt's new ski jacket was about to transform his recovery process. We knew that the profits from it would go to the CR Johnson Healing Center, which is a centre to help winter sports athletes who have suffered life-altering injuries. As CR's story had been such a huge inspiration during Matt's recovery, we really wanted to contribute something. Written on the jacket were the letters ENEFCT. I thought these must stand for something and I was determined to find out what. I initially wrote to Armada and they informed me that it was what CR had been intending to call his clothing company had he lived. I still didn't know exactly what they stood for, though, and that was bugging me, so I wrote directly to the Healing Center. Little did I know what I would be starting with the sending of that email.

I received a reply from Roy Tuscany of the High Fives Foundation in Truckee, California. It just oozed enthusiasm and positivity. He said that he was excited by our positive attitude towards Matt's injury, which *resonates with the positive work we are doing with the High Fives Foundation*. Such was the energy emanating from the email that I felt I had to reply and tell him more about Matt, and so started a series of emails flying back and forth across the Atlantic.

I never did find out if ENEFCT actually stood for anything other than the proposed name for his clothing company, but I did find out all about Roy and the High Fives Foundation. Roy was a young man who had been well on his way to becoming a professional skier when he went one jump too far and broke his back. He was warned that he might never walk again, but he was determined not to get down about it. He decided to force all the medical staff to 'high five' him when they approached his bed. This forced them to make eye contact with him and relax more. Realising that his professional skiing career was over, what did he do? Weep, wail and feel sorry for himself? No way. Firstly, he worked hard to ensure that he would walk again. Having achieved that goal, Roy decided he must put something back into life or, as he puts it, 'pay it forward'. The local community had got together for him to make sure that he had sufficient funds for his recovery, and he would now spend his life helping other winter sports athletes who had also suffered life-altering injuries. He would show them that there is a way forward using the power of positivity and believing that everything is possible. So together with two other young men who had also been affected by illness or injury, Adam Baillargeon and Steve Wallace, Roy set up the High Fives Foundation. They work tirelessly to raise money to support injured athletes. The events they organise to raise funds are fun and crazy and effective. As an organisation, it is growing all the time and reaching out to more and more people. I have never in my life come across anything like it before or indeed anyone like Roy. I always thought Matt was positive, but for Roy you need to multiply that by ten. I would rate him as the most positive person on the planet.

So now here was Roy taking a genuine interest in a young, injured British skier, who was not a professional and who had injured himself, not in a skiing accident, but by falling through a roof. He insisted on sending Matt the CR ski helmet and goggles so that he could 'rock' those as well as the jacket. This was seriously generous and unexpected and Matt's grin was as wide as wide could be.

This further reinforced my already strong belief that there is something amazing about the ski community. What is it about these skiers? They have life-altering injuries (usually spinal or brain) and then they somehow bounce back twice as positive and full of life. The love and support that they have for each other is quite something. From the men and women operating the ski lifts at Le Tour to the instructors in the ESF (École de Ski Français) to Roy Tuscany and crew in Truckee, it's been quite overwhelming. We even received a lovely email from CR's sister, which was very touching. 2013 was already turning out to be quite a special winter season!

On Friday 18th January, it went up a further notch when Matt left the slopes of Le Tour to graduate up to Lognan for the first time since his accident. Lognan is the ski area just below the legendary Grands Montets in Chamonix. Matt had already declared his intention of skiing the black runs of les Grands Montets before the season finished, so this was his first step on the way. Once again, he was skiing with Maeva, who was perfect for him. She seemed oblivious of the fact that he had had a serious head injury and was quite happy to take him anywhere, which was a good thing as far as Matt was concerned. He hated people fussing over him and being overprotective. They skied all the way down the long, steep red slope known as Pierre à Ric, which leads back down to the bottom of the mountain, and it is a lot longer and tougher than its equivalent in Le Tour. This was quite a challenge for a still-wobbly young man. Every single new achievement was like another brick in building Matt's recovery, adding to his confidence and optimism.

Matt became fairly obsessed with his goal of skiing les Grands Montets. As more than one person has commented, Matt doesn't exactly set his sights low; only the highest will do for him. At some point during every single ski lesson he had, he would say, "Okay, tomorrow, we ski Grands Montets." And I do mean every single lesson. I know it drove the instructors mad. This was a good example of how his brain would get stuck on something in the same way as an old-fashioned record needle would get stuck in the groove of a vinyl record and just keep going on and on and on. His persistence has a way of paying off, though. He wears people down. On the 24th of January, when we met Magali to go skiing, she called me into the instructors' inner sanctum to talk to her and Fabien. Fabien was the head of the Le Tour ski school and we have known him for years.

I went into the little room where the instructors kept all their kit and we sat round the long central table, which was covered in food. They obviously need a lot of fuel to get through the long, cold days. After the customary kiss on each cheek, Fabien started to explain. "Matt really wants to get up to les Grands Montets, doesn't he?"

"It's all he ever talks about. It would be amazing if he could somehow do it, but do you think his skiing is up to it? I don't want another accident!" I replied with my mum hat on.

"No, no, nor do we!" Magali reassured me

"Okay," said Fabien, "I really can't promise anything. We have the rest of the season to get through, but he seems to be making good progress. If we think he's skiing well enough by the end of the season, we can get a group of instructors together and take him up there. It will be difficult getting him down all those stairs to get to the slope. We'll have to carry him down, I think."

"What! Do you think you could do that safely?" My mum hat was even more firmly on now.

Fabien laughed at my concern. "Don't worry. It's been done before. I'll make sure it's all arranged beforehand. It'll be okay. We won't do it unless the conditions are perfect – good snow and good weather."

"That's fantastic! Can I tell him that it might happen?"

"Of course, but warn him we'll only do it if his skiing is good enough and conditions are great."

"Thank you! Thank you both so much." I just threw my arms around the two of them, while they grinned at me with delight. Once again, people were going the extra mile for Matt, who was now known as *'le Mascot du Tour'* (the mascot of Le Tour). I just wish I'd taken a photo of Matt's expression when I told him about it – it was a mixture of disbelief and sheer joy.

We also heard from Roy T. I had jokingly said to him that Matt was having difficulty getting people on board for his Grands Montets ambitions. So never fear, Roy was here. He told us that he had contacts in Chamonix whom he would reach out to for Matt. It had now become his personal goal to get Matt up there. He was also sending Matt a prototype CR t-shirt. I was getting the distinct feeling that Matt now had a guardian angel in the form of CR Johnson. I really felt he was somehow looking out for Matt, especially when he was wearing his CR ski jacket. I did feel very strongly that CR's spirit was with him and getting him through, which was a little strange for me, as I didn't think I believed in that sort of thing. We'd never met CR, but we had looked at so many of his ski movies and seen his incredible strength of spirit that I guess he was just in my head. I know that Matt felt the same, as he swore that he would never update that jacket. It had become his lucky charm, and in Chamonix, he was widely recognised because of it.

Once a week, the High Fives Foundation sent out a newsletter and that year they had a weekly Inspiration Station. Matt was very privileged to appear on it with his Torch Relay story. All these things gave us such a boost. Life was pretty good on the whole.

Matt was also going great guns with his physio in Chamonix. He went four times a week at the end of the day. Neil was proving to be quite a find and was constantly finding different ways of challenging Matt. This, combined with the skiing, was doing him so much good. He had so much more stamina than last year and could manage a full two hours of skiing now.

February is always an extremely busy time on the slopes because of the school half-term holidays. The long queues and crowds are pretty impossible for Matt to cope with, so we decided to return home.

*

Back in Bognor, Matt was continuously winding up Lisa by constantly harping on about Neil and how wonderful he was. Lisa has been Matt's neuro physiotherapist since the beginning and she has put her heart and soul into helping him. She has been wonderful and Matt knows it, but that doesn't stop him from teasing her mercilessly.

I decided to go on a two-day Brain Injury Workshop that I had come across, and found myself to be the only non-professional there. Most of the other attendees were therapists looking after TBI patients. It was an interesting couple of days, but what I remember most of all is the session on 'denial'. The speaker spoke of families refusing to see the injury for what it was – life-changing – and how they need to be prepared to reassess their life goals and realise how a person's abilities have changed. According to him, these families were living in a permanent state of denial. I couldn't help myself; my hand shot up.

"Ah, Anne. Ladies and gentlemen, this is Anne. She is with us today as her son suffered a serious TBI a couple of years ago. I am sure she will have some insight on this for us." He didn't really sound that keen on hearing that insight.

By now, about twenty-five pairs of sympathetic eyes were fixed on me as Exhibit A – a real live carer-mother.

"I just wanted to say that what you describe as denial, I would describe as hope. My son's progress has been slow, but it *is* progress and as long as we see even the tiniest bit of progress we'll keep hoping. I don't think you could get through this without hope. If we reach a stage where it's obvious that Matt is not going to advance any further, I think we'll recognise it and deal with it then. You can't start with no hope, though. Sometimes hope is all you have."

The expression in the eyes had changed now. I think they now all saw me as a prime example of a relative in denial, but I stuck to my guns. I had seen someone give up in rehab. That someone was a person who had been generally reckoned to stand a good chance of recovery. I saw them a year later, still in their wheelchair, looking dreadful. Matt had no intention of giving up, and we had no intention of telling him to be realistic and lower his expectations.

In some ways, it was quite a depressing couple of days, as all the worst outcomes were highlighted. Don't these people ever know any good stories?

It was not only the professionals who cast doubt on Matt's future abilities, sometimes friends did too, and who could blame them? We never really saw Matt as disabled, merely injured. It would come as quite a shock when someone would say something that indicated very clearly that they were seeing a disabled person in front of them.

There was one occasion when a well-meaning friend asked me, "Have you given much thought to the future? What will happen to Matt when you're too old to look after him anymore?"

I couldn't have been more shocked if they had thrown a bucket of ice-cold water over me. I remember thinking to myself, *What a weird question. That's a long way away. We don't need to worry about that just yet.*

My actual reply was, "Well, we'll just have to see where we are by then."

I then got 'the look'. 'The look' was something I would see plenty of as time went on. It was always an intense gaze of real concern as they saw a poor deluded woman who needed to get real. Although I became more accustomed to seeing it, it always shocked and always hurt.

I am sure that any professional reading this is totally horrified by our stubborn refusal to plan for the long-term future, but neither Nick nor I could even begin to think like that. Planning for the worst-case scenario would have seemed like we were giving up. We were seeing improvements, no matter how tiny, and while they were still happening, we would continue to reach for the moon and beyond.

I felt that our approach had been vindicated by everything we had learnt about High Fives. Their whole philosophy is based on believing that anything is possible. Roy once reminded me that 'impossible' spells 'I'm possible'. Over the coming years, I would read the stories of their recovering athletes and how they all looked to the future with optimism, in the belief that the future would hold good things for them. Their adventures would continue, but maybe in a different way. Someone in a wheelchair can still speed down mountains and even do tricks with the right equipment. You cannot keep these people down; their zest for life is just too great. Finding out about High Fives had cleared the way for Matt to achieve his dreams. We were not crazy or in denial.

During our time back in the UK, as well as physical exercise, we also did plenty of other things to stimulate Matt's brain. The Nintendo Wii proved to be a very valuable tool for this. We spent many hours playing virtual golf, bowling or football. They had used these games in Donald Wilson as a form of therapy, so we knew we were doing the right thing there. We also played a lot of board games to exercise his brain, and discovered that Matt still hated losing as much as ever.

*

At the end of March, we returned to Chamonix. Matt had made a second appearance on the High Fives Inspiration Station by then, with pictures of him in his CR jacket, helmet and goggles.

Our friend Magali had done a wonderful job getting Matt back to skiing, but she confessed that she had found it quite stressful. She has known Matt since he was nine, so he is much more than just a client, and she was constantly worrying about the responsibility – what if he fell on his head again? It was all a bit emotional for her and, as soon as I realised that, I felt quite guilty for having put her through it. We therefore decided to relieve her of the stress and opted for a couple of younger instructors – Fabien and Stephanie. They became like his big brother and sister. Fabien is the same Fabien who was planning to take him to les Grands Montets – he has the same daft sense of humour as Matt, and the pair of them were constantly in fits of giggles. He and Stephanie pushed Matt a lot more and constantly drilled him to improve his technique. It was looking better and better. We will always be so grateful to Magali for having had the courage to take him on right at the beginning. It really can't have been easy.

While we were in the mountains, we would often immerse ourselves in the world of freeskiing. This is the sort of skiing that is a world away from traditional downhill skiing. Freeskiers are to be found out in the wild backcountry doing enormous jumps and tricks off cliffs on frighteningly steep terrain. They also inhabit the snow park where they use the jumps, rails, boxes and half-pipes to push themselves to the limit with tricks such as 720s, 900s, truck drivers, double corks, switch corks and tail grabs. Or they can be spotted in a more urban environment skiing off the roofs and walls of buildings, steps and railings or any other man-made structures that present a challenge to them. I hasten to add that Matt and I weren't actually out there doing any of this stuff (!), but we would watch these amazing young men and women on Matt's seemingly endless supply of ski movie DVDs.

I learnt a whole new range of vocabulary. If it was good, it was 'sick'. They would 'shred' their trails, which were often 'gnarly'. My personal favourite was 'shredding and schralping' and, in my own way, I like to think that I can do a bit of that! The word 'awesome' featured a lot, as did 'stoked'. They had 'bluebird' days and it all got a bit 'rad'. For these freeskiers, life is for living. They don't worry unduly about material wealth. They're not there to become rich. Their lives are all about finding the perfect run on the perfect day and going for it. Life is fun and they are doing something they love. There is a tremendous camaraderie and I think they have got it right. Whereas a lot of us have lost sight of what matters, they haven't. Above all, life is for living, not for stressing about your next promotion or whether your neighbour has more money or a bigger car than you. I think we could all learn a lot from them. To these freeskiers, skiing isn't just a recreational activity or sport; it is their life and their family. I can totally understand how these movies inspired Matt.

As I watched these skiers with my jaw hanging open in awe, I would wonder how on earth they did what they did. Why weren't they terrified? Why did they seem so supremely confident? Well, once again, it's all down to the brain. Extreme athletes have the ability to enter what is known as 'flow state', which is when their brains become hyper-concentrated on the job at hand to the extent that all outside distractions are blocked out. They know exactly what they are doing and don't allow any doubt to creep into their heads. Free climbers, for example, practise, practise, practise until their skills and movements become hardwired into their brain circuitry. Free climbers do use ropes to protect against injury during falls, but they don't use them to assist progress. Within free climbing, there is, however, a subset known as 'free soloing'. This involves a very high risk as they climb using just hands, feet and body without any rope or protective equipment. So how on earth could anyone do that? Well, they too are completely confident in what they do and go into automatic pilot as they climb. Unlike the rest of us, they do not look down and think, *What am I doing? I could kill myself if I fall,* and then have a panic attack. They are 100% in flow state or 'in the zone'.

I believe that this practice, practice, practice which leads to things becoming hardwired into the brain is why Matt found skiing easier than walking. He was an ace skier before the accident, the sort of skier who you would stop and watch as they descended the mountain, and wonder how they could make it look so easy and relaxed. I remember one day, pre-2010, skiing at my very top speed downhill, when, to my dismay, Matt caught up with me and overtook. Normally, I would have expected this, but on that occasion he was skiing backwards (or as I should say in ski lingo, 'skiing switch') and still going so much faster than me! Such is his love and passion for skiing that it is now written into the hardware of his brain and, thankfully, that bit is obviously still functioning. People often refer to this as 'muscle memory', with the skills obviously not actually stored in the muscles, but the brain.

During that winter of 2013, the correspondence with Roy continued as he persisted in his goal of finding Matt the right person to get him down les Grands Montets. Once Roy is on a mission, he is a fairly unstoppable force. This time, he had set his sights on Dean Decas, a top-rated ski instructor from the US, who just happened to be spending some time in Chamonix. He has been described as a 'ski ninja' and sounded an awful lot like a genuine dude to me. Matt and I were very excited when he arranged to meet us in Le Tour to ski with Matt.

Dean (or Deano) is normally found taking people out of their comfort zone into the wild backcountry of skiing. If you are a good skier but don't quite have the confidence to launch yourself completely off-piste, Deano is your man. He'll get you there. I am quite sure that the relatively tame slopes of Le Tour were not his natural habitat.

We waited by the ski school in Le Tour where we had agreed to meet Deano. When the bus arrived, we figured out straight away which of the descending passengers was Deano. He had to be the one with the long hair and bandana. Fabien was also there, as he was quite curious about this ski ninja. I went up with them on the lift to take a few photos for my album and then left them to it. This was Matt's special day and I didn't think it was appropriate for his mum to trail along behind them (although I was very tempted). They set off at 13.30 and came back down at 15.30, which was Matt's longest ski to date. Deano even had him doing the most difficult red run in Le Tour, which was another first since the accident. I later concluded that there is something about Deano that somehow takes your skiing to another level. He is very calm and gives you the feeling that nothing could go wrong when he is around.

He came back with Matt to the chalet afterwards for a bit of a chat. They had obviously had the very best time. He seemed to be impressed by the obvious affection and respect that Matt had from the lift operators and other people working up on the pistes. He described Matt as 'inspirational', which was pretty high praise coming from him.

When Roy heard that it had all come together, he was so excited. To quote from his email: *This is so awesome. What a crazy storyline, a simple email from you to me has turned into one of my biggest ski heroes and legends helping Matt out with his goal. Totally awesome.* When I forwarded Roy the video that Deano had taken, this too ended up on the Inspiration Station.

Matt was having the time of his life. We were just living in the moment. Life was good and we didn't really worry too much about what the future might hold. I now had a strong feeling that whatever happened as far as Matt's recovery went, it would work out all right. At the end of the day, people liked him and wanted to help him. He seemed to bring out something in people and I just felt that somewhere there would be a role for him. He was still wobbly and stooping forward when he walked, but the minute he smiled, he could light up any room, and he was always smiling.

Shortly after his skiing with Deano, Fabien invited Matt up to les Grands Montets ski area for its 50th anniversary celebrations. When I picked Matt up at the end of the day, he was full of it. "Fabien took me to the snow park, but don't worry, we didn't go fast or do any jumps." He was beaming. "Guess who was up there too."

"I don't know, Matt, who was up there? Steph, Magali, Maeva?"

"No, guess again." I knew this could go on forever. Matt usually makes you guess at least ten times, before he'll give in and tell you.

"I honestly don't know. You tell me."

"Deano. I spent ages talking to him. It was great. There were loads of bands and food and drink and stuff."

It was all quite amazing; what could have been the worst time of our lives was turning out to be the best. The local community were embracing Matt and he was so happy. Whatever may happen in the future, we were all building up a store of great memories to treasure forever.

With the help of Fabien and Steph, as the season continued, Matt went from strength to strength. He was skiing and/or doing physio every weekday, and his skiing was coming on in leaps and bounds. That CR jacket *definitely* had a little bit of magic attached to it. It is so distinctive with its big yellow lion on the back that Matt is instantly recognisable from quite a distance. Complete strangers came up to him to say *"Bonjour, Matt,"* and seemed to know his story.

As April continued and the end of the ski season approached, the temperatures soared into the 20s centigrade, and the prospect of skiing from the top of the mountain at les Grands Montets seemed to be highly unlikely. However, on 16th April, Fabien went up there on a recce and declared that Thursday, 18th April, 2013 would be Grands Montets Day. Coincidentally, that evening, Nick, Matt and I were meeting up with Deano for a meal to thank him for his help with Matt. As soon as we told him what was due to happen on Thursday, he changed all his plans and declared that he would be there too.

On 18th April, we woke up to a gloriously sunny day – a bluebird day with clear blue skies. In a word, perfect. My stomach was in knots. This was a huge thing that Matt would be doing. Needless to say, he was full of confidence. At the top of les Grands Montets, there are only partially groomed black slopes (the most difficult), and once you start off, the only way is down – you can't zip off to a convenient lift or stop for a break in a café; you just have to keep going. It had always been Matt's favourite ski area and he couldn't wait to get back up there.

Unfortunately, Nick had hurt his knee and couldn't ski that day. He went up by cable car to the mid-station at Lognan and waited for us there. This would be our start and finish line. Matt and I met Steph and went up by chairlift and then skied across to the main arrival point as a warm-up or 'échauffement'. By the time we reached the meeting point, it was 12.30, and there waiting for us were Nick, Deano, Magali, Carole (another one of Matt's lovely instructors) and Fabien and his young daughter, Lily-Rose. It was quite a team and it was touching to see them all there for Matt. They all seemed just as excited as we were. Or maybe they were just glad to be able to do it at long last, as it might put a stop to Matt pestering them all about it the whole time!

So, finally, we got into the cable car that would take us all the way up to the top of the mountain. Our adventure was about to begin. As soon as you get into that cable car, you know that this is going to be no ordinary ski. All the other passengers just looked more hardcore and ready for adventure. Most of them would probably head for the far off-piste areas as soon as they got out of the car, leaving us on our own. The cable car swings high above the mountain as it goes through the giant pylons on the way up, and I could feel my stomach churning in anticipation. With all those instructors accompanying us, I knew it would be fine really, but this was to be the first time I'd been up there in a while, and I was always a bit apprehensive, as conditions continually changed up there and you never quite knew what you might find on arrival.

Once you arrive at the top, the first thing you have to do is walk down approximately 200 metal steps to the ski area. These have since been replaced, but we had to do it tough! They were all worried about Matt exhausting himself on the stairs before he started skiing (that's if he could even have done it, which was doubtful), so the plan was to carry him down the stairs. Fabien had organised a chair on which to take him down. I had imagined that this would be some sort of special chair that would somehow fit onto the stairs and slide down them – a bit like a home stairlift. It actually turned out to be far less technical than that – it was just a pretty basic plastic garden chair that needed to be physically carried down by two people. Fabien and Deano drew the short straws for that. Fabien was behind holding the back of the chair and going down facing the stairs. Deano was at the front holding the seat of the chair and going down backwards. Both of them were wearing their cumbersome ski boots, which was an added handicap. Even in normal circumstances, those stairs are not easy. I tend to hang on to the bannister for dear life as the thought of tripping and hurtling down headfirst is quite terrifying. The female instructors carried the men's skis as well as their own. To me, they were all heroes, but I definitely think that Fabien and Deano went above and beyond the call of duty on that day. How on earth they succeeded in carrying Matt down those stairs without dropping him or breaking their own necks, I will never know, but succeed they did, and for that I will be eternally grateful. Needless to say, Matt sat there beaming, obviously delighted.

Sadly, by the time they had reached the bottom of the stairs, Magali had to shoot off to teach a lesson, which was a real shame, because she really deserved to be there with us all. She was the person responsible for getting Matt back on skis and down those slopes. How many other instructors would have given it a go last year when Matt couldn't even walk unaided? Most people would have dismissed him as crazy (as many people did). Fortunately for him, Magali already knew what a determined young man he is and what a passion he has for skiing, and she has supported him all the way.

So there we all were, finally, at the bottom of the stairs ready to ski. It is beautiful up there. You feel like you're on top of the world with snow-capped mountain peaks all around you. On that particular day, it felt like the mountains were welcoming Matt back and had put on their Sunday best especially for him. The first bit of the descent is a very steep, but short, slope that then opens out onto quite a flat area. It's the bit that I always dread because it is like a wall and can be very icy. That day, though, it was still steep, but not icy. Fabien and Steph were on either side of Matt helping him down and then he was away. Deano was following along behind, filming it, so we would have a record of the day. The only other bit that Matt really needed help with was a rather narrow steep traverse. Once again, Fabien and Steph were there protecting him. I really felt my heart would burst with pride.

It was a truly perfect day. There was not a cloud in the sky and the deep blue of the sky provided the perfect background for the dazzling white snow. It was one of those days just made for skiing – the mountains were magnificent and Matt was having the time of his life. As we neared the end, his legs were obviously getting incredibly tired. A couple of times, they sort of collapsed under him, but he just got up and got on with it again. Towards the end, Steph, who had been leading the group, suggested that

Deano should take over at the front. Matt followed him while he worked his magic (combined with the CR jacket, of course) and he seemed to get a whole new lease of life. His strength and energy surged and he suddenly upped his game and skied brilliantly.

The last bit of the return to the mid-station is a long, fairly narrow road where it is possible to gain quite a lot of speed. Added to that is the fact that people coming down from les Grands Montets are mostly very good skiers who like to ski fast, so it can be a bit like being on a Formula 1 track. In my early ski days in Chamonix, it was another place I found terrifying – everyone just seems to hurtle past you at high speeds. I needn't have worried for Matt, though. Fabien skied behind him holding on to his jacket to prevent him from gaining too much speed and they both skied in snowplough. Steph and Deano were one in front and one behind so that he was well protected from the mob. I tootled along behind, feeling a little bit emotional about how these people had put so much effort into making sure that Matt had succeeded in skiing down his favourite run.

At the bottom, Fabien just dragged him across, using his ski poles, to the café where Nick was waiting. All in all, it had taken about one and a half hours to complete. In his previous life, Matt could probably have done it in about 10 minutes. It didn't matter, though – it was mega! There was much hugging and back-patting. Everyone was so excited. It had been absolutely magical and we were so fortunate to have experienced such a day. That's the upside of a really traumatic experience – your senses become heightened, and when the good times happen, you appreciate them more than you will ever have appreciated anything else in your whole life. There are no words that could describe my emotions on that day. I could just have exploded with joy.

None of the instructors would take any money for their time, so we just bought them all celebratory bottles of champagne to open at their leisure and look back on a day when they had made one young man's dream come true. The words 'thank you' are simply not enough on such occasions – nothing is really. They all knew what it meant to us, though.

After a much-needed refreshing drink at the mid-station bar, we were forced to make a fairly rapid exit. The temperature was still soaring and the authorities were seriously worried about the consequent avalanche danger, so the mountain was closing at 3pm. Thankfully, we all got down unscathed and once again said our thank yous and, sadly, our end-of-season goodbyes.

I think this is one memory that Matt will have no trouble in storing.

*

Every time I organised skiing with an instructor, I'd always (half-jokingly) say, "Cool, we'll go do Grands Montets tomorrow." Only to get a dismissive laugh in return. The top of les Grands Montets is at 3,300m, with a 2,000m vertical drop down to Argentière. There are many routes down from the top, but none are easy skiing. Skiing from the top of les Grands Montets all the way down to the car park at the bottom has always been my favourite run.

One day in April 2013 – after an afternoon with Steph – she and Fabien had a little discussion and then gave me the incredible news: "Tomorrow, if the weather's okay, we'll ski les Grands Montets." (But they said it in French.)

The next day, the weather was way more than 'okay'. There wasn't a cloud in the sky. Deano's aim was to get me to ski les Grands Montets, so there was no way he'd miss it. I had been bugging Magali since those days on the kids' slope of the beginners' slope, so she came. Carole came too with Steph and Fabien (of course). My mum was a welcome addition to the crew! Dad had a bad knee, so he'd meet us at the end.

You have to get another cable car to the peak at les Grands Montets and then you have to tackle over 200 metal stairs. Because everyone knew that I'd need all my energy for the skiing, we needed a way to get me down the stairs without wasting any! So Fabien and Deano sat me in a plastic garden chair and CARRIED me all the way down. I do often wonder what people must have thought seeing that. There's this guy who can't walk that well, with five instructors, getting carried down the stairs like some sort of princess!

Fab and Deano did a heroic job of getting me down those stairs. When I got to the bottom (very well rested), I clicked in and started to follow Steph. I wasn't at all nervous about the fact that this was by far the most difficult skiing I had done since the accident. This was exactly what I had been dreaming of in my hospital bed. After asking daily for two whole seasons, I was finally skiing les Grands Montets!

The instructors took it in turns to lead me down and some had to leave to teach other lessons. I know I have skied it way better and a million times faster in the past, but because of the circumstances and all the hard work, it really was the best run of my life.

*

The next day, Matt and I set off for England. Nick and the dogs would be driving back in a couple of days' time, after having collected Tim from Nendaz in Switzerland at the end of his season. Matt and I were flying home. Even that was not without a little bit of excitement. On the bus that ferried us out across the tarmac to the plane, an Australian lady approached Matt and declared, "Oh, you were skiing with Deano yesterday! He was so stoked that you did it!" So many people in Chamonix had been aware of Matt and his goals and were genuinely pleased for him. I have decided that human nature is pretty good on the whole.

Once we were back home, we received some great videos and photos from Deano, which I forwarded to Roy, the man who had cheered Matt on from California. Yet again he made the Inspiration Station under the heading, *Matt Masson skiing Grands Montets with the legendary Dean Decas.*

So there we were at the end of the ski season and Matt was exactly where he wanted to be. He had made it to the top of his mountain, and on the way, he had cemented some extraordinary friendships. He immediately announced his next two goals, which were:

- Get his ski instructor qualifications
- Run a marathon

Who knew if he would ever be able to achieve these goals or not? One thing is for sure, I wouldn't recommend betting against him succeeding once he sets his mind on something.

EIGHTEEN

THE HIDDEN INJURY

When we arrived back home, it was time to take stock of the situation. What should we do next? Matt was obviously a bit deflated after all the excitement of the winter, and Nick and I just felt inadequately equipped to deal with it all. How could we direct Matt when we had no idea of the direction he should be going in? What I really wanted was a local High Fives Foundation, full of lively, positive Californians. It was tailor-made for Matt – a foundation run by skiers with life-altering injuries for other skiers in the same situation. Unfortunately, they haven't opened a UK branch yet.

One of the hardest parts of living with a brain injury in the family is that it's not very easy for people to understand what you're going through. For the first few months, especially in intensive care, it was obvious to everyone that Matt was very ill. Friends and family were fantastic and they still are, but it's harder for them to understand now. This is, in large part, our own fault. We made the choice to be super positive and upbeat, thereby giving the impression that everything in the garden was rosy. They don't see the sheer exhaustion, the anxiety about the future, and no one really knows what Matt is thinking about his own situation. He maintains his happy exterior, only rarely letting the mask slip. Let's face it, no one likes a miserable moaner, so it's much easier to simply reply that "It's fine" when asked how it's all going.

Brain injuries are known as the 'hidden injury' and, because of that, it is easy for people to ignore them. Consequently, there have been several occasions when friends have made insensitive remarks that have been very hurtful. They have meant no harm and doubtless remain completely unaware of the hurt that they have caused. Sometimes it's easier just to stay away from people. Even just hearing friends talking about their highly successful children, with their high-powered jobs and partners, can be painful. Of course, I don't want them to stop telling me things. I certainly don't want a 'don't mention the war' sort of situation, but sometimes it just hurts. I hate the fact that my son has lost all of his mid-twenties, but I know I can't dwell on it or I will get bitter, and that won't do at all. I guess that's why I latched on to the High Five people. They truly understand. They've been there and are still living with their life-altering injuries. Above all, they have gone on to make something of their lives despite their injuries, and I know that Matt will too.

Matt has had very obvious physical signs that all is not right with his limp and balance problems, but there are many brain-injury survivors who are able to walk perfectly and have no physical signs of any injury. However, they can struggle greatly with their thinking processes, emotions and social skills. In some ways, this might be even worse. Other people will have no idea of why they are perhaps behaving badly and completely misjudge them. Life can be very tough for them, and a better understanding is needed of their plight.

I vividly remember one incident that I found quite upsetting. I was out walking with Matt and the two dogs at West Wittering beach. West Wittering is an extremely 'nice middle-class' sort of place. Matt was a little way ahead of us and he was having quite a wobbly day. Also, it was not easy for him to walk on sand and dunes. That was the whole point of doing it – to challenge his balance by walking on different surfaces.

So, there we were, minding our own business and bothering no one when one of the wardens came up to me. He pointed at Matt. "Do you know that chap?" The way he said it suggested that he was suspicious of 'that chap'.

"Yes, I do. He's my son." I waited to see how he would respond to that.

"Oh," he spluttered, "it's just that we've had trouble in the past with someone who matches his description."

"Well, it won't be him. He's had a brain injury and that's why his walking is wobbly, in case you think he's been drinking."

He looked rather startled, bewildered, and at least he had the good grace to look a bit embarrassed too. I could almost see the 'does not compute' messages that must have been flashing up in his brain. There was me, an innocuous dog walker and quite acceptable for West Wittering, but then there was this long-haired 'drunk' with me. How did that happen?

I honestly don't remember if he even apologised or just scuttled off. Why could that man not see what I saw? A courageous young man, who was doing something that was very difficult for him and still doing it despite that. Unfortunately, it's just one example of the huge amount of ignorance surrounding brain injury. People need to look beyond what they think they see and consider that there might be another explanation. I caught up with Matt, who asked me, "What did he want?"

"Usual thing, Matt. I think he thought you were drunk."

"Oh well, never mind." As always, my good-natured son took it in his stride with an accepting smile.

Matt has plenty of support around him, but I do worry for people who don't have that. When I see an unkempt, probably homeless, man wobbling around and often confused, I now wonder if they have had a brain injury. Without a lot of support, especially in the initial stages, it would be very difficult to get through this experience. I fear many of them do end up homeless, with drugs and alcohol as their only 'comfort'.

The problem is that the brain controls everything we do: all movement, thinking, emotions, sight, hearing, speech, taste, balance. Literally everything is dictated by the control centre that is the brain. Even the best neurologists in the world don't seem to quite know exactly how it all works. They can't really intervene to fix it once it's broken. Fortunately, due to the ingenuity of those brain cells that remain intact following an injury, as already mentioned, they can reroute. Matt's brain cells seem to be doing a pretty good job on that front. They've diverted metaphoric traffic onto the metaphoric B-roads of his brain, and we're hoping that eventually some of the super highways might also reopen. But one thing is for sure, once you have had a brain injury, you absolutely cannot afford to bang your head again.

All these thoughts were going through my head at the end of April 2013 as we tried to map out our future course. At some point, Matt needed to try and re-enter the real world and get some sort of job. Was it time to do that? Nikki, the neuro physio, had already advised that we go all out that year with the rehab exercises, so that's the decision we made. Better to spend time now working on the recovery in order to give Matt the best chance of reaching his goals. We decided to up the amount of physio. We had not yet used any musculoskeletal physios in England, so, following the success of Neil in France, we decided to recruit a couple. We managed to find a Dutch lady called Petra, and a colleague of Neil's recommended a South African called Brett. Our little team was growing.

Of course, life was not all about therapy. As Matt was getting fitter, he was able to be more independent and catch the train to various places to see friends, who always met him at the other end. He was under strict instructions to text me once he was safely in their care. Nick and I would not have been at ease if we thought Matt was wandering around London on his own.

I guess in many ways we had the same approach with Matt as you might have when releasing an injured animal back into the wild. We were very protective of him and doing it little by little. When you have nearly lost someone you love, you can't just throw them out there and hope for the best. On the other hand, you can't keep them locked up, either. (Tempting as it was to do just that!) You have to take a deep breath and let it happen slowly and safely. We didn't want any setbacks at this stage. He was doing so well, but he still occasionally got confused. You could see the puzzlement in his eyes, as he couldn't quite remember what or when something was going to happen. We still had a way to go, but we were certainly well on our way. The various therapists seemed to be genuinely excited as they could see real progress happening. You could never fault Matt's own determination and effort. If we tried to hold him back and stop him doing something, his favourite riposte was, "What do you think would have happened if Mrs Armstrong had said no to little Neil when he told her he was going to go to the moon one day?" That soon put us in our place.

I felt that my belief in the principles of never giving up and always believing had been totally vindicated when I read an article in *The Times* newspaper in September 2015. It tells the story of a man who fell off a mountain 21 years before who had not been expected to live and, even if he did, according to the doctors he would be 'a cabbage' (their words, not mine). His parents believed him to be a fighter, and they have been proved right as, 21 years after the accident, he has just succeeded in taking his first few steps after years of being in a wheelchair. He had refused to give up and he has now been rewarded.

The doctors don't always get it right and, more importantly, they don't know the patient. For most of the time that Matt was under the care of the Royal London, he was asleep, so they had no idea of what sort of person was inside that body. The hospital medical staff admit that they rarely know what happens to their patients once they are out of their care. They see these patients at their worst and get them to a stage where no more medical intervention can be of use to them. They are often discharged in a wheelchair or even (as Matt was) in a bed by ambulance to another unit. They don't know whether that patient subsequently remained in a wheelchair or went on to play football. They love it when an ex-patient comes skipping back in to say hello. On those occasions, they often don't recognise them, such is the transformation.

In June, it was Matt's twenty-sixth birthday – his third birthday since the accident. For this, we bought him a wonderful machine called The Skier's Edge to help him with his skiing (unsurprisingly). This was added to all the other gear spread out all over our house. A session on this was included in his nightly exercise regime, which lasted about half an hour and was entirely his own plan. He ate his supper, waited about half an hour and then sprang into action. He never missed a night. I can't recall ever hearing him say, "I don't feel like doing my exercises today." As far as he was concerned, they were his way forward. Quite right too.

He had now begun to treat his nutrition really seriously and was on an 'athlete's diet'. He had cut out all junk food and only ate and drank healthily. Water is a key ingredient, as he believes (quite correctly) that 'hydration is key'. Gone are the sugary breakfast cereals, to be replaced by eggs and smoked salmon on rye bread. Snacks such as crisps are replaced by fruit and nuts. Lots of vegetables, chicken and steaks are consumed. All this from the young man who used to declare that Ribena and Walker's crisps were the perfect diet for him!

Growing up, his diet was a nightmare. He was one of those little boys who refused to have anything to do with anything green. The best we could do was to sneak chopped-up vegetables into things like spaghetti bolognaise, but even then he would spot them and spend hours picking them out. Despite that, he seemed to grow up fit and healthy and did lots of sport at school.

It wasn't until his 2009/10 trip to Sydney, when he met a blue lady on stilts at a cricket match, that he really started eating fruit and vegetables. She was a fortune-teller and had foreseen serious trouble ahead healthwise unless he improved his diet. In retrospect, she might have got this a little bit wrong. It wasn't a lack of vegetables that had ultimately caused serious health problems. Nevertheless, this mistaken forecast did the trick regarding diet. Unfortunately, when he woke up from his coma, he couldn't remember having changed his diet and thought I was trying to trick him when I insisted that he did now eat fruit and vegetables. We weren't quite back to square one, as he would still eat salad and fruit, but not many vegetables. But now he was on his athlete's diet, so the variety in his diet was back on.

That summer, I read James Cracknell's book about the traumatic brain injury he had suffered, *Touching Distance*. He had been cycling across America when he was clipped by one of the wing mirrors of those huge trucks and knocked off his bike. The book is an excellent account of his experiences and is co-written with his wife. They have had a tough time as, in complete contrast to Matt, he made a good physical recovery but was left with lots of emotional problems and personality change. A lot of the book made me chuckle, as he had so much in common with Matt, such as an initial obsession with poo (yes, really).

When you are recovering from a serious injury or illness, everything is obviously closely monitored, and this includes your bowel functions. Matt was highly delighted during his stay in Donald Wilson House when he discovered that there is an invaluable aid to checking the quality of your poo known as the Bristol Stool Chart. This is a beautifully illustrated document listing seven different categories of poo. In an ideal world, categories 3 to 4 are the ones you'd want to have. When I arrived to visit Matt on the day when he had been shown this document, he grabbed the nearest passing nurse and implored her, "Please show my mum the Bristol Stool Chart. Go on. Show her, show her, please!" He found it so hilarious that the nurses presented him with his own laminated copy a couple of days later. If only they had given it to me secretly, I could have saved it for Christmas and gift wrapped it for him and then saved a fortune on Christmas present-spending. Nothing could have topped that!

Apart from that, James and Matt also seemed to have shared a love of sweet chilli sauce, and the qualities of wanting to prove themselves and never giving up. Mr Cracknell coined a wonderful phrase. He experienced, as we did, a lot of discouragement and he describes these people as 'dream stealers'. I know exactly what he means.

In October, Matt, the dogs and I once again went to stay in Le Tour for 10 days and, while there, he had a few sessions with Neil. Much to Matt's delight, he took him down to the athletics track in Chamonix because Matt wanted to see if he could run. Again, this was something that he would pester people about, constantly asking them, "Do you think I will be able to run again?" As always, no one knew. At that stage, running was certainly still way beyond Matt, but he was determined to give it a go, so Neil let him 'run' 100 metres. It was quite terrifying to see. The best way I can describe it is that it was like watching a demented drunk lurch forward uncontrollably, with two very worried people alongside him! Matt was delighted as he set a personal best of 81 seconds. Usain Bolt's record is safe for the time being, but watch out Usain, Matt is on the move.

Being up in the mountains led to a renewed discussion about the ski instructor's course, which Matt was still refusing to give up on. This was such a difficult subject. We all knew how much he wanted to do it, but he still wasn't anywhere near ready for something like that. Everyone else on the course would be fast, fit and strong, and he would hate not being able to keep up. He got very upset in front of Neil and blurted out, "I can't stand being stuck at home in England with my parents anymore!" This was at first very hurtful for me, but I like to think it was more to do with him wanting to get back out into the real world, rather than hating us. That should be interpreted as a healthy sign, as it wouldn't be normal if he happily accepted everything. It was good that he was making a stand, even if it did make me feel very upset. Luckily, Neil, Fabien and Stephanie all agreed that it was not the time to attempt a ski instructor's course and suggested that maybe it might be a good thing to work in Chamonix that winter. After a furious argument, Matt came round and saw that would be a good compromise. I was happy too. Nick and I really wanted Matt to get back to a normal life and Chamonix was the perfect place to do it. We just needed to figure out what job he could do and how to get it.

NINETEEN

A SEASON IN CHAM

We were all in agreement that Matt needed to get back to real life again, and on the 10th of December 2013, Matt and I boarded a plane bound for Geneva and then travelled on to Chamonix in search of jobs and accommodation.

If Matt wanted to be independent, Chamonix was the place to go. He knew enough people there to act as support if necessary, there is an excellent physio clinic in the town and, most importantly, they understand injuries there. That last observation may sound a bit strange, but it really worried us that people might not recognise Matt as someone who had been injured, but instead as just another drunk. Chamonix is the extreme sports capital of the world and they are well used to accidents and their consequences. They don't look at Matt as an oddball; instead, they respect him for his determination and Herculean efforts at recovery. Chamonix and Matt are made for each other.

It was a bit of a chicken and egg situation. Which should we tackle first – the job or the flat? As it happened, we had a stroke of luck with the flat when the ladies at La Clinique du Sport told us about an American lady who was looking to sub-let her flat while she went back to the States for a while, and he could move in virtually straight away. The flat was in the very centre of Chamonix town, which was perfect for him. All he needed now was a job. He was confident that would come.

On the following Saturday, I once again took a deep breath and flew home, leaving Matt out in Chamonix on his own. Not for the first time I found myself questioning my sanity – was I completely mad leaving him there? Surprisingly enough, Nick, who is usually much more of a worrier than I am, was quite relaxed about it and felt sure that Matt would be fine.

At least Matt and I had spent several hours getting him equipped with the right footwear to tackle the ice and snow of Chamonix. It was a bit like Goldilocks trying out the chairs and beds at the Three Bears' house. He tried Nick's new snow boots that had some device that pulled down to provide studs on the heels. He didn't like those. We bought two sets of crampon-like attachments to put over his ordinary shoes. He didn't like either of those. In the end, he opted for a pair of Sorel Caribou boots, which are THE boots to buy for snow and ice. They were just right. He was now confident that he could walk around the town without fear of slipping. The previous year, there was no way he would have walked around on his own without someone's arm to lean on, so this was another huge step, both figuratively and literally. He later told me that when it was very icy on the pavements, he would simply ask a passing stranger for the use of their arm, and they were always happy to oblige. It seems that very few people ever say no to Matt, especially in Chamonix.

On arriving back in England, I went through a whole range of emotions. I was very happy that Matt had the confidence to do this. I felt afraid in case it didn't work out (as in the Scilly Isles) or, God forbid, that he had an accident. I was all over the place

– sad, happy, frightened, anxious, proud. You name it, I felt it. I knew that I just had to have confidence in my son. He certainly sounded very happy when we spoke to him on the phone. He was managing to get around and seemed to be getting to know just about everyone in Chamonix. Finding a job was not proving easy, though, as most places had already found their staff for the season.

After a couple of weeks, Matt was thrilled to be able to inform us that he had landed a job as a glass exchanger in a local bar. Never having actually heard of this particular occupation before, we were intrigued to find out what it involved. Basically, Matt had to stand by the door and when someone attempted to go outside with a glass, he had to take the glass glass and pour the contents into a plastic glass to ensure that all was safe outside and there was no risk of broken glass outside or of anyone walking off with the glass glasses! His other duty was to make sure that no one was smoking anything dodgy by his pub. If they were, he had to politely request that they go somewhere else to do it. Now, I realise that this job was not exactly high powered, but it was his first step towards real independence and we couldn't have been prouder. The hours were from 11pm to 2am, which weren't ideal for brain-injury recovery, but it was only at weekends, so he would survive. The important thing was that he had done it all by himself; he took it very seriously and he was coping well with life in general. In fact, on Christmas Day, he was invited to two Christmas parties, and he was also invited to Fabien's house and to Magali's, so he was certainly not sitting at home alone.

He was still working hard on his fitness; attending Neil's clinic for physio, and skiing with Steph.

The previous year, Matt had been very reluctant to get on a crowded bus, even if accompanied by someone. This year, he was catching the bus up to Le Tour and down again by himself. The ski school had kindly agreed to let him leave his skis and boots there overnight so that at least he didn't have to carry them onto the bus, which would have been more difficult, if not impossible, for him. When he went skiing by himself, there would always be someone around to help him get to the top of the stairs in order to catch the lift to the ski area. Needless to say, his friends operating the lifts were, as ever, happy to see him and ready to help too. There was a very nice young lady in the office of the ski school, and Matt had an arrangement with her to call when he returned to the bottom of the slopes and she would come across and help him with his skis. I must say that he did a very good job of organising his team of helpers.

On the 27th of December, after a quiet Christmas at home, Nick and I set off for Le Tour. Tim was again in Nendaz teaching skiing and snowboarding for the winter, so the Masson family were once again all within an hour of each other in either France or Switzerland.

As we entered this new phase, we all had to make adjustments. Nick and I had to try and back off and let Matt get on with it. It was very hard, though, to just cut off like that and step back. I know that we drove Matt mad by constantly trying to help and offer advice. However, Matt also had to realise that after three years of running around doing everything for him, it was difficult for us to adapt to our new role of ordinary parents, as opposed to carers. Also, as a brain-injury survivor, Matt doesn't always see the true picture. For example, we can see how he changes when he's tired – slurred speech, wobbly walking, and he gets a look of puzzlement on his face, which is a complete giveaway that he is not thinking clearly. He will always deny this and insist that he is not tired. That's when it becomes a worry. We don't want him on his own with impaired judgement, but what can we do? If we play the heavy-handed parents, we risk alienating him more and more. But what if we ignore the situation and he risks injury due to a further accident because of tiredness? Sometimes I feel we just have to trust the guardian angel who has got him this far.

It was all very stressful, though, and once again I began to feel very down. I had read about the post-rehab slump, when the patient has finished the intense rehab and is back out in the real world, only to find it's not that great. I think that is where Nick and I found ourselves at the beginning of 2014. I desperately needed that non-existent crystal ball to see what the future would hold. I had a feeling that the ups were about to get a whole lot steeper and the downs were about to get a whole lot deeper. We were now on an ultra-roller coaster. Matt was making it increasingly obvious that he didn't want us fussing around him or trying to help. This was very unlike him, and it was as if he couldn't see how hurtful he was being.

At the beginning of 2014, brain injuries were very much in the news as Michael Schumacher, the legendary Formula 1 racing driver, had suffered one while skiing. As he lay in a coma, the newspapers were full of speculation, and various neurological experts were putting in their opinions about the various possible outcomes: the extent of his disabilities should he wake up, the possible changes in his personality, the fact that he would be a different Michael Schumacher post-accident. It was all depressingly familiar to us. Matt was also reading all this on the internet and was very upset to read that brain-injury survivors were three times more likely to die prematurely than other members of the general public. He didn't mention this to us at first, but just brooded over it. He did eventually tell Neil, who reassured him that they would be referring to TBI survivors who turned to drink or drugs, or who became depressed and didn't look after themselves, or didn't have supportive friends and family, or were maybe just adrenalin junkies who continued to take risks after their first brain injury. None of that applied to

Matt, thankfully. When Matt told me about it, Nick and I were also able to reassure him that statistics shouldn't always be taken as given truths. I just hope that Mrs Schumacher and her family were firmly ignoring all of these articles.

While we were out in Chamonix, Nick and I watched *Crash Reel* with Matt. This is an excellent DVD about a young snowboarder, Kevin Pearce, who suffered a TBI while training for the 2010 Winter Olympics. He had been widely tipped to be in line to win a gold medal for the USA and, because of that, he was being filmed during his training. His accident was captured on film as he crashed heavily in the half-pipe. Subsequently, they went on to film his recovery process. It is a must-see film for any young brain-injury survivor and their family. There was a particularly interesting section when he visited someone who had gone on to have a second brain injury and, frighteningly, that young man had lost all reason and couldn't distinguish right from wrong. He actually ran his brother over with a golf cart for fun. Luckily, his brother suffered no serious injuries. I can only begin to imagine the stress his poor mother was under. We also saw Kevin's family dealing with some of his decisions. They could see the direction he was heading in was impossible but, as is often the case with the brain-injury victim, he refused to see it. He has an extremely loving and supportive family and you can see the strain they are under as they struggle to help someone who thinks they don't need help.

However, as time went on, Kevin began to realise that some of his goals were unrealistic and even potentially dangerous (such as going back to the half-pipe), and he now devotes a lot of time going into schools and talking to young people about the importance of safety in extreme sports and especially to always wear a helmet. So his story has a happy ending. He has found a fulfilling role while still keeping in contact with the sport he loves.

I found the film strangely comforting, as I realised that Kevin was treating his parents exactly as Matt was treating us at that time. It was as if all empathy had been destroyed in their brains. They simply couldn't see how their actions were affecting those closest to them, who, after all, had also been through a very tough time. As I watched Kevin's mum in tears with the stress of it all, I no longer felt quite so alone. Other families were also going through this. It seems that none of us can get through the aftermath of a brain injury scot-free, although we hadn't done too badly. I guess the rewiring will short-circuit occasionally. We just had to hope that it would eventually sort itself out.

Halfway through January 2014, while we were still up in Le Tour, we received a phone call from Matt with some unexpected news: "Hi, Mum. I've just entered the Amsterdam Marathon."

"Have you? When is it?" I was surprised to say the least. Anyone would find 26.2 miles a very long way – let alone someone who can't walk very well.

"It's on the 19th of October this year. So it'll be fine. I've got nine months to improve my walking – I'm not running it, obviously! My aim is to do it in seven hours and I've looked at all the marathon courses and Amsterdam is definitely the flattest, so that's good."

"Are you just going out there on your own? What if it's harder than you think?" A few alarm bells were going off in my head imagining all sorts of potential disaster scenarios.

"I've asked Sam and he says he'll come with me. He does Ironman and all sorts, so he'll be able to help me. He's done loads of marathons."

"He won't run off and leave you behind, will he? He might want to be with the faster runners."

"No, of course not. He's already agreed that he'll walk too."

"Okay. What does Neil think about it?" Maybe Neil would talk him out of it.

"He thinks it's a great idea." That was that then. It looked like it would happen and he had obviously thought it all out and enlisted help before telling us. Very smart. "And, Mum, the main thing is, I want to raise money for High Fives." I couldn't really argue with that ambition. I wasn't quite sure what to think. With Matt, you can never say never. He constantly surprises us. Who would have thought he would have been back on skis a year after his accident? He told us all he would do it, but there were plenty of doubters. He proved them wrong, but would it be the same with the marathon? Could this be a challenge too far? The only thing I could be sure of on this one was that Matt would throw himself 100% into the challenge. Deep breath time again!

At the beginning of February, Nick and I returned home feeling very down. We had seen Matt the day before we left and he had been very grumpy, very rude, and just ignored us. The fact that he was normally so easy-going and happy meant that it came as a complete shock to us and it just crushed me. I was very weepy for the next few days. I couldn't understand how he could suddenly be so cruel. Once again, though, I realised that maybe I was blowing it out of proportion. In just over three years, we had had two grumpy outbursts from Matt. That really wasn't very much. As with the heated ski instructor discussion, Matt was really behaving normally. Everyone has their grumpy moments. It was just that we were so unused to him having any. Maybe his brain had continued rerouting and had successfully got the grumpy area going again, so that was a good thing. A day or so later, he phoned to apologise and explained that someone had upset him. Fortunately, the grumpy area didn't make too many repeat appearances after that – just when we drove him around the bend because of well-meaning overprotectiveness.

TWENTY

"NO HEAD INJURY IS TOO SEVERE TO DESPAIR OF, NOR TOO TRIVIAL TO IGNORE"
HIPPOCRATES

As Matt's recovery process continued, I found myself becoming more and more attuned to any news or articles about brain injury. It was as if I had a little antenna that picked up anything to do with head injuries. As I was learning more and more about the brain and the different ways it could be affected when injured, it made me think that I needed to do something to raise awareness of head injuries, and is one of the things that spurred me on to write this book.

The United States seem to be way ahead of the game compared to the UK. Most of the really interesting reports that I came across originated from across the Atlantic. If I searched for statistics on various aspects, there were invariably many more that were US-based. It's time we caught up.

Of course, there are all sorts of scenarios for head injuries – a fall from a height, car accidents, falling down stairs, slipping on a paving stone, a heavy object falling on you. The possibilities are endless. It struck me, though, that there are two areas of activity in particular that are gradually causing people to sit up and take notice. These are sport and war.

In sport, people are realising that wearing a helmet to protect your brain is a very good idea. You rarely see a cyclist without a helmet these days. It's not hard for people to imagine the impact that a head hitting a hard road surface might have. According to the RoSPA (Royal Society for the Prevention of Accidents) website, in 2016, 3,499 cyclists were either killed or seriously injured in the UK. The actual numbers may well be much higher, as these figures only cover those accidents that are reported to the police, and many go unreported. Hospital data showed that over 40% of cyclists involved in accidents suffered head injuries. An international study led by the University Of New South Wales, also in 2016, found compelling evidence that wearing a cycle helmet reduces the risk of serious head injury by almost 70% and fatal head injury by 65%. That is why I absolutely hate seeing any cyclist without a helmet. It might not be glamorous, but it could save your life.

There is now a very long list of sports in which helmets are routinely used, including the relative newcomer to helmet use: sailing. As racing yachts get ever more technical and move ever faster, head injuries are occurring more frequently. A whack on the head from a fast-moving boom coming across the boat can cause very serious injuries. As a consequence of this, helmets are now being worn by many crews at the top end of sailing.

Unfortunately, a helmet is not always a guarantee against injury; after all, your brain can still bounce around in your skull following a severe impact even with a helmet, and it is the motion of the brain banging against the skull that will damage the brain. In an accident involving velocity, the brain will keep moving in the skull after an impact brings the rest of the body to a halt. Imagine dropping a shatterproof bowl of jelly from a height. The bowl will stop when it hits the ground, but the jelly will still keep wobbling around in it after impact. Your brain in your skull is much like that jelly in the shatterproof bowl. The wearing of helmets will help, though, and there is no doubt that many lives have been saved because of helmets. If your head hits a sharp object, such as a rock or something similar, the helmet can prevent what could have been a very severe injury if that sharp object had penetrated the skull. Many helmet manufacturers are working flat out to come up with ever more advanced helmets that can absorb shock to minimise the impact on the brain. The problem is that so many sports are going ever higher and faster, and our skulls were just not designed to protect the brain under such circumstances. Mike Douglas, a pro skier from Whistler, British Columbia, was quoted in *Outside* magazine as saying, *Our sports are supersizing. It's all about going higher, farther, faster. It's just not sustainable.*

You only have to look at how high the freestyle skiers and snowboarders go up above the rock-hard, icy surface of the half-pipe in competitive events in order to 'get air' to realise that, if they don't land it properly, they run a high risk of getting seriously injured.

It's not just the one-off major impact injuries that we need to worry about, either. Dr Bennet Omalu, a forensic pathologist, carried out an autopsy on an American footballer called Mike Webster who died in 2002. He had died of an apparent heart attack at the age of fifty but, from what he had heard about Webster's behaviour, Dr Omalu decided that it might be worth having a look at his brain. Following an autopsy, he concluded that the human brain cannot cope with an unlimited number of traumatic impacts, or even mild concussions, such as occur in many contact sports, including American football. Axons can only be stretched hard once, or lightly many times, before eventually rupturing. When they do, brown balls of tau protein form in the pathways, shutting down communications. This results in chronic traumatic encephalopathy or CTE. CTE exhibits symptoms such as memory loss, impaired judgement, depression and dementia. Unfortunately, this disease can only be diagnosed posthumously, and 110 out of 111 former NFL players who have donated their brains to medical science have been found to have CTE.

The world of action sports sat up and paid attention in February 2016 when Dave Mirra, a BMX legend, committed suicide, and a subsequent autopsy revealed that he too had been suffering from CTE. During his BMX career, he had suffered numerous concussions and bangs on the head. Suddenly people involved in other action sports, such as skiing or snowboarding, where bangs on the head are also 'part of the job', began to wonder if they too might be at real risk. Any activity with the risk of repeated concussions or even trauma at the sub-concussive level has a greater likelihood of resulting in CTE.

However, while CTE is a very real thing, we mustn't get too carried away. Dr Rahul Jandial, neurosurgeon, acts as the voice of reason in his book, *Life Lessons from a Brain Surgeon*. He points out that the study of former NFL players' brains involved players who had exhibited possible symptoms of CTE. The vast majority of NFL players do not have CTE, despite possibly having had concussion.

The message is to treat concussion with the respect it deserves and watch out for symptoms such as dizziness, confusion, nausea, headaches or visual disturbances. Check them out and give yourself time to heal. The likelihood is that there will be no lasting effects, BUT getting a second concussion is to be avoided. Multiple concussions are definitely not a good idea.

Nobody is suggesting that people should stop these sorts of sport, but they need to realise what measures they should take to safeguard themselves. They cannot afford to simply sit down for five minutes after such a knock and then get up and do it all again.

As more and more elite athletes are taking this message on board, it should hopefully filter through to the general public enjoying sport on an amateur level. Education is the key to preventing this. This is where sporting bodies and coaches can play a key role. In the US, the High Fives Foundation has launched a program called B.A.S.I.C.S. (Being Aware Safe in Critical Situations) where they go to sports clubs and schools and instruct them as to how they can participate safely in the sports they love.

Thankfully, in the UK, other sports are also sitting up and taking notice, which is why rugby and football players are now taken off the pitch if there is any suspicion of even a minor head injury. Both the RFU and the FA have produced excellent 'return-to-play protocols' for teams to follow when a concussion has occurred. They set out six distinct stages before a player can return to the field of play. For adults (over nineteen), there is a minimum of 19 days before the player can play again, and for those under the age of nineteen, the minimum period is 23 days. Obviously, the more serious the concussion, the longer that period will be. There will always be the macho alpha male types who think they are immune to brain damage and that this is all a big fuss about nothing but, hopefully, in time, even they will see the light. I just hope that it won't be too late for them by then.

Various sporting bodies have also collaborated to produce a pocket recognition tool for concussion, so those involved in sport can keep it with them to refer to when concussion is suspected. The organisations involved are the International Rugby Board (IRB), the International Football Federation

(FIFA), the International Ice Hockey Federation (IIHF), the International Federation for Equestrian Sport (FEI) and the International Olympic Committee (IOC). They are all working hard to get the message out there and, at long last, it does seem to be getting there.

The other major area that has helped to raise awareness of head injuries is war. The conflicts in such places as Iraq and Afghanistan have made us well aware of the serious injuries that are sustained by our soldiers on the field of battle. Unfortunately, in battle, there is plenty of scope for traumatic brain injury. Bombs and bullets are obvious dangers, but even the blast waves from an explosion can cause severe trauma as they travel through brain matter. This sort of injury can often leave no outward physical signs of the internal damage. The US military's own statistics state that as many as 20% of all returning veterans may have some degree of brain injury.

Naturally, any nation seeing its soldiers returning from conflicts with such devastating injuries will want to find them both the very best medical treatment and then, subsequently, the very best therapy to enable them to get back to the best quality of life possible. The work done by neurosurgeons and therapists on these soldiers is no doubt adding further knowledge to the world of trauma injury, including brain and spinal cord injuries. Any advances will, of course, filter through to non-military medicine.

Being the sort of people they are, these soldiers love a challenge and we have all seen our wounded heroes taking part in various adventures and sporting activities as they fight a different sort of battle in order to overcome their injuries. The two worlds of sport and war are linked through events such as the Paralympics, which now numbers injured former soldiers amongst its athletes, and also the Invictus Games, which is specifically for wounded soldiers.

The athletes who are missing limbs have clearly been seriously injured. Don't forget, though, that the ones you see out there apparently walking normally on their two legs, with both their arms, who seem unscathed, are probably just as seriously, if not more seriously, injured as the others. They may have suffered a TBI. We can all understand that to lose a limb must be devastating. However, the physically intact soldier with the damaged brain may never be able to think clearly again or live independently again. What will make it especially hard for them is to hear people say (and they do), "What's he/she doing in this race/challenge? There's nothing wrong with them." Before making such statements, people should make sure to engage their own brain and have a think about what might have happened to these people. Sometimes the damage done to a brain can have a far more devastating and far-reaching effect than losing an arm. Just because you can't see an injury, it doesn't mean it's not there.

TWENTY-ONE

CALIFORNIA SKIING
ON A WINTER'S DAY

Following our rather troubled departure from Chamonix in January, Nick and I stayed in the UK until the 14th of March, when we returned to Chamonix to pick up Matt for a very special trip. Just before Christmas, we had decided that it was now or never for a visit to Truckee, California to meet our new friends at the High Fives Foundation in person. We were all looking forward to it so much. I know that I was ridiculously excited. It felt so important to meet these super-positive people who had defied the odds and battled back from life-altering injuries. We also wanted to see the CR Johnson Healing Center where so much good work is done.

We left England on Wednesday, 19th March to fly to San Francisco. I was actually quite nervous – what if these people didn't meet my expectations and the High Fives Foundation turned out not to be what I believed it to be? There was only one way to find out and we were doing it. In a couple of days' time, we would be face-to-face with them. We spent the night in San Francisco and that afternoon had a chance for a stroll around. We saw the Golden Gate Bridge and Alcatraz and got a little taste for the place. It was a lovely spring evening and the people of San Francisco were busy getting fit by jogging and biking along the seafront. Others were busking and playing various styles of music for the enjoyment of passers-by. There were lots of restaurants, many of them featuring seafood specialities, which are no good for Matt as he is seriously allergic to shellfish (which just gives Nick and I something else to worry about when Matt is off on his own). All in all, it seemed a pretty buzzy place and provided a good introduction to California.

The next day, we collected our hire car and set off for the Sierra Nevada Mountains. California was experiencing a severe drought and there had been very little snowfall over the winter. That, combined with rising unseasonable temperatures, did not bode well for the ski slopes, but we weren't too concerned about that. As we got nearer to our destination, the scenery got more and more stunning with beautiful pine forests set against snow-capped mountains. I guess in a normal year the snow would have been a lot lower down and it would have been magical had all these forests been dusted with the white stuff. As it was, it was still pretty special, and it was obvious we were not in Europe. It just had that big, spacious American feel to it.

As this was to be a once-in-a-lifetime trip, we had booked ourselves into the luxurious Ritz-Carlton Hotel at Northstar, Lake Tahoe. It is a beautiful mountain-style building right on the slopes at Northstar, nestling amongst the pine trees. The exterior of the building featured lots of stonework and wood. Inside, there were huge roaring log fires and comfy chairs and sofas. Outside on the terrace, there was a big firepit where guests could gather round to roast marshmallows. There was snow on the ground when we arrived, but not a huge amount. It looked like it would be enough for us to ski on, though, and even if it wasn't, we didn't care. We were there to meet some incredible people – snow or no snow.

We were now in the region where many of Matt's ski heroes had grown up or spent a lot of time, most notably CR Johnson and Shane McConkey. We were just down the road from Squaw Valley, which features heavily in many of Matt's ski DVDs. When we were snuggled up in Le Tour watching those DVDs, we would never have guessed that one day in the not-too-distant future we would actually be there. It's strange how life works out. That's why you have to sometimes let yourself go with the flow and have faith that somehow things *will* work out.

On our first night in the hotel, we had invited the High Fives crew to join us for dinner. They all rolled up on time – Roy, Adam and Steve, together with Luka, who was a new recruit to the team. Roy and Steve had both broken their backs, which had put a stop to their skiing careers. Their injuries had left them both with limps and difficulty walking, but they were both mobile. It was immediately obvious that the one thing they all had in common was a huge zest for life and an overwhelming desire to make life better for others. I needn't have worried about being disappointed, as they were just as I had expected them to be – full of life, enthusiasm and brimming over with positivity.

We spent a wonderful evening chatting with them all and hearing their accounts of the many inspiring people that they had met and helped on their way after terrible accidents, mainly involving spinal cord or brain injuries. They show people that there is life after injury. Not everyone will be able to get back on their feet, but by providing adaptive equipment, they can be given the chance to at least get out there and enjoy whatever it is they enjoy doing, but in a different way. If you've ever seen anyone hurtling down the slopes on a 'sit ski', you'll know how fast they go and how much fun it looks! They also put them in touch with, and give grants for, all sorts of therapy that again will help in giving them a fighting chance of recovery. At the very least they are giving back to seriously injured people some sort of quality in their lives that they may never have dared hope for until the day they encountered High Fives and opened the door to all sorts of possibilities. Roy and Steve are living, talking, walking proof of how good life can still be once it has changed forever. It may not be the same life, but it can be pretty good and sometimes even better. I know that both Roy and Steve were really good skiers before their accidents, but what they have achieved since and what they have given back to others is immeasurable.

There is a whole group of people who have suffered life-altering injuries and quite possibly thought that life was going to be pretty dire from then on, but through the High Fives Foundation, they have been taken in all sorts of unexpected and wonderful directions. They've taken people heli-skiing in Alaska, on adaptive surf trips in Hawaii, and even adaptive fly fishing. It seems that you can adapt just about any activity to make it possible for severely injured people to participate in. For example, people who are completely wheelchair-bound can be put into a machine resembling a passive stander in order for them to stand up and take golf shots. If a disabled person has a favourite sport, the chances are there will be a way back to it using adaptive equipment. Just take a look at all the sports featured in both the winter and summer Paralympics.

They also visit schools and clubs talking to them about the importance of staying safe on the slopes, hopefully preventing many accidents from happening in the first place.

For me, it's not really about the amount of money they raise (although that is obviously important); what I find amazing is the time and effort High Fives take to visit and meet people and convince them that a positive, worthwhile future lies ahead of them. Money can't buy that – it's priceless. We are a good example of that. Roy never failed to answer an email, and from afar, he offered such encouragement to Matt and cheered him on as he reached his various goals. The feel-good factor in all his emails gave us all such a boost. You just believed that if Roy thought it was possible, then it must be.

At the end of the evening, I was delighted to find that Nick had also been really impressed with them all. He had been discussing with Steve the more serious aspects of actual fundraising and how the Foundation worked, and was very struck by their obvious professionalism. Matt, of course, had had the best time. I only needed to look across the table to see him laughing and joking with them all to know that. I also knew we were in for a great time in California.

The next day, we opted for a quiet day while we were still getting over our jet lag. We had an exploratory ski around Northstar, which was a beautiful area. All we had to do was step out of the back door of the hotel onto the slopes where the ski valet had laid out our skis in readiness for us. What luxury! At the end of the day, we just had to step out of them and they were put away for us. It was a far cry from the usual hard slog we had carrying our skis up the car park in France! The lift operators were very Californian and wishing us 'nice days' left, right and centre. Matt and I had a little chuckle as we thought of our friend Jean-Luc in Le Tour doing things very much his way – wishing people a nice day didn't feature too highly in his *modus operandi*. The Californian way was lovely, but the French way made us laugh more.

At the end of the day, we went for a drive to have our first look at Lake Tahoe, which is a beautiful lake surrounded by mountains. It was a little reminiscent of Lake Geneva, but with no big cities on the edge of it, just small communities and some stunning homes and lovely forests. We stopped off at the village in Squaw Valley and had a little look around. It was definitely the place to be, with many dudes strolling around in their baggy ski pants. Matt managed to get a commemorative Shane McConkey glass, which he was thrilled about. Shane McConkey was another extreme skier who is no longer with us. He did all manner of crazy things, but he did them well. He died in a wingsuit accident in Italy doing what he loved. He was a larger-than-life character who packed more into his 39 years than anyone else could in 139 years. They say that you should judge someone's life by the impact they leave behind, much like throwing a pebble into a lake. Some people leave barely a ripple. Shane McConkey left a tidal wave and, in my opinion, the world needs more people like him.

The next day was a Saturday and there was a ski competition on in Squaw Valley. Roy invited Matt to join him there for the day, and he certainly didn't need to be asked twice. Roy seemed to know every single person in Squaw and Matt had the time of his life. (To be added to all the other times of his life he keeps having!) The highlight of the day had to be meeting Tanner Hall, another of Matt's ski heroes. He is a friend of Roy's and I would have loved to have seen the expression on Matt's face when Roy said to him, "Turn around and say hi to Tanner." Talk about living the dream – that is exactly what Matt was doing.

On Sunday, we decided to head out to the resort of Heavenly for a ski. This is to be found at the south end of the lake and gave us the opportunity to drive right around the lake. This was our first view of the whole lake in all its glory, and it is truly glorious. On that day, the sun was shining and the lake was the most wonderful shade of azure blue. Add to that the majestic mountains and the pine forests and you could imagine yourself in paradise. No wonder those Californians are so happy! The pistes or 'trails' (as they say in the USA) were long and wide and we had a fantastic day up there. We had travelled down one side of the lake to get there and we returned via the other side, so that by the end of the day we had circumnavigated the lake. It was absolutely beautiful.

We decided to go back to Heavenly on Tuesday to explore the other side of the mountain. On Sunday, we had been on the Californian side, so this time we went to the Nevadan side. The mountain was much the same, but the view was very different. Now we were looking down on a huge expanse of very flat, arid-looking plains, which would eventually end up in desert. An interesting fact is that, although Nevada is largely desert, the name Nevada is actually Spanish for 'snow-covered'. The first Europeans to explore the region were Spanish, and they chose the name because of the adjacent snow-covered mountains. We had another good day of skiing on those very same snow-covered mountains. That night, snow fell and on Wednesday, we woke to fresh snow in Northstar and perfect skiing conditions. Matt was skiing really well and was on top form.

During one of his conversations with Roy, Matt had mentioned that his big regret was that he had never done a backflip on skis before his accident. Roy approached Nick and I the next time he saw us. "You know, Matt's been telling me that he really wished he could've done a backflip on skis before his accident."

"Yeah, it's a shame, I guess," I replied, not really thinking it was that much of a shame.

"It's not too late. We can make it happen for him."

Oh no, we should have known that Roy the Great Fixer might have the answer. Nick and I looked at each other nervously.

"Do you not think this might be tempting fate a bit, Roy? He's just got away with one accident. Maybe a backflip in the snow is not such a great idea."

"Please, Mum." Matt's eyes were shining with excitement.

"It's okay, you guys. It won't be on snow. We can train him in a safe environment, with a special coach. It'll be fine. We won't do it if you guys are really set against it. It's up to you."

We figured that this was what High Fives is all about – making things happen that seemed out of reach since an accident. We couldn't be that mean to Matt, and we trusted Roy to do no harm. Besides, I don't think Matt would have ever forgiven us if we'd said no.

"Okay, if you really think it's safe, we'll go for it." We were rewarded by the expression of sheer joy on Matt's face.

So it was that on the following Thursday, Matt and I set off with Steve for the Woodward Tahoe Bunker at Boreal. Nick was still a little worried and felt it would be better for him to stay away in case Matt picked up on his nerves.

The Woodward Tahoe Bunker is described as 'an innovative action sports training camp' and also 'quite possibly the raddest place to train'. It is basically a huge building, a bit like an aircraft hangar, and to be found under its roof are Olympic-sized trampolines, skate parks, foam pits, ramps and anything else you might need to practise all sorts of tricks and flips. It's a place where professional BMX riders, skateboarders, skiers and snowboarders can go to train safely. The advantage for the skiers and snowboarders is that they can perfect their tricks in the foam pits and then go straight onto the outdoor slopes and try them out on the snow. When we arrived there, Matt was introduced to a young coach called Jamie, who was standing by to take him through his paces. Roy and Adam joined us there to witness events and Adam was filming it all. We had a lovely surprise when CR's sister, Kahlil, turned up with her little boy. Matt had to do well now. It was the first time we had met her in person and she was every bit as nice as we expected her to be. Really friendly, open and generous, and happy to meet CR's number one fan.

Jamie started Matt off on his warm-up and checked out what he could and couldn't do. I have to say that this was the only place on earth where this could have happened. I could not imagine anyone in England encouraging Matt to do a backflip on skis. It did seem slightly crazy. The first thing he had to do was to simply jump onto his back onto a big foam square and tuck his legs in. That alone was quite a tricky manoeuvre to carry out, but he did it well. From there, he progressed onto a big round roller where he had to again jump onto his back and tuck up his feet, but then carry the movement through and do a backward somersault into the foam pit. Quite amazing. Then he had to get out of the foam pit, which was almost his greatest challenge. A foam pit is a pit full of big chunks of foam, and scrambling out is hard enough for anyone, as there is nothing static to get a grip on, so for Matt it was almost impossible. Thankfully, with a little help from his friends, he made it with a delighted expression on his face. After having done those things for quite a while, I actually expected him to be exhausted and give up, but of course he didn't. There was no way he was leaving until he had progressed further in his training. It was definitely the hardest training I had seen him do since his accident, but he was finding extra energy and strength from somewhere. I think a lot of it was to do with the fact that not only did he believe he could do it, but the High Five guys and Jamie also believed that he could do it. He was surrounded by positive energy and that goes a long way. If there is one thing I have learnt from this whole experience, it is that positive thinking really can work. Being surrounded by people who believe in your abilities can go an awfully long way. It was totally inspiring and enabling for Matt.

The next stage of training was slightly scary for a watching mother. He was taken over to the ramp area where the skateboarders and BMX riders train and he then put on a pair of wooden skis with small wheels attached. Jamie grabbed hold of his t-shirt and ran up and down the ramp with him and then, when he felt he had gained enough momentum, he let go, and Matt launched himself into the huge foam pit at the top of the ramp. He then took Matt up to the top of the large ramp and let him go by himself! He shot down it, up the other side, and launched himself into the pit fearlessly. Matt worked hard, but I have to say that Jamie was a total hero. He ran up and down that ramp I don't know how many times, keeping close to Matt. We were there for over two hours until exhaustion finally caught up with Matt and he crashed at the bottom of the ramp. Thankfully, no harm was done, apart from winding himself (and nearly giving me a heart attack). He had really made a superhuman effort that afternoon. Jamie was convinced that Matt would achieve that backflip and was willing to do the whole thing again if possible, so we planned to go back there on Saturday and give it one more go. All this was done as a favour. Roy explained that Tahoe is a community and a community helps each other, and the Woodward people were doing this as a favour to High Fives. Once again, we were experiencing the kindness that still exists in the world today, despite all the awful things we are continually reading about in the papers. I also know how hard the High Fives people work and yet they gave up an entire afternoon to support Matt.

The following day, they spent even more time with us as they joined us on the ski slopes. Kahlil came too in her green Armada CR Johnson jacket to match Matt's. She was skiing on a great pair of CR Johnson skis in the Rasta colours, with another big lion on them. It was quite amazing to see three people who couldn't really walk that well (Roy, Steve and Matt) whizzing down the mountain on skis at speed. Once they were on skis, they were transformed. I said to Kahlil, "You know, time was when Matt would have gone straight down, without putting in a single turn. It's weird seeing him putting in all these turns."

"Yep, that was then – different times now." They were the heartfelt words of someone who had been through the same experiences as we had. She had given up her job to return home to help her brother with his recovery, so she understood only too well the recovery process from a brain injury. It was a fun day and at lunch, they announced that they were giving Matt a pair of the CR skis to take home with him! The generosity of these people truly knows no bounds.

Later that afternoon, we went to the High Fives offices to collect the CR skis. The offices are in the same building as the CR Johnson Healing Center and the walls there are covered with bright murals featuring CR, painted by a local artist. Also on the wall is the jacket that CR had designed himself, that then inspired the jacket that Matt and Kahlil had. It is the jacket he was wearing when he died. It was very sobering looking at it and all the other reminders of that remarkable young man, who was one of the best skiers of his generation and who has continued to inspire countless other young skiers, including my son. He has had such a huge effect on Matt's recovery. It was thanks to him that we first really believed it was all going to work out. I really wished we could have thanked him in person. He certainly has a wonderful legacy in the Healing Center. It is an amazing facility with all sorts of therapists and equipment available to help injured athletes fight their way back to fitness or, at least, the very best they can be. You can feel the positivity and optimism surrounding you there.

Steve and Adam were in the office and, together with Kahlil, they presented Matt with his skis. To say Matt was thrilled would be severely understating it. That night, back in the hotel, he just kept looking at them, and photographs were sent back to all of his pals. I can picture him now with a look of almost disbelief on his face. It was as if he was trying to figure out why all of his dreams were suddenly coming true. He is indeed a very lucky young man. Fate may have dealt him a cruel blow on that night back in November 2010, but ever since, it really does seem to have been trying hard to make it up to him. So many good things have happened.

That night, Roy and Adam were over in Squaw, where Roy was in charge of a charity auction for the Shane McConkey Foundation – another cause supporting young skiers. All of these skiing foundations interact, helping each other. They are a shining example of community spirit and a lesson for us all.

Saturday was our last day in the Tahoe area and Matt was due to try his backflip. Unfortunately, the weather was not on his side. It was absolutely bucketing down with snow. Undaunted, we set off for Boreal, but the highway was in chaos and jammed up with people stopping to put chains on their cars. In order to continue, you needed either chains or winter tyres, and our hire car had neither, so we had to exit the highway and return to Northstar. Matt was disappointed, but at least he had the satisfaction of knowing that Jamie had firmly believed that he would have succeeded, given the chance.

We went back to Northstar via the High Five offices to say goodbye to our friends there. They were all getting ready for their next fundraising event, which was to be on Monday. It was the Skinny Skiathon. People were sponsored for skiing laps on old-fashioned skinny skis, dressed in '70s-style gear if possible. They continually think of and arrange fun events that will raise lots of money to help their High Five athletes. Every week, there is something going on. Their activities also extend to the east coast ski areas. They just never stop working to raise funds. They keep coming up with fun ideas and they attract more and more support all the time. They certainly have our support.

Our last night was spent with Kahlil and her little boy, Thomas, who is quite a little character. It was good to spend time with her and she was quite happy to talk to Matt about CR.

She is so proud of her brother, as indeed she should be. Matt was delighted to find out that CR had difficulty in managing a knife and fork after his brain injury – this is something that they had in common! After a very good evening, it was time to go to bed and dream about the amazing time we had spent in the Sierra Nevada Mountains before heading home on Sunday. We had met some very special, big-hearted people during the last ten days, and Matt was now more motivated than ever to complete his marathon and raise lots of money for High Fives. We had had the most wonderful holiday with many memories to treasure and look back on in years to come. I think we all hoped that we would return one day; after all, we still hadn't managed to fit in a ski session in Squaw Valley, nor had Matt completed his backflip. In the meantime, we also hoped that our new friends would come and ski with us in Chamonix before too long.

On the drive back to San Francisco, in contrast to the journey out, the surrounding forests and mountains were covered in snow and, as I had suspected they would, they did indeed look magical. Thankfully, it was no longer actually snowing, so the roads were clear for the journey as we headed back to the airport to start our journey home. Once we got home, we would have to start thinking about where Matt would go next on his path, but for now we could just enjoy looking back on our best holiday ever and the special people we had been privileged to meet. We now believed more than ever that the seemingly impossible could be possible. In Truckee, we had undoubtedly seen the power of positive thinking in action. I'm not saying that positive thinking can work miracles, but it definitely boosts confidence and self-belief, and that is so important.

TWENTY-TWO

MARATHON TRAINING

Matt returned to Chamonix for the last two weeks of the winter season, and he had set himself one final challenge before returning to the UK for the summer. He was going to walk up from Chamonix to Le Tour, which is 14km straight up a mountain. I am happy to report that he did in fact succeed in this goal. Accompanied by his Australian friend, Nicole, they did it in 4 hours 40 minutes, walking on bumpy, narrow mountain paths, going up all the way – a tough call for anyone, even if fully fit.

I have to say that Nicole deserves a medal for this, as Matt tells me that he was gripping hard on to her arm for support during this expedition and she was probably left with a few bruises. Why didn't he use a stick? Well, the physios had suggested this and it didn't work, because using a stick is multi-tasking. In order to use a stick successfully, you need to get into a rhythm with your arms swinging in coordination with your legs. That involves a lot of brainpower and, at this stage, Matt's brain couldn't handle that. All of his brainpower was focussed on putting one foot in front of the other and moving forward.

On the 16th of April 2014, Matt returned to England to start his marathon training. As always, on his return to England, we decided to tweak his regime to see if we could bring about further improvements. We invested in a juicer and mixer to start making fresh fruit smoothies and juices. We also added Pilates to his training regime in an effort to try and improve his posture, which would in turn fully engage his core muscles. For that we had found an Australian Physio called Trish, so our team was getting increasingly international!

The priority now was the Amsterdam Marathon. By the 19th of October, Matt had to be capable of walking 26.2 miles. We kept Monday, Wednesday and Friday afternoons clear of appointments. These were to be our training sessions. We did a lot of research in order to find good surfaces to walk on where we could measure the distance and monitor what we were doing. Mostly it was Matt and I walking, sometimes it was Nick and Matt and occasionally it was the three of us.

We discovered the Centurion Way in Chichester, which is a cycle path that follows an old rail track. It has a good surface, it's quite wide, it's quiet and we knew exactly how long it was. On Matt's first attempt, he walked 2 miles and took 2 hours and, by the end, he was very wobbly and leaning heavily to one side. By the 5th of May, he was already doing it in 1 hour 32 minutes without the wobble or the lean. Our other favourite place for walking was West Wittering. There, the sandy beach and the big estate also allowed for some good walking surfaces with measurable distances. Twice a week, we would do moderate distances between 2 and 4 miles, but once a week we would try and increase the distance. By the 29th of June, Matt could manage 7 miles relatively easily and had even done a 10-mile walk with Nick.

All of his physios were supporting him in this venture, with Petra taking a particular interest, as she is Dutch. She was also teaching Matt a few words of Dutch during their physio sessions, which might come in useful in Amsterdam. One Sunday afternoon, she took him off for a 13-mile walk as part of his training.

Even the weather was on our side. The summer of 2014 was turning out to be one of the driest and sunniest in a long time, which meant that our training schedule was rarely interrupted. Some of the coastal paths that we walked on would have been very difficult in the rain, as mud would not be great for Matt's walking. As it was, we had optimum conditions for most of the time. I was intrigued to observe that, on a long walk, Matt's walking just got better and better. Apparently, this is because the brain picks up on the repetitive pattern and it would therefore get easier the more it was repeated. Due to the slow, unpredictable nature of the brain-healing process, this was not completely carried over from walk to walk, but the amount of walking that we were doing was certainly beneficial for us all. Matt was undoubtedly getting stronger and fitter and even I was feeling very much fitter!

At the end of August, we went to Le Tour for high-altitude training. Tim came over from Switzerland to join us with his new girlfriend, Tina. We all went walking up on the mountain and Matt managed very well. Surely after the mountain paths of the Alps, Amsterdam was going to be a doddle. Our neighbours in Le Tour, Philip and Maria, were also in residence, and Maria took Matt off on a very long walk up the mountain. They were gone for over 4 hours on the steepest paths and he came back in remarkably good shape. I think Maria was quite impressed.

On our last day in Chamonix, Matt was back on the athletics track ready to break his 100m record. The previous year, he had done it in a blistering 81 seconds, so now he needed to knock at least 5 seconds off that. Tim and I accompanied him down to the track. Tim was the starter and official timekeeper. I was the cheerleader and trotted alongside him in case of any wobbles. It was a lovely sunny afternoon and there were plenty of people sitting around the track. Matt's first attempt was a bit of a muddle, as we didn't quite get the start right, so we reran it. By this time, the watching crowd had figured out that something a bit different was going on and they cheered Matt on as he lurched forward: "*Allez! Allez! Allez!*" (Go! Go! Go!) They will never know, but they were actually watching a very impressive run. Matt had smashed his previous record by 20 seconds. He did it in 61 seconds, much to his delight.

Matt's fundraising page on Crowdrise was now up and running. He had set a target of $5,000 to raise for High Fives, although we were all secretly hoping for a lot more. We needn't have worried; in the end, it was to get up to over $12,500. Every day, there were fresh donations. People were incredibly generous, both with their cash and their kind comments. His friend Sam had lived up to his promise of signing up to walk the marathon with him and all the necessary flight and hotel bookings had been made. Tim and Tina were planning to surprise Matt by going out to Amsterdam to support him. His friends Chris, Foxy, Steph, Dan and Pruden were also booked up to be there. Even Petra, his physio, was going.

September and the first two weeks of October were spent training hard. Not a session was missed. The highlight for me was the 19th of September, when we walked 20 miles. We started by the Canal Basin in Chichester and followed the towpath down to the sea, then along the coastal path to West Wittering, on towards East Wittering, back along the beach and round the estate to make 20 miles. I must confess to wanting to give up at 15 miles. It had not been a particularly easy walk. The coastal path section had been really quite difficult, with many tree roots in the way and a very uneven, muddy path. I thought that by walking 15 miles, he had already proved that he could walk a long way. "You know what, Matt, I think we could stop now. You've done brilliantly today," I said hopefully. I should have known better.

"It's fine, Mum, *you* can stop now if you like. I can't, though. My target for today was 20 miles and that is what I'm going to walk. You wait here for Dad, and I'll call you both when I'm finished and you can come and pick me up then."

"Yes, but it's only another 5 miles and it's obvious that you *could* do it, so we might as well call Dad now and he can come and pick us both up. If your hip is hurting, it's probably a good idea to stop." I was pushing it now.

"No, I have to do 20 miles. I'll see you later," replied Matt with a note of impatience in his voice.

"*Okay*, I guess I can keep going too. If you're determined to do it, I'll do it with you," and so I staggered on.

He had planned for a 20-mile walk and he was jolly well going to walk 20 miles with or without me. He had made that quite clear! He did it all unaided too. His hip was really hurting by the end, but he walked through the pain. We all knew then that he would succeed in the Marathon. Unless he physically collapsed, he would complete it.

The level of excitement mounted until finally the big weekend arrived. On Friday 17th October, I put Matt on a train and he set off to meet Sam in London. The next morning, they were to get on a plane bound for Amsterdam and the greatest challenge of Matt's recovery so far. Nick had commissioned some special t-shirts for his supporters, listing the many people who had helped him get this far. On this occasion, Nick and I had decided that this was something for Matt and his friends to do without us. Much as I would have loved to be there, it was time for him to do it alone without his anxious parents loitering in the background. I have to say, over the course of the weekend, I came to regret that decision. It was agony not knowing what was going on! As I wasn't there, it's up to Matt to tell his own story now.

TWENTY-THREE

THE AMSTERDAM MARATHON

I went up to London on the Friday night to stay with Sam, ready to fly from London City Airport on Saturday morning. We went for a quiet dinner and then an early night so that we would be fresh for a pretty big weekend that lay ahead!

We travelled to the airport on the tube. Sam carried my bag (I think I overpacked a bit). We got there no problem and checked in. The only thing of note was the lady at security who asked if I had a bad leg and needed a wheelchair. I just smiled and said, "No, thank you." On the plane, I asked the girl sitting next to me if she was going out for a holiday (I can't help talking to literally everyone I sit next to on planes, trains and buses). She told me that she was going out for the half-marathon and when I told her I was going out for the big one, I think she was a bit surprised, because she had obviously seen how I was walking.

When we landed, we got a cab to the stadium to get our bibs. There were lots of stands from the sponsors selling clothing, equipment and nutrition. After we had got our bibs, Sam went off to get some energy drinks and gels and I snuck off to the Mizuno stand. There were lots of people looking at the running shoes, taking the whole thing very seriously, but I saw some special edition Mizuno slippers. They were bright orange clogs, so obviously I had to buy a pair! When I found Sam and showed him, weirdly enough, he thought they were a bit ridiculous. I love them and am actually wearing them as I write this.

Next, we needed to check into our hotel. Mum texted me while we were on the tram and asked where we would be in an hour's time. I replied that I hadn't got a clue! When we got to the hotel, we went straight to the restaurant. We were just looking at the menus, when a loud voice said, "ALL RIGHT, GUYS!" It was Tim and Tina. Turns out they had wanted to surprise us at the airport but had missed us. That was why Mum had been texting me. Sam said that we had to try and just 'do nothing' for the afternoon, so we just sat there and met Tim and Tina later for a quiet dinner. They then went off to meet Chris, Nick, Dan, Steph and Pruden, my friends from Windsor who had come out on a later flight.

Sam and I booked a cab for the morning. The girl on the desk at the hotel said that a few roads would be closed, so most people would be walking there as it was, "only a few miles away." I explained that, as I would be walking 26.2 miles that day, I'd rather not add unnecessary mileage. She agreed and booked us a cab, then we went to get an early night so that we'd be fresh for the big day.

Sunday, the 19th of October, 2014 was Race Day, and I woke up with a sore jaw! I took a painkiller, but when *we went down for breakfast, I couldn't eat anything, as I couldn't open my jaw enough – not the best start to a race day. We got our cab with an English guy, who was also running the marathon. He had done a few different ones, but I think he was impressed with us walking it.*

Tim had wanted to meet up to take photos of us all in our t-shirts for High Fives, but I think they might have been out late, so weren't up for the start. We got a stranger to take a photo of me and Sam. The start was in the Olympic Stadium and, after the photo, we duly made our way in. There were a few thousand runners, so there was a big queue to get inside the stadium. The runners were separated by expected times, fastest go first, and so on. We were obviously in the last group. (We probably should have been in an even slower group!) While we were waiting to start, Tim and Tina called us from the stands. It was good to know that we had some support from the start. I think because we were in the 'slow runners bit' (not sure that is the official name), everyone was pretty relaxed and friendly. I didn't hear any official call, but everyone started to shuffle up to the line, so we followed suit.

I had decided that I might as well go for broke and when the gun went, I'd just go for it. Ha ha! In my head, when the gun went off, I would start walking but then speed up until I was doing a very good impression of Mo Farah. Oddly enough, when the gun went off, I just stumbled forward like normal, obviously as fast as I could go, though. Maybe this would be quite a long walk after all.

So, as everyone jogged past us, a few people could see how I was walking and they patted me on the back (as they ran past). I think our pace was quite good. Sam had one of those GPS watches that measures speed, distance and stuff. He said our pace was over 4 miles an hour, which would be quite a good pace if I could keep it up. As we left the stadium, there was a big crowd of supporters and suddenly I heard my physio, Petra, scream "MATT!" I knew she was coming, but I didn't expect to see her so early on.

The course went from the stadium through the streets. Obviously, we were quite far back now, but we could still see a few stragglers in the distance. There was a man on a motorbike who was hanging back with us. He asked if I was hurt, so Sam explained. I think he was quite impressed. Sam chatted to him, but I couldn't afford to waste any time chatting – I was in a race!

As we went along a straight road, we saw Tim and Tina again (second of many appearances throughout the day). There were now other marathon runners coming back down on the other side of the road (there were barriers splitting the road in half). A few were clapping us; that was cool. People in the crowd were cheering and clapping. They all said, "Success!" Ha ha! I said to Sam that we were definitely the people's champions. We were about 6 miles in and I asked Sam if I could lean on his arm. I think maybe I'd started a bit fast, so I was a bit tired. The first thing that goes when I'm tired is my balance. Leaning on Sam's arm meant that I didn't have to worry about balance and could pick the pace up again.

By now, we were definitely just on a leisurely stroll through Amsterdam – everyone else was LONG gone! In the distance, I could see the Windsor lot. There were five of them, plus Tim and Tina. They were all laughing and making 'hilarious' jokes about us being a bit slow and everything. Dan said that I looked like a Vietnam veteran in my headband. I thought I was actually looking pretty dashing. We couldn't stop for a chat, so we just kept on going and said that we'd see them later. A few minutes further down the road, I could see a few people running out of a café. They were yelling, laughing and squeaking. It was my best friend from Geneva, Greg. Complete surprise! He was with his girlfriend and his sister and her boyfriend (Taylor, Jess and Paul). They had driven through the night to be there. I hadn't seen them for a couple of years and wanted to stop and have a chat, but I told them that I was on a mission, so we'd catch up later. I told them that Tim was a couple of minutes back down the road, but we needed to keep on going.

After that excitement, we had to do a big loop down the canal. Sam looked at his map on the phone and saw that we had to go pretty far down one side of the canal before crossing over and coming back down the other side. It was at this time that I told Sam my 'halfway theory'. This is that the second half of anything goes quicker than the first. This theory works for physio exercises, push-ups, etc. However, I now know that it's not quite the same with marathons. As we went on, I was apparently leaning harder on Sam's arm, so we tried me walking 'freestyle' for a bit (that's what I call anything I can do without help these days). That didn't go so well. I was a bit wobbly and it REALLY slowed me down, so we compromised and I switched to lean on Sam's other arm. I'm not sure that he was too excited about another 14 or so miles like that! As Sam had his hands free for a bit, he had the chance to get some of those tubes of energy gel out. I'm not 100% convinced that they are quite as effective as people had told me, but I quite liked the taste, so I wasn't complaining. By now, we had started to come back down the other side of the canal. The sweeper bus passed us and asked Sam if we *were okay, and told us we would be too late to finish. "We know. We're fine."*

He then sent Petra a message. To this day, I have no idea what he said, but a few minutes later, she came cycling along. She looked very Dutch (she is Dutch), which made me feel safer on the mean streets of Amsterdam. Well, actually the mean streets alongside the canal just outside Amsterdam. It was good, because Petra obviously had a bit more of an idea of where we should be going, rather than just following a tiny map on Sam's phone.

We could no longer see any other runners. To be honest, we hadn't seen any for a while. The sweeper bus was long gone and it was a quiet road alongside the canal, so it was just me, Sam and Petra. Then we saw Tim and everyone walking towards us. I think we needed that boost. I'm not sure how much fun it would have been, just me and Sam plodding along mile after long mile. Now there was Petra, Tim, Tina, Greg, Taylor, Jess, Paul, Chris, Nick, Dan, Steph, Pruden and obviously me and Sam. So now it was a bit of a party! Everyone was laughing and joking, and one added bonus was that Sam could now rotate to rest his aching arm. As people took turns for me to lean on their arm, it was good because I could catch up with them. I then had a brainwave – with all these people, what if I had someone on each side? Then I'd be done in a few minutes! Well, we tried it and I can tell you that if Usain Bolt was allowed to run like this, he'd do the 100 metres in a couple of seconds! This new technique was faster and I didn't need to think at all about balance now.

As we got nearer the end of the road along the canal, there were a few houses. People in their gardens were asking us what we were doing. Sam explained and they clapped, cheered and wished us luck. The locals were still encouraging us with the same phrase: "Success!"

I've just realised that I haven't really been keeping you updated with times as I'm telling this story. I think as we got to the end of the canal, it was about five and a half hours since the race had started. As we got back on the main roads, most of my friends went off to get lunch, leaving me with Sam and Tim on either side, plus Petra on her bike. They were now opening the road after the marathon – everyone else had finished or just given up. There was a big truck with people on the back who would stop and collect the barriers from the road. We were able to follow this for a bit as we were travelling at about the same pace. When the workers hanging off the truck saw us and figured out that we were still doing the marathon, they clapped and cheered, which was nice.

As we headed back into the city, Sam said that we were 5 miles from the finish at the Olympic Stadium. At this point, Petra offered Sam a little break and swapped with him, so Sam had a little rest by riding the bike for a bit. Now I wouldn't have thought that 20 miles into a marathon would be a very good time for a physio session, but Petra thought it was. For a few steps, she held my hands and walked backwards trying to get me to do various little exercises. I just smiled and said that I could just about put one foot in front of the other now, so I couldn't exactly do little exercises. She agreed and I just kept plodding along.

Meanwhile, Tim had a call from Chris. They had finished lunch and said that they would wait on a bridge for us a mile or so ahead. As we reached the bridge, Greg gave me a full rundown of the football scores. United weren't playing until Monday, so I wasn't that distracted. We were getting tantalisingly close; I could almost hear the *roar of the stadium. Not really! Everyone else had finished a few hours ago. As it was getting late, Petra went to take the rental bike back to the shop before they closed. She told us that the route passed through the Vondelpark, which was only a mile or so from the end, so she would meet us there.*

Limping through most of a marathon had obviously done a bit of damage, because my knees and especially my hips were killing me now. I was conscious not to whinge too much about the pain. Well, I say I was conscious of it, but that didn't stop me letting everyone know just how much pain I was in! Coincidentally, Steph is also a physio, so she gave me a bit of advice and a few stretches, but neither of us thought that this was the time or place for a massage.

As we ticked the miles off, I was getting more and more excited and people continued to take it in turns to let me lean on them. Taylor obviously hadn't planned to be walking a few miles of the marathon when she had left Geneva the night before. She was wearing a pair of high(ish) heeled boots. Her feet had suffered a bit, so she had stopped in one of the souvenir shops to buy a pair of clog slippers. They were not dissimilar to my own new pair back at the hotel, just a bit less orange. We saw the gates of the Vondelpark and I knew that we were only a couple of miles from the end now. I'd love to tell you that I put one final little burst on, but by now my hips were so bad that I was just about managing to hobble slowly forward! As we were going through the park, we saw a girl who had obviously completed the marathon. "Ha ha! You guys are STILL going!" At that point, Tim politely told her how I had been in a coma and had walked the whole thing. She went bright red, said that she was sorry and wished me luck.

Petra had now caught up with us again and asked Sam how far we had gone. He told her that, thanks to a little unintentional detour earlier, we had already done 26.2 miles. "Oh, then you have done a marathon now. The stadium is less than a mile away, so you can stop now."

I replied, "I'm finishing in the stadium." I think everyone knew that I wouldn't compromise!

So we left the park and it was just a couple of left turns. I was just going where I was told. It was dark, I was getting cold and my hips were really hurting with every step, but I had been training specifically for the marathon for months, since that walk from Chamonix to Le Tour with Nicole in April, although really I had been training ever since the accident, because at the end of the day, I had had to relearn to walk. This marathon was me proving to the world that I had succeeded! It was now VERY dark and as we went along the last long road, we saw people heading out for dinner. I then realised that I had been walking nonstop for 9 hours! About a mile from the end, Tim and Chris ran ahead. By now, my hip was hurting so much that I didn't really notice them at the time. I later learnt that they had gone on to check that we would be able to get in. They had had to persuade the security people to open the gates for us.

I could now see the floodlights of the stadium and, as we got closer, the gates into the stadium were also open. Tim and Chris were there holding a bit of toilet paper across as a finish line, like they do in the opening scene of 'Cool Runnings'. As I hobbled through the line, all I wanted to do was find somewhere to sit. Dan gave me a piggyback to a bench (I don't think my legs were working anymore). I sat down and borrowed someone's phone to ring my mum. She had given me strict instructions to ring *her as soon as I finished. She said she was very proud and asked how I was feeling, I think I just laughed! Tina then came along with a nice surprise. She had gone and found some people who worked for the marathon and got me a medal. Officially, you didn't get a medal if it took more than 6 hours, but Tina explained and they were more than happy to give me my medal. As we were all sitting on the bench, Sam had a look at his sat nav watch thing and told me we had actually done almost 27 miles! It had taken us 9 hours and 37 minutes.*

So, I think the marathon was a bit of a metaphor for the last 4 years: tricky, tough at times, sometimes a bit painful, pretty funny the whole way through and it all came together at the end!

TWENTY-FOUR

MATT DECIDES
ON HIS FUTURE

So there we were at the end of 2014 with the marathon, and the all-encompassing effort that had taken, now behind us. What would Matt's next goal be? I was very conscious that November 2015 would mark the fifth anniversary of the accident. Five years seems to be a very important milestone in recovering from a serious injury. The High Fives Foundation website frequently featured their athletes with their 'Five-Year Redemption'. The fifth year often seemed to be the year that everything changed and rehabilitation gave way to getting back to as normal a life as possible. Young adults who had been forced by circumstances into living back at home with their parents were desperate to get back out there after five years!

So many things had been achieved by Matt over the last 4 years. He had worked like crazy to get as far as he had. We had put together a great programme of therapy, but now there had to be more to life than that. He needed to get some real substance back into his life. He needed to get back to full-time employment, but what sort of job? His life before had been perfect for him, involving travel and working with like-minded people and a lot of fun. Sadly, watersports and ski instructing were no longer viable options, at least at this stage. He needed to be a lot stronger and less wobbly for both of those. I couldn't see him working in a shop for the rest of his life, nor being office-bound. Even working in a bar or restaurant wouldn't be suitable at this stage – he'd drop the plates and glasses.

He needed something a little bit out of the ordinary that would involve his love of sport and not be the same old routine day after day. Maybe he needed to completely retrain for something? Perhaps return to university? But how would his brain cope with academic demands? Once again, it looked as if we were about to take a huge leap into the unknown. This time, we really needed to get it right and plan for the long term. It had to be something that would keep him connected to his old life, but not as physically demanding. Somehow, Matt came up with the idea of sports journalism, specialising in skiing, of course. Funnily enough, this was something that had come up strongly in a career's aptitude test that he had done at school.

Once again, Matt was fired up about something and determined to make a go of it. He knew that he already had the right grades from his schooldays, but he was acutely aware that he was no longer exactly the same person he had been then. He wanted people to meet him to see for themselves how he was now. He chose his shortlist of universities and rang the various admissions offices to arrange meetings or telephone conversations with the appropriate people in order to talk it through with them. He then did the rounds of university open days and seemed to always find the right people to talk to, who turned out to be very encouraging. Once again, he was impressing people with his spirit and determination. Having assured himself that this was something he could do, he went ahead with his applications and in the end opted for Southampton Solent University, who seemed to have an excellent course available to him.

*

2015 now seemed to be a year full of promise. In September, Matt would be starting a new life. At the end of 2014, Tim and Tina announced that they were expecting a baby in June 2015. Suddenly the light at the end of our tunnel was shining very brightly indeed.

The winter of 2015 was spent once again skiing and receiving excellent physiotherapy from La Clinique du Sport in Chamonix. His skiing was even better, as he was getting stronger and stronger. Still not vintage Matt, but pretty good. After her first ski with Matt that season, Steph came up to me and, in her best Arnold Schwarzenegger voice, declared, "Matt is back!" She was obviously very impressed with his level of skiing that year. Walking around on snow and ice still remained a problem, but once his skis were on, there was no stopping him.

In April, it was back to the UK and the last chance for intensive therapy. It was our final 'throwing the book' at him.

We also needed to sort out his driving. One of our greatest challenges had been dealing with the DVLA in order to reclaim his driving licence, which he had been advised to hand in after the accident. He had already had one test on the road and the examiner had felt he wasn't quite ready at that stage. We had, therefore, started the process again a year after that. However, following two years of unbelievable bureaucracy, in the end they just returned it to him after a rather perfunctory medical examination at our GP's surgery and no practical test in an actual car. We really weren't sure how capable of driving he was and above all we wanted him to be safe.

Once again, it was up to us to figure it out, so we searched for a professional driving instructor. We finally found the right instructor in the form of a very jolly Irishman who was perfect for Matt and, when the time was right, was able to reassure us that Matt was indeed ready to drive again. His confidence grew and we decided the time had come to buy him a little car. He was now able to drive himself to his various sessions locally. I was rapidly becoming redundant.

On 25th June 2015, baby Maja was born to Tim and Tina and we were all delighted. Uncle Matt was the most excited uncle on the planet and never stopped talking about her!

*

Back in April, Paul had asked Matt if he wanted to be in a team that Nikki, the neuro physio, was putting together for some sort of triathlon event. It was not going to be a full triathlon, but a paratri for athletes with disabilities. It was a shortened version of the traditional triathlon involving teams of three, with each person doing a short stint. Various patients of hers would be participating, with one doing the swimming, one doing the cycling and the other doing the running. Matt was going to do the 'running', except, of course, he couldn't run, so he would be walking the required 5km. Should be a doddle after the marathon, so we didn't bother too much about intense training. At least we didn't until a few weeks before the event, when we suddenly became aware that this wasn't just a fun jaunt that Nikki had put together, but a major event. It was to be the inaugural Tribal Paratri held at Dorney Lake in Eton. This had been the venue for the rowing events at the London 2012 Olympics and would be a very iconic setting for the competitors. We needed to get on with some serious training after all, so it was back to Centurion Way in Chichester where we had trained for the Marathon, and back to serious walking.

The 9th of August 2015 was Paratri Day, and it was a beautiful day. It has since occurred to me that all of Matt's 'special' days had taken place in glorious sunshine: the Torch Relay, skiing les Grands Montets, the Marathon and now the Paratri. Paul and Nikki were both going to be there and Paul was actually going to walk alongside Matt as his designated helper. We arrived there at almost exactly the same time as Paul and his daughter Ellie. We made our way to the registration tent to get Matt's race number, where there was a real buzz as all sorts of people were waiting for their chance to compete in the various races.

There were people there in wheelchairs, people with prosthetic limbs, people with oxygen tanks to aid their breathing, older people, young children, all with varying degrees of disabilities ranging from minor to severe. There were also some elite Paralympians there, including the gold medal-winning Paralympian David Weir. What they all had in common was the desire to prove that, although they might be classed as 'disabled', in reality they were all quite able to compete and live their lives to the full. The feel-good factor was everywhere. I don't think I have ever seen so many happy, smiling people in one place before. Seeing the children competing with such determination and enthusiasm would have melted even the hardest heart. Some of them were being pushed along in their wheelchairs by beaming parents. One little boy, who couldn't have been any older than seven, was running on prosthetic legs, grinning from ear to ear. It was obvious what the day meant to them all.

It was a wonderful venue, with the five Olympic Rings on the bridge reminding everyone what a privilege it was to be there, in the same place as all those elite athletes who had competed there only a couple of years previously. Channel 4 was there recording the event and listening to the many stories that were there to be told. A few weeks later, there would be a half-hour programme about the Paratri and, much to our delight, one of the final shots would be of Matt, Nikki and Paul crossing the finish line.

When it was time for Matt's race, he and Paul waited in the transition area for their team's cyclist to hand over to them and then they were off at a cracking pace. Ellie and I were cheering them on and once they were out of sight, we found ourselves a spot close to the finish line so that we would be in a prime position to cheer them across the line. Eventually, I spotted them, but as soon as I confirmed to myself that it was indeed Matt on the homeward straight, he disappeared.

"Oh God! Ellie, Matt's fallen. Did you see him? He was just there with your dad and then he disappeared. I'm going to get Nikki," and I ran off in a bit of a panic. "Nikki! Nikki! Matt's fallen and I can't see him." Nikki raced off to the rescue down the track.

"It's all right, Anne! I can see him and Dad now. They're heading this way, back on track," yelled Ellie. "Look, Nikki's with them now."

I needn't have worried, as he was soon up and running/staggering along. Nikki ran on to the course to help, so he now had Paul on one side and Nikki on the other and Ellie and I cheering on the sidelines! With support on both sides, he was able to speed up quite a lot and they came storming across the finish line and, once again, emotions got the better of me as I felt myself welling up with tears of pride. I don't have a clue what position they came in the race; it didn't matter. Everyone was a winner that day. It was brilliant. Nikki declared it to be one of the best days of her life, up there with her wedding day and the arrival of her boys. It was yet another wonderful memory to file away for the future and look back on. The picture of the three of them crossing that line was to feature on the website for the Paratri event.

I get the sense that, following the success of the 2012 Paralympics, people are slowly realising that being disabled doesn't preclude you from anything. Seeing those people at the Paratri, I felt very humbled and thought that really there is just no excuse for any of us to say that we can't do something. Sometimes you just need to dig a little deeper, but you'll get there if you want something badly enough. I think maybe most of us never really discover just what we are capable of. Sometimes it's not until everything is taken away from you that you find those hidden reserves and realise just how far you can go. That event was just joyous, as all of those competitors proved that despite any problems they might have, they were still unstoppable.

The next day, we set off to France for a final session with Neil. Matt had to do his 100m on the Chamonix track and once again slashed his time. He got his time down to 40-something seconds, although I forgot to record the exact time. He's getting closer to Usain's record...

On the 19th of September 2015, life once again changed for us all as Matt went off to Southampton to start the next phase of his life. He allowed me to help him up to his room with his stuff, but then I had to make a swift exit. It was marvellous to see that he was so confident and ready to regain his independence, but a part of me felt a little sad that I was no longer needed. For five years, we had been very close and worked hard together on his recovery. Now he was going to spread his wings again and fly. It's bad enough when your children fly the nest once, but to go through it twice with the same child is a bit tough, especially in these somewhat unusual circumstances.

After a couple of anxious weeks wondering how it was all going, it became obvious that he was well able to cope with the new demands that university presented. It had been a leap in the dark and could have been catastrophic had it all gone wrong.

I was worried in case his battered brain would have problems absorbing all the new information that it would be presented with. Fortunately, it was not a problem. He soon had a new gang of friends and people who would help him if needed. He did admit that he got very lost in the first few weeks going to and from university. Also, he was still being stopped by people who suspected he was drunk, but he was able to take it all in his stride. The most important thing was that he was happy and, in complete contrast to his time at Bournemouth University, he was working very hard. One of his lecturers even said to me, "I wish all of my students had the same work ethic as Matt. He works hard and never misses a lecture or tutorial." I did wonder if he'd got the right Matt. Of course, the difference now was that this time Matt was on a mission to prove to the world that his damaged brain was now firing on (nearly) all cylinders and he was ready for full-scale independent living.

Who could have guessed that it would take a fall through a roof, resulting in a traumatic brain injury, to eventually lead Matt to take up the career recommended for him in school? It just shows that life is a funny old thing, and sometimes the strangest twists of fate can take you all over the place until you reach your goal. Sometimes the darkest of places can eventually lead to the brightest of lights.

TWENTY-FIVE

LONDON'S AIR AMBULANCE

There is no doubt in my mind that one of the main reasons for Matt's good recovery was the amazing work of London's Air Ambulance at the scene of the accident. Without their rapid intervention, it is highly probable that Matt would have suffered secondary brain damage due to lack of oxygen to the brain, and then his prognosis could have been very grim indeed.

In May 2016, Nick, Matt and I went back to Whitechapel to visit the air ambulance, which is now based on top of the new Royal London Hospital. This is the very modern seventeen-storey blue-glass building that was still in the final stages of construction back in 2010. The bright red helicopter has been flying from its new helipad since December 2011.

To enter the new building, we had to walk past the old hospital, which will always be very special to us. It was now all boarded up and stood there, silent, awaiting its fate. All of its fascinating history, experiences and the extraordinary things that must have happened there over the centuries are contained within those old walls, which will keep those secrets. It reminded me of some venerable old lady keeping a dignified silence, while a brash young teenager stands behind her attracting all the attention. I have recently learnt that it will now be transformed into a Civic Centre for Tower Hamlets Council, which is okay, I think – better than luxury flats; at least it will still be serving the community. The good news is that, although much of it will be demolished and transformed, they are keeping the Georgian façade, so the old Royal London Hospital won't be disappearing completely.

Since 2010, I had read quite a lot about London's Air Ambulance, as I knew we owed it so much. Originally known as the Helicopter Emergency Medical Service (or HEMS), it was established in 1989 in response to a report by the Royal College of Surgeons, which had concluded that seriously injured patients were dying unnecessarily because of the delay in receiving treatment.

In 1990, LAA was the first air ambulance in the UK to include a senior doctor and paramedic in the crew, which obviously made a huge difference to the level of treatment that could be given. As it is too dangerous for the helicopters to fly after dark or in adverse weather, in 1999 the first rapid response car joined the service, which allowed for the expansion to nighttime operation. It initially only operated for four nights a week, but since 2010, the cars (there are a number of them now) have been operating 24/7, which was just as well for Matt. These cars have the same equipment and drugs on board as the helicopters and, more importantly, the same experienced crew of a senior doctor and advanced trauma paramedic.

The service was further enhanced in January 2016 when a second helicopter joined the team, which meant that the helicopter service need never be out of operation due to routine maintenance or repairs.

On our arrival at the Royal London, we were met by Frank, the patient liaison nurse – another fairly recent innovation and one that we would certainly have welcomed back in 2010. We were whisked up to the seventeenth floor by the very efficient modern lifts. We then walked up the ramps to the helipad and, just as we were peering into the helicopter, the alarm sounded, which meant that someone needed their help. We scuttled back down the ramp to a safe distance and watched the crew get into the cab.

Later on, I would think about that ramp and how those crews would run up it, knowing that whatever they would find at their journey's end, it would be far from routine. There would be somebody somewhere in a critical state needing urgent attention. Sometimes they are in the middle of complete chaos. Whenever there is a terrorist attack, bombing, stabbing or disasters such as the Grenfell fire, these brave men and women are there saving lives.

On the day of our visit, they put on their stab vests, as they had been alerted to the fact that they would be attending a stabbing. It then transpired that the incident was not as serious as it had first appeared and they came back quite quickly. This gave us the opportunity to go back up to the helipad and meet the crew as they got out of the cab. The crew consisted of two pilots, a senior doctor (who is usually of consultant level) and a paramedic. On that day, there was also an additional doctor who was being trained. Matt had been able to video the helicopter as it flew back in and then take pictures of the crew. Incidentally, the 360° view from up there has to be one of the best in London.

The crew spent some time chatting with Matt and very patiently answering his many questions. They said that they love to see returning patients. They pick up these very broken people and once they leave their care they often have no idea what happens to them. To see patients coming back weeks, months or even years later able to walk, talk and lead a good life makes it all worthwhile.

After a good chat with the crew, we went back down to the seventeenth floor where Frank fished out Matt's medical records and talked us through the events of that fateful night. He explained how vital it is that they have the ability to carry out various procedures at the scene. The presence of that senior doctor, a highly trained paramedic and all that equipment means that, in effect, they have a mobile operating theatre available on site. The helicopters and cars are all packed with state-of-the-art medical equipment. Any urgent life-saving treatment can be carried out in advance at the scene before they are even loaded into the ambulance. I asked the rather stupid question, "Aren't you worried about germs at the scene?"

Frank pointed out to me that, "If we're called out, then it's already a critical life or death situation, so germs are really the least of our worries. By that stage, anything's worth a try."

The patient will normally be taken to the nearest appropriate hospital by road in a standard ambulance, unless it is too far away, in which case they will be put on board the helicopter. The waiting A&E team will have been informed in advance of any treatment given at the scene and will know exactly what needs doing on arrival, thus saving valuable time in situations where every second really does count and could prove to be the difference between life and death. I am sure that you have heard of the 'golden hour' immediately following a serious injury – I think it is fair to say that these people have provided thousands of 'golden hours' to ensure the survival of people who might not otherwise have made it.

Meeting and speaking with Frank really brought it home to me just what a remarkable recovery Matt had made. More than once, he told us that to make such a recovery from an initial GCS score of 3 was 'superhuman'. That was not the first time I had heard this term used in connection with Matt, but hadn't really paid too much attention, as words such as 'superhuman' and 'inspirational' do tend to be overused these days. Hearing those words come from someone who was dealing with life and death situations on a daily basis did really mean something, though. A bit of research on my part further reinforced this. There are many, many studies on the consequences of a TBI combined with a GCS of 3. The mortality rates are high and the prognosis for those who survive is not great, either. Once again, I would emphasise that the remarkable work carried out by London's Air Ambulance must have played a huge part in Matt's subsequent recovery. It is they who are the true superhumans. They are a cutting-edge, innovative force in emergency medicine.

Some of the medical milestones in the history of London's Air Ambulance are:

- December 1993. The first open heart surgery was carried out by the team at the scene of an accident.
- March 2012. It was the first air ambulance in the UK to carry blood on board, thereby allowing for transfusions to be carried out at the scene.
- June 2014. The first pre-hospital REBOA (Resuscitation Endovascular Balloon Occlusion of the Aorta) was performed at the scene. This is when a balloon is fed into the bottom end of the aorta and inflated, thereby temporarily cutting off the blood supply to damaged blood vessels to stop patients bleeding to death before even reaching the hospital.

All pretty amazing stuff!

Frank spent two hours with us, talking us through everything. Matt had been patient number 25,327, and between then and May 2016, a further 10,000 or so patients had benefitted from the services of the teams.

The pilots, doctors and paramedics are, needless to say, the best of the best. Due to the extreme stresses of the job, the doctors can only work with them for a period of 6 months, and the paramedics for a period of 9 months. They must be prepared to have anything and everything thrown at them during this time. Despite that, people from all over the world are queuing up to join the service because of the unique and invaluable experience that they can acquire here.

Frank was able to inform us of the names of the doctor and paramedic who had attended Matt on that fateful night. They were Dr. Louisa Chan and Paramedic Michael J. Nolan, both of whom have since moved on to continue their work for other HEMS. Matt managed to make contact with Mike recently. In his reply to Matt's email, Mike wrote that, "You won't remember me as you were in pretty bad shape when we last met, but I was the one who drove it like I stole it when we got the call for you down Camden Market!" For that, the Masson family will be eternally grateful.

It comes as quite a surprise to many people when they are told that this essential service is actually a registered charity and heavily dependent on donations. Thankfully, there is a team of dedicated people working hard to raise funds for them, and they receive huge support from Londoners who understand just how vital their service is.

We left there feeling thoroughly inspired and privileged to have met these wonderful people. It's always good to know that, with all the bad stuff that is out there, there are still big-hearted, courageous men and women who are willing to go out, in often very challenging and dangerous circumstances, and save the lives of complete strangers. Our family certainly has a lot to thank them for.

TWENTY-SIX

"I BET I'M THE ONLY PERSON ON MY UNI COURSE TO EMPTY THE CLIP OF AN AK-47 ON THEIR WORK EXPERIENCE!"

I was happy with the way my recovery was progressing (between you and me, as long as I could ski, I could deal with anything else), but my balance and stuff was nowhere near good enough to go back to instructing sports. So, I decided that a way to stay close to the sports I love was to be a sports journalist.

I started my course at Southampton Solent in September 2015. It was very exciting to sort of go back to a bit of normality. I know that I'll probably have to keep ticking over with physios for quite a while and that's fine. I enjoy chasing down different goals. I really enjoy writing and the work. I've also made some good friends.

I had to do a certain amount of work experience on each year of my degree. During my first year, I did work experience on the Isle of Wight, followed by an internship in London that summer. I thought I'd go big for my final summer internship in 2017 and arranged a two-week internship at The High Fives Foundation with Roy in Truckee, California. Although it's not a newspaper or anything, I asked my lecturers and they said that as long as it's relevant, I could do it. I was going to write for the High Fives' website, capture images/footage in the gym and do general office work.

My friend Kahlil Johnson (CR's sister) said that I would be welcome to stay at her house while I was there. Roy invited me on an adaptive fly fishing trip that he'd organised in Montana. I was already excited about California, but now I had a trip to Montana to get excited about too. I headed out on the 15th of June. My birthday is on the 21st of June, so I'd be turning thirty in California, which I was pretty happy with!

Truckee is like Hollywood to me, but rather than movie stars, there are amazing skiers and snowboarders that I have been watching since I was a kid. On one of the first nights, Kahlil and I went for a pizza and Tanner Hall just happened to be there waiting for a pizza. People use the word 'legend' a bit too much these days, but Tanner really is a freeskiing legend, with eleven medals at the Winter X Games (including seven golds) and countless classic movie segments, and he co-founded Armada in 2002 and was best friends with CR. I used to have his pro-model ski goggles, so to be chatting to him while we waited for our pizzas was a bit surreal.

After a week of work, training and acupuncture in Truckee, it was time for our fishing trip to Montana. The trip was a joint venture between Access Unlimited (a company specialising in adaptive outdoor adventures), High Fives and Craig Hospital (a neuro rehabilitation hospital in Denver).

We stayed in an amazing lodge in the middle of nowhere: the Silver Bow Lodge. That's the thing about High Fives – they help all these amazing people who've had life-altering injuries to get back to all these active sports, but through High Fives' and Roy's connections, they are even more exciting versions of these sports than most 'normal' people get! The lodge was enormous and decorated with stuffed wild animals, eagles, fish and a massive grizzly bear.

I met one of the guides, Donny Wackerman, that night and he looked like he could have killed that grizzly with his bare hands. He is a huge, loud and friendly cowboy. He's a Vietnam war veteran and Roy told me that he used to be Willie Nelson's bodyguard. He is the most American person that I have ever met. Donny and Roy told me that they would 'Americanize' me over the weekend and, as far as I could tell, this would involve fishing, hunting, guns and hats!

Before the trip, I was asked to research the High Five athletes who would be on the trip. There was one name on that list that I already knew all about. Riley Poor is an action sports filmmaker, who has captured some amazing footage of the world's best skiers. After filming Simon Dumont winning a ski competition in January 2009, they went back to celebrate at a house in Vermont. Riley was a brilliant freestyle skier, which is what makes him such a good filmmaker; he really understands the sport. But after years of taking risks on skis, his life changed when he dived into a swimming pool. He broke his neck and is now *a quadriplegic. Riley didn't let that stop him, though, and he now works as an executive producer at Nike.*

Most people on the trip had suffered spinal injuries, either skiing or snowboarding, and there was me with my brain injury. Between us, we pretty much covered the whole spectrum of mobility – all the way from motorised wheelchairs to walking quite smoothly and everything in between. One thing everyone had in common was the huge smile on their faces.

We were split into groups for the fly fishing. Me and my roommate, Trevor (who broke his back snowboarding a couple of years ago), went with a guide called Tommy. We would all be on boats that just drifted down the river, one seat in the front and one at the back with the guide in the middle. Tommy taught us the basics and me and Trevor shuffled into our seats. I'd not done much fishing in my life, but drifting down a river in Montana seemed to be just about the perfect fishing trip. My 'Americanization' continued with Trevor giving me some plasticky meat snack for lunch while he and Tommy proudly told me their best American jokes, and I even saw a bald eagle in a tree. You can't get much more American than a bald eagle!

When we got back from our day's fishing, just by listening, you would never have guessed that anyone had any difficulties. The laughing and joking as we all compared our fishing stories was probably heard by our next-door neighbours. Remember, this was Montana, so that could have been 10 miles away! I caught two fish, which I was very proud of until I went and told Riley. He's pretty calm and had been very patient with me asking about all his famous skier friends. "Oh, two. That's pretty good." I thought I was now Angler of the Year 2017. I asked him if he got any. "Yeah, I got a few." His girlfriend, Andrea, told me that they each got four!

That night, we went to an Access Unlimited fundraiser at Dillon, Montana. A great night, great food and many funds were raised. The good people of Dillon were incredibly generous, with a live charity auction. Roy showed his awesome talent for auctioneering. With the crowd buzzing off his energy, he managed to raise $18,500 in about 10 minutes for an Action Trackchair (an off-road powered wheelchair).

I met a local called Austin who'd suffered a TBI two years ago. I spoke with his dad about my recovery experiences. They told me that Austin never missed a physiotherapy or cognitive therapy session and was always motivated. I told him that, in my experience, that's the key. Just stay motivated, stay positive and never stop working to get better with your exercises. I like to think it was good for him to meet someone who had been through a similar injury and recovery.

The next day was (apparently) the last phase of my 'Americanization' – shooting. Now I won't lie, I've never really been attracted to guns, but I had heard many rappers mentioning AK-47s in their songs. So when we got to the shooting range that was all I wanted to shoot. Me and Andrea were taken to learn the basics, as we were the only beginners. Not sure I was the best shot, but I hit a few targets with a little gun, then it was time to move on. The instructor told me that children can shoot AK-47s, which was not only worrying but a bit disheartening, as I couldn't really figure out the loading, cocking and aiming bit of it! There were a few targets set up across the valley. After trying and failing to hit any of them, I just decided to pull the trigger and vaguely shoot towards them. When Roy came to congratulate me on 'Being an American', I told him that, "I bet I'm the only person on my uni course who emptied the clip of an AK-47 on their work experience!"

We headed back to Truckee for the last week of work in the office. My thirtieth birthday was on the 21st of June, and I was about to receive the best present I will ever get. I was writing up my piece about Montana when everyone came in singing 'Happy Birthday' and carrying a plate of cupcakes with candles in them. That was a nice enough surprise, but then Roy came in with a big parcel. I thought it was just something to do with High Fives, nothing to do with me.

In this package was a jacket that CR Johnson had stitched a design onto. I had seen a painting of this design on the wall at High Fives and I thought it was cool that he actually made it. Roy then got Steve to film me (bit suspicious now); he then gave me the jacket!

CR has been my number one inspiration during my entire recovery. This whole thing: meeting Roy, Kahlil, High Fives, even (indirectly) me deciding to train as a sports journalist – it all started with that Armada CR memorial jacket. Now I had been given a jacket that CR had actually owned and customised. That night, I asked Kahlil what she thought I should do with the jacket – frame it or wear it? I wouldn't want to damage it! She replied that it was made to be worn, so I should 100% wear it. She actually tidied up the last bit of stitching using CR's sewing machine.

I imagine that CR would be happy to know that his jacket will be skiing in the Chamonix Valley from now on.

I was looking forward to my flight back to England via LA – I had big plans for a quick trip to Compton in my

2-hour layover. Then Roy offered me a chance that was even better than Compton. If I could take a later flight, I could go with him and watch a NASCAR race in Sonoma, California. NASCAR is an American, very quick stock car racing series. That was an offer I couldn't refuse.

Roy, being Roy, treated me to a pretty unique NASCAR experience. We drove a few hours in his fancy pickup truck to the middle of California wine country. We were greeted by plenty of flags, barbecues and cowboy hats, and we would be staying in an NFL team owner's RV (campervan). There were ten of us in our group, including Red Bull's chef and a pro skier!

We set up our camp (with hundreds of flags flying!). Then, on race day, we got pit passes, watched from a box and even had a visit from one of the drivers – Joey Logano. Joey signed my Logano shirt and we all went to see the cars in the pits and had photos taken with the pit girls.

The whole thing was delightfully American. I had a corn dog, and red, white and blue fighter jets screamed past during the national anthem. My Americanization was well and truly complete.

Due to my change of flight, my layover switched from LA to Chicago, so I never got to visit Compton, but thanks to Roy and everyone connected with High Fives, I had an unforgettable experience of the USA!

*

Roy made me chuckle when he sent Nick and I a little note after Matt returned from Truckee. It was regarding his 'Americanization'. I should just explain that in 2016, we had been to a family reunion and Matt was delighted to find out that his great-grandfather had lived for two years in Jamaica.

He seized upon that fact so he could instantly claim Jamaican nationality to add to all the others he had previously laid claim to. Roy worked it out as follows:

"I think Matt is at least 5% American now, which makes his make-up, according to him, 50% Jamaican, 5% American, 25% Chamonix and 20% Swiss. Not sure if these are correct but that is what I believe is the make-up of Matt's roots. However, I know for a fact that he has 100% heart of a lion."

TWENTY-SEVEN

THE WOBBLY JOURNO

Matt graduated from university in July 2018 with a 2:1 in Sports Journalism and we were incredibly proud of him. Nick, Tim and I were all there to cheer him on, as well as Lisa, who had done so much to get him this far.

If there had been a prize for the funniest graduate, Matt would surely have won, as by the time he had scrambled his way up onto the stage to shake hands with the Chancellor and receive his diploma, his mortarboard had slipped onto one side of his head, completely obliterating his face. All you could see was a very wobbly young man clutching his hat against one cheek to prevent it from falling off completely. We have the posed, professional-looking photos of Matt taken before the ceremony, but to me the one snapped of him as he lurched onto that stage, completely dishevelled, with a rather startled expression on his face, shows the real Matt we all know and love.

When it was all over, we were once again in the position of wondering where to go next. We needn't have worried, though, for Matt's lucky streak was definitely back with a vengeance. His story came full circle as he made a video for his final uni project entitled *Skiing Before I Could Walk*. It tells the story of his recovery. Remember way back in 2011 when Matt was so thrilled to receive a signed photo from Jacob Wester, one of his ski heroes, and then met him in London later that same year? Well, Jacob came up trumps again when he agreed to be part of that video. He appeared in the video with Matt in Chamonix, helping him to try that backflip that had eluded him in Truckee, this time on snow. If you want to know how it worked out, you'll just have to look it up on YouTube: *Skiing Before I Could Walk – Matt Masson*.

That video also led to him getting his first bit of freelance work as a journalist, when it was spotted by the editor of a ski website. He then started to pick up bits and pieces of work from other websites and magazines. In March 2019, he was sent on his first assignment to Austria, shortly followed by another assignment reporting on the Freeride World Tour final in Switzerland. He is continuing to pick up more assignments and work and, in the process, meeting some of the top freeskiers in the world. He is making freeskiing his speciality and, as far as he is concerned, there is not another job in the world that would give him more satisfaction than the one he has now.

For me, perhaps the best illustration of Matt's sheer guts and determination was the day that he went off to Verbier in Switzerland on assignment. I was in Le Tour at the time and offered to drive him there. It's only just over an hour away by car but, no, he was determined to get there under his own steam on the train. This would involve a change of train once he was down the mountain and then at the end of that second train ride, he would have to walk to a cable car to get up to the ski station. He also needed to take skis, poles, boots, backpack with technical gear in it and another bag containing clothes for the weekend. I was allowed to take him to the little station in nearby Vallorcine, where we unloaded all his stuff. His backpack we put on his back, his boots we hung around his neck, he pulled his overnight bag along behind him and he somehow carried the skis and poles.

"Can I at least help you carry something into the station, Matt?"

"No, Mum, I have to be able to do it on my own."

He resembled an overloaded pack mule. As soon as he took a step, the boots fell to the floor and we had to load up again. As I watched him literally wobble his way towards the station, I felt such a mixture of pride and despair, and I admit to shedding a tear. This was so difficult for him, but he would not give up. I knew people would help him along his way, but all of a sudden, it just seemed so unfair that he should need any help. Needless to say, he made it there and back, and I know he was just thrilled to be off doing this on his own, and he would have approached that journey with his 'can do' mentality, and he would have hated the fact that his silly mum was fretting about it. I guess that's what we mums do, and I do have complete faith in him and his abilities – it's just that he looked so very wobbly.

As I write this in the summer of 2019, the highpoint of his career to date was in May this year when he spent a week with the Armada team in the Armada House in Sweden interviewing the various members of the team. The person responsible for recruiting him for this assignment was the same Tom who had written me a letter and sent me the goodies for Matt back in 2011 when he was in the Neuro Rehab Unit relearning his life skills. How crazy is that? Matt's whole story has been about coming across the right people at the right time, who have then often popped up later on when needed. One link has led to another, building a strong chain throughout Matt's recovery.

He and I have also managed to do our bit for raising awareness about head injuries. As well as the video, we appeared on BBC Radio 4's programme *Ramblings* with the TV presenter Clare Balding in September 2018. For that, we walked down Centurion Way with Clare, reminiscing about how important a role those training walks had played in Matt's recovery. It reached a wide audience and I hope some good will have come of it. We certainly had some good feedback from surprised friends who heard it, having had no idea that we were doing it!

Matt's story is also now on the Headway website, where, again, we hope it will do some good and help others who are going through the same bewildering experience.

Everywhere Matt goes he meets new people and widens his network of contacts. In the ski world, where injuries are all too common, he is gaining a huge amount of respect for his attitude and, more importantly, praise for his journalistic skills. To say that Nick and I are proud of him doesn't even begin to describe our feelings. I still feel slightly anxious every time he sets off on a new venture, but hopefully these feelings of anxiety will diminish over time.

His wobbliness has become part of his character now and he has embraced it. It's often a good conversation opener, as he explains to people just why he is so wobbly. So when he had to think of a name for his website, he knew straight away what it would be – The Wobbly Journo, of course. Quite where the Wobbly Journo will end up is anybody's guess, but one thing's for sure – he'll have fun getting there!

TWENTY-EIGHT

SOME FINAL THOUGHTS AS WE LOOK TO THE FUTURE

There was a time in the dim, distant past when I never used to worry about Matt at all. I firmly believed that he was one of those people who had been born lucky. No matter what happened, he always seemed to land on his feet. Then came the day when, instead of landing on his feet, he landed on his head. However, it seems to me that for a while now he has been back to landing on his feet.

On the 27th of November 2010, Matt had become one of 168,539 people who were admitted to hospital with a head injury that year. Between 2005 and 2018, 1,936,396 people altogether were hospitalised with head injuries according to statistics available on the Headway website. These injuries will have ranged from mild concussion to severe traumatic brain injury, and their levels of recovery will also cover a wide range. Matt is still working as hard as ever on his recovery, and there is still scope for further improvement. As always, only time will tell.

If someone were to ask me that fashionable question: "What would your 2020 self say to your 2010 self?", I know exactly what my 2020 self would say. If she could have walked into the ICU and spoken to that bewildered woman sitting beside Matt's bed in November 2010, she would have said:

"Anne, the most important thing you have to understand is that you have to allow time for a brain to heal, and there is no way of knowing how much time is needed. Sometimes all the time in the world will make no difference and you'll have to accept that no recovery is possible. Over the coming days, weeks, months or even years, you might meet or read about people who have suffered severe TBIs who recover so much quicker than Matt, and you must learn not to resent them or feel despondent. It's okay – that's just what happens. Every brain injury is completely unique. You, Nick, Tim and Matt will all have to learn the art of extreme patience. Hopefully, you will start to see tiny little improvements, which will all add up and amount to a huge improvement over the course of time.

"The doctors are telling you the truth when they say that they can't make any predictions – they really can't. You and your family will have to live one day at a time and have faith that what will be, will be. Just don't even think about giving up too soon – believe in your amazing son."

The only problem is, I doubt whether my 2010 self would have listened.

I am sure that there are still many good things ahead for Matt, but I think this is a good place to end his recovery story as he starts to build up his new career. He has certainly reached the top of this particular mountain, but I am sure that ahead of him lie roads that will lead to even higher summits, and they too will be conquered. So, how would I sum up these past few years?

The first words that spring to mind are: challenging, exhausting, rewarding, emotional, exhilarating and often a lot of fun.

A lot of people have helped Matt on his way and we couldn't have got this far without them. However, I am proud to say that most of it is down to Matt himself. He has remained so positive and determined all the way through. Any down moments have been few and far between. I am really not sure whether or not, in the same situation, I would have had the emotional strength to maintain such a huge degree of effort over such a long time, especially with the improvements happening so very slowly. He did explain it to me right at the beginning of his recovery. As he sees it, he just doesn't have a choice. He wants to recover, so he has to get on with it. There is no point in wasting any time on negative energy looking back on what might have been or what has changed for him. He has to deal positively with what is happening right now. He really can't understand why so many people find that so amazing.

Of course, Matt is not unique in his determination to get better. We know from all the stories on the High Fives website that there are many young men and women out there who adopt this ultra-positive approach to recovering from life-altering injuries, and that it works. However, I do worry for other young adults with life-altering injuries who don't have access to a High Five. I know that many formerly active, fit young people finding themselves with a serious brain or spinal injury are totally overwhelmed by the change in their lives. This is hardly surprising. One minute, the world is their oyster and they are pursuing their dreams, whether big or small, and then suddenly they find themselves confined to a hospital bed and nobody can tell them how long they will be there for. That is precisely when I believe they need hope and encouragement to look forward to the future. Not false hope, but to see that, even in a wheelchair, these days life can be fun if you dare to accept the challenge.

Once they have sunk into depression and anger, it is very difficult to motivate them. There are many sporting organisations out there who do excellent work with disabled people, but you need to seek them out. If you're sitting in a dark hole, you're not going to be bothered to do that.

It goes without saying that my role model and benchmark organisation for aiding recovery from a life-altering injury is the High Fives Foundation. My focus throughout this book has been unashamedly on young adults, as that is what I feel I know about now. My dream would be to have a similar centre (or centres) of excellence here in the UK aimed at adventure-seeking young adults, with all the various therapies available and where they would be encouraged to participate in all manner of exciting activities within their new abilities. This would be a charitable organisation, which would have connections with all the sporting organisations who help the disabled. The most important thing is that this would be a totally upbeat and positive environment designed to take people as far as they can safely go. All neurosurgeons would know about this and recommend it to those patients who they feel could benefit from it. Let's hope that one day it might become a reality.

One thing that really struck me was that both Kahlil Johnson and Roy Tuscany on separate occasions have told me that the take-up by TBI survivors of the services offered by the Healing Center and High Fives has been very low compared to spinal-injury survivors. I wonder if this is because, due the very nature of their injury, a TBI survivor is not thinking clearly. They need others to fight for them, especially in the early stages following an accident. That is so important for family and friends to bear in mind. It is really up to them to try and guide the survivor along the right path following their accident. Sometimes that won't be easy, as they can be very unreasonable. You will need to become masters of distraction, so be prepared.

I know that many people will question our encouragement of Matt's skiing, but that is what he loves to do. If you took that away from him, there would be a huge hole in his life. His skis have been his way back to life. He knows that he has to be careful and he can't leap off cliffs or off the ramps in the snow park. His skiing these days is quite genteel and he actually puts in a few turns on the way down, instead of straight-lining as he did before. He always wears a helmet, of course. When I look back and consider how much the skiing community has done for Matt over the last five years, I can't help but wonder if his recovery would have been half as good without them. It certainly would have been a lot less fun. They have all been 100% behind him, cheering all the way. They are magic.

We are still fighting the battle that my Chinese lady assured us we would win, and we will not give up. We have been through all sorts of emotional experiences following Matt's accident and have had many highs and lows, but funnily enough, the highs greatly outnumber the lows. We have learnt the importance and value of friendship. We have seen the power of positive thinking in action and how it succeeds. We have seen how Matt can set seemingly impossible goals and then achieve them. We have found that there are a great many good people out there, who have helped us on our way. My faith in human nature has certainly been restored.

As for me, I do understand now that it is impossible to predict the level of recovery from a brain injury. A damaged brain is quite different from a broken leg. No one can know how well, or if, it will heal. I can therefore understand the reluctance of the medical profession to give a positive prognosis at the beginning. However, I do maintain that a positive, determined effort is essential in order to achieve the best chance of any recovery potential that may exist and to keep hoping for the best. Matt has more than proved that. I have stood in awe and watched him in his battle and we are all very proud of him. As always, I must qualify that last bit by saying you must also be prepared to recognise when that recovery is not going to happen.

Perhaps one of the most surprising things that I have learnt from this whole experience is the way that many people who have suffered a life-altering injury feel about it. The ones who have managed to emerge out the other side with a different, but good, life, mostly declare that they wouldn't change a thing – Matt included. I can only conclude that this is because it is truly an experience like no other, and senses are heightened; and the tiniest things are subsequently appreciated like never before. They have all been on the ride of their lives.

I still spend a lot of time researching and reading about brain injury and its consequences. It is a fascinating subject and still proving challenging to many people in the medical world as they seek to unravel its mysteries. Now that we have survived the worst of our roller-coaster ride, it is easier for me to face up to exactly what happened to Matt. When I look back over the last 9 years, I realise how very, very lucky we have been and how much worse it could have been. We have also been privileged to witness something quite remarkable.

It was a horrible accident, but Matt had a lot of things in his favour following it. He was in excellent health at the time of his accident and that, combined with his youth and fitness, gave him the very best chance of recovery from a devastating injury that could so easily have been fatal. The rapid intervention of London's Air Ambulance also improved his chances hugely. Add to that his fighting spirit and sheer optimism and his chances improved further. Then bring in a group of loyal and brilliant friends who have stood by him the whole way and kept visiting him, even when he was totally unresponsive, and who continue to keep in touch to this day. Next we further added to the mix by finding a team of wonderful therapists who all seem to have gone the extra mile for Matt and have all been equally determined that this cheerful, cheeky chappy should make the very best recovery possible. They have put up with all of his eccentricities and crazy ideas and his incessant chattering! Then there are all the people he has met along the way, who have started out as strangers intrigued by his story and ended up as friends. Last, but not least, we mustn't forget CR Johnson's magic jacket and all the good things that came from that. All these factors combined to ensure that Matt has just kept on improving and, hopefully, will continue to do so. As a family, we can now face the future with real optimism and, as his mother, I am eagerly anticipating what new adventures it might bring.

One thing that I have learnt for sure is that there is a lot of what our Californian friends would refer to as 'awesomeness' out there. People with battered brains and spines who just do not let life get them down and, against all the odds, still climb mountains, sail the seas or trek across vast landscapes!

I just want Matt's story to give people permission to hope. Without hope, it would be very difficult to progress. We took the attitude that if no one knows the prognosis, why assume the worst from the beginning? If we go for it and fail, at least we won't spend the rest of our lives wondering if we should or could have done more. We have done everything. Matt might not make a 100% recovery, but he will definitely be the best he can be. So what if he still wobbles a bit and has a limp? Compared with what could have been, we'll take that any day.

Matt worked incredibly hard to obtain his degree in Sports Journalism. You will never see him in a suit presenting the sports news. That's not really his style. Whatever he decides to do, he will do it his way, and it will no doubt be fun and quirky. The Wobbly Journo is now more than ready to go out into the world and challenge perceptions.

This has been our unique story. We chose to tell it because we wanted to let people know that a life-altering injury doesn't necessarily have to mean the end of everything – sometimes you just have to change the road you were on.

•

It seems only right that Matt should have the last word. So what does he think?

Whenever anyone asks about my accident, I always tell them it was much worse for my friends and family. I woke up in hospital, couldn't walk, talk or even move much, but I had friends coming from all over the world – some of them I hadn't seen for ages – and they were all bringing me presents!

Unlike an illness, my recovery has been almost just physio and training really, which I have loved. I have also loved setting goals. There was no pressure here because most people probably didn't think I would do them, so there was no expectation. Skiing before I could really walk and doing the marathon before I could even vaguely run were both pretty cool. Everyone was really supportive when those goals were set, especially my mum, who has walked and skied miles with me, as well as being my unofficial chief physio! I know it's a bit of a cliché, but I actually liked it when people doubted that I could do something – it just motivated me even more.

Obviously, there have been times when I've seen friends going on holidays, living and working in all these cool places and I've thought, "I could have been doing that." But then I think of all the amazing things that I probably wouldn't have done: the Olympic Torch Relay, the Amsterdam Marathon, High Fives/Roy, meeting pro skiers and even training to be a sports journalist. I loved my life before, but I think I would have just gone from summer season to winter season until I got to my mid-thirties, when I would have thought, "What do I do now?"

Now I can, hopefully, go back to a similar sort of lifestyle, but with an actual career still based around the sports that I love. Every step since I woke up in January 2011 has been quite enjoyable. I'm now a fully trained journalist and on the night I left Southampton I got an exciting email...

I had put my video on the forum of Newschoolers (freestyle ski website). The editor sent me an email saying that he loved the video and if I sent him some of my writing, "I can't make any promises, but I'll see what I can do." So, of course, I sent him some of my writing about skiing and since then I have started freelance work with them and already interviewed many of the best freeskiers in the world, with many more lined up, and even been on assignments in Austria, Switzerland and Sweden!

It's funny how things work out. Who would have thought that a traumatic brain injury would be my ticket into the world of professional freestyle skiing!

So, while it has been tough at times, and obviously I would never have specifically wanted to have the accident, if Marty McFly were to pull up in his time-travelling DeLorean, I don't think I'd go back and not have the accident.

AFTERWORD

This has been the story of recovering from a serious brain injury sustained at the end of 2010. Currently, as you have learnt, it can be a long, slow, laborious process. Hopefully, however, this might not always be the case. There is great hope for the future as teams of scientists from all over the world are working hard to unlock the mysteries of the brain. It is very hard to see into the brain, as you can't just go poking around in it without risking great harm. Whole new technologies are being developed that may well allow scientists to do just that in the future, though. Billions of dollars are being spent worldwide on various research projects, employing some of the brightest brains on the planet.

In 2013, President Obama announced the BRAIN Initiative (Brain Research through Advancing Innovative Neurotechnologies). He proposed a decade-long effort to examine the workings of the human brain and to try and map it in order to understand just what all those billions of neurons in the brain do. The proposed initial expenditure during the fiscal year 2014 was $110 million. On 2nd April 2013, President Obama said: "We have the chance to improve the lives of not just millions, but billions of people on this planet through the research that's done in this BRAIN Initiative alone. But it's going to require us as a country to embody and embrace that spirit of discovery that is what made America, America."

There are now many leading technology firms, academic institutions and scientists involved in this project, and by September 2014, over $300 million had already been committed to the initiative. This is a collaboration between public and private funding, and its future seems secure. Although President Obama launched this initiative, thankfully it has survived the change of president and it is still looking very healthy. Funding of more than $434 million was proposed for the fiscal year of 2017, immediately following President Trump's election, and it continues to thrive. It is growing all the time as more and more scientists and technologists seek to join the mission of unlocking the many secrets of the brain.

At the same time, in Europe, the Human Brain Project was launched. This is planned to last a decade from 2013 to 2023 at an estimated cost of 1.19 billion euros. It described its mission as follows:

> *Understanding the human brain is one of the greatest challenges facing 21st century science. If we can rise to it, we can gain profound insights into what makes us human, build revolutionary computing technologies and develop new treatments for brain disorders. Today, for the first time, modern ICT has brought these goals within reach.*

This project is co-funded by the European Union, who are responsible for 50% of the budget; the other 50% is funded by member states and private funding sources.

In 2014, Japan announced its own project to run parallel with the US and Europe ones. This is known as Brain/MINDS (Brain Mapping by Integrated Neurotechnologies for Disease Studies).

It doesn't end there. All over the world, other countries are also pursuing their own projects, including Australia, China and Russia.

If all of this research can lead to a dynamic understanding of brain function, we could be on our way to uncovering the mysteries of brain disorders such as Alzheimer's and Parkinson's diseases, depression and traumatic brain injury. Through the integration of neuroscience, technology and physics, researchers can use high-resolution imaging technologies to observe how the brain is structurally and functionally connected in living humans.

The significance of these projects is every bit as huge as the Apollo Space Program or the Human Genome Project. As Dr William Newsome of Stanford University said when comparing the US BRAIN project to those two projects: "The goal of the BRAIN Initiative is much more complex. Our own brains are trying to understand themselves. That is a deep scientific voyage, not an engineering project."

It's all exciting stuff and who knows what amazing breakthroughs may be on the way right now? Of course, all these scientists don't work in isolation. They share information and work with each other. In December 2017, at the Australian Academy of Science in Canberra, representatives from Japan, Korea, the USA and Australia announced a formal declaration to work together to speed up progress on cracking the brain's code. It was known as 'The International Brain Initiative', and brain research initiatives from other countries and regions were also invited to join them. The subheading of the 'Declaration of Intent to create an International Brain Initiative' is: *It takes the world to understand the Brain*. I can't argue with that.

To be able to really understand the brain with all its complexities would be incredible. Who knows? Maybe one day it will actually be possible to fix a damaged brain as easily as fixing a broken arm. Now, that would be something.

GLOSSARY OF TERMS

Axon   The 'cable' that connects neurons and carries the
             electrical inputs from one neuron to be received by
             other neurons

CT Scan   Computed Tomography Scan: uses X-rays and a
             computer to create detailed images of the inside
             of the body; a CT scan can provide more detailed
             information of a head injury than regular X-rays

ECG   Electrocardiogram: measures the electrical activity
             of the heart

EEG   Electroencephalogram: a test that detects electrical
             activity in the brain

GCS   Glasgow Coma Scale: a neurological scale to
             measure the level of consciousness

HDU High Dependency Unit: one step down from an ICU, but providing more extensive care than a normal hospital ward

ICU Intensive Care Unit: specialised hospital ward providing treatment and monitoring of people who are very ill

ICP Intracranial pressure is the pressure inside the skull and thus in the brain tissue and cerebrospinal fluid (the fluid found in the brain and spinal cord)

ICT Information & Communication Technology: all devices, networking components, applications and systems that, combined, allow people and organisations to interact in the digital world

Neurons The fundamental units of the brain and nervous system that receive sensory input and send motor commands to our muscles; their interactions define who we are as people

PTA Post-Traumatic Amnesia: a state of confusion following a TBI with no continuous memory

TBI Traumatic Brain Injury: an injury to the brain caused by trauma to the brain

ACKNOWLEDGEMENTS

So many people have played their part along our long road and I really hope we haven't overlooked anyone:

Dr. Louisa Chan and Paramedic Michael J. Nolan, the crew of LAA's rapid response car, who saved Matt's life on that fateful night

The wonderful medical teams in the ICU and HDU at the Royal London Hospital in Whitechapel who made sure he stayed alive

My brother, John, and his family, Sally, Charlotte and Charles, who ferried us around, fed us, provided a roof over our heads and kept our spirits up over the first six weeks

Dr Bradley and team at the Donald Wilson Neuro Rehabilitation Centre in Chichester for teaching Matt how to do everything all over again

Lisa Featherstone, neuro physio, and Paul White, personal trainer – our dream team who stuck with Matt for several years

Gavin Learmonth of Definition Camps who put Matt back on snow a year and a day after his accident

BMW for allowing Matt to show off his walking to the world by carrying the Olympic Torch in 2012

The magnificent men and women of La Compagnie du Mont Blanc operating the lifts in Le Tour, Chamonix

The ever-patient instructors of the ESF Argentière, who got Matt back on his beloved slopes – especially Magali Devouassoux, Fabien Cartier, Stephanie Parizet, Carole Tairaz and Maeva Martin

Roy Tuscany and the High Fives Foundation, who proved it was okay to be stubbornly optimistic and so much more

Dean Decas – 'nice, nice, nice!'

Kahlil Johnson for her kindness and generosity

Jacob Wester, who has always taken the time to help Matt

A long list of physiotherapists, including:

Rich Holmes at Donald Wilson

Nikki Penny at the Nikki Penny Stroke and Neuro Clinic, Hurstpierpoint

Petra Tanner at the Oving Clinic

Trish Formby of Trish Formby Physio

Jane Haydon at the Boxgrove Clinic

Neil Maclean-Martin, Janie McCorriston and Malin Samuelsson at La Clinique du Sport, Chamonix.

Southampton Solent University – "I told you freestyle skiing was a sport!"

Tom Suesskoch and all at Armada Skis for being general all-round good guys

All the many pro skiers who supported Matt as he embarked on his new career

Twig at Newschoolers, who gave Matt his first opportunity to be a paid Wobbly Journo.

Clare Balding for a lovely *Ramblings* in Chichester; we didn't get very far, but we had plenty to say

Headway for being an invaluable source of information throughout Matt's recovery and for this book.

The Book Guild, who allowed us to fulfil our dream of publishing our book

Our friends and family for being there

Last, but certainly not least, Matt's many, many friends who have always been there for him. Some of them appear in the book, but you all know who you are!

Huge, huge thanks to all of the above and lots of love from:

Nick, Anne, Tim and Matt xxxx

REFERENCES AND SOURCES CONSULTED DURING THE WRITING OF THIS MEMOIR

A lot of the information in this memoir was picked up by talking to and quizzing the various medical professionals who looked after Matt in the hospitals and rehab.

I also found the following books and websites particularly useful and informative:

Head Injury – A Practical Guide by Trevor Powell
The Brain – The Story of You by David Eagleman
Life Lessons from a Brain Surgeon by Dr Rahul Jandul

Headway.org.uk – the UK's leading head injury charity has a huge amount of really helpful information on its site, together with some inspirational stories. It also has a lot of very useful brochures dealing with all aspects of brain injury from the early days right through to living with the after effects. It also has various support groups all over the UK.

Synapse.org.au – the Australian version of Headway, which I also browsed for information.

My interest in head injuries as they relate to sport and war started when I read a couple of articles a few years back:

After the Crash – A closer look at the rising incidence of brain injury by Marc Peruzzi in *Outside* Magazine 7/11/2013.

A Special Report – *Battling Traumatic Brain Injury* by Maryann Brinley 19/09/2011.

To learn more about London's Air Ambulance:

Londonsairambulance.co.uk

For inspirational stories about life following a life-altering injury:

highfivesfoundation.org

An outstanding documentary movie about brain injury is *The Crash Reel,* telling the story of the talented young snowboarder Kevin Pearce.

To catch up with what the Wobbly Journo is up to:

www.thewobblyjourno.com

facebook.com/thewobblyjourno

instagram/thewobblyjourno